Extraordinary Tide

The Extraordinary Tide
New Poetry by American Women

EDITED BY

Susan Aizenberg
and
Erin Belieu

Jeremy Countryman

ASSISTANT EDITOR

Columbia University Press   New York

COLUMBIA UNIVERSITY PRESS
NEW YORK

Columbia University Press
Publishers Since 1893
New York   Chichester, West Sussex
Copyright © 2001 Columbia University Press
All rights reserved

Library of Congress Cataloging-in-Publication Data

The extraordinary tide : new poetry by American women / edited by Susan
Aizenberg and Erin Belieu; assistant editor, Jeremy Countryman
      p. cm.
    ISBN 0-231-11962-3 (cloth: alk. paper)
    ISBN 0-231-11963-1 (paper: alk. paper)
      1. American poetry—Women authors.   2. American poetry—20th
century.   3. Women—Poetry.   I. Aizenberg, Susan.   II. Belieu, Erin.   III.
Countryman, Jeremy.

PS589 .E96 2001
811'.54089287—dc21

                                               00-064439

∞

Casebound editions of Columbia University Press books are printed on permanent and
durable acid-free paper.

Printed in the United States of America
c 10 9 8 7 6 5 4 3 2 1

⁓for Margaret Crews Belieu and Edith Latman Singer

Contents ～

Madeline DeFrees

Toi Derricotte

Deborah Digges

Rita Dove

Nancy Eimers

Lynn Emanuel

Angie Estes

Kathy Fagan

Jane Kenyon

Mary Kinzie

Carolyn Kizer

Maxine Kumin

Ann Lauterbach

Dorianne Laux

Cleopatra Mathis

Gail Mazur

Heather McHugh

Lynne McMahon

Sandra McPherson

Jane Miller

Susan Mitchell

Thylias Moss

Lisel Mueller

Laura Mullen

Carol Muske

Foreword ∼

As what is now the last century drew to its close in December of 1999, a rare conjunction of three signal events took place: on December 21, a full moon— that is, the moon aligned with the sun respective to Earth—coincided with the perigee of the moon's orbit, that point at which it comes closest to Earth, enlarging it in our eyes. And those events coincided with the winter solstice. So it was that on the longest night of the year at the very end of the twentieth century, the moon as bright and as large as it ever appears to us, the tides— drawn by the moon's pull, reinforced by the pull of an aligned sun, and amplified by the moon's nearness—were exceptionally high.

Though astronomical coincidence is no respecter of human calendars or events, such a heavenly configuration tempts metaphor, reading as an over-head projector of our own meanings: the conjunction of presiding forces at the turn of the century seen as similarly conspiring in the production of unusual brightness in an extended night, bringing on an extraordinary spring tide—the one that, quoting Alicia Ostriker, has given this volume its title.

Speaking as one of the poets represented in this collection, and feeling its publication as a celebratory occasion, one that appropriately inaugurates a new century in poetry and locates a powerful source of its reinvigoration, I feel at the same time the need to question the premise of this assemblage, and to ask, at the outset, just why we are here together, and on what grounds we can call ourselves by so collective and intimate a pronoun as that first person plural. For we are, as poets, so patently, dramatically, prosodically, philosophically, experientially, temperamentally, stylistically—as many ad-verbs as there are kinds of unlikeness—different from one another.

We, who see those differences so vividly, who rankle at attempts to homogenize our disparity, nevertheless feel our connection, and honor it. How then to understand this connection, one which indicates a commonal-ity while resisting a category? A category is a division in a scheme of classification, it divides and encloses; a commonality underlies and connects, it indicates something shared.

In our case, or so it seems to me, it is a commonality powerful enough to supercede both our differences and an uneasiness that necessarily accom-panies a women-only anthology. This uneasiness is a sensitivity inherited from a history of being members of an historically excluded or secluded group, a history that precludes ease of conscience about exclusions, while raising fears of a ghettoized seclusion. Yet, despite such hesitations, I have no doubt that there is reason and value in the premise shaping this anthology's selection.

There is something undeniable and of literary significance in this particular "we"; something begun with a xx chromosome, but no longer crucially about our biology, which we not only experience quite variously, but which, for many American women, birth control and other advances—both medical and social—have made simply a fact and no longer a fate. What we, as poets, with our heterogeneous backgrounds, aesthetics, concerns and voices, have in common; what matters, whether consciously acknowledged or not, to all of us for whom the published poem is a voice made manifest and public, is the immense silence at our backs. It is a public silence so profound, of so long a duration and carrying so great a mass of human talent and experience, that its effect is crucial in the production of this great spring tide of contemporary poetry by women.

Whether we will or no, that silence moves us—and here I use the word *us* with a singular assurance. I do not mean that it is thematic to our poetry; I mean it is the ground of it. Even as we have a language in which our tongues are formed; even as we have the same great male poets as do our brothers as our sources, traditions and influences; so do we also have the Great Silence of those unheard women, the would-have-been poets, who are also our ancestors, and just as powerfully our influence.

We have, really for the first time, several generations of women poets (in numbers unprecedented, and rapidly increasing) alive and writing at the same time; the search for foremothers mixing now with the "anxiety of influence," that anxiety creating freshness, frictions, fruitful discord, creative resistance and painful ingratitudes; the youngest group already bemused (and a bit bored) to hear what sound like fables about the Time Before, when women did not, by and large, publish—except notices of birth, marriage and death; when the femme designation for poet ended in the spongy squish of "-ess," allying her with soft soap, tears and madness. Of course there were exceptions; largely because of feminist criticism, the revised anthologies of the past have begun to sprout them. And exceptions, so goes the commonplace, prove the rule.

How new and how inspiriting for that very newness is this presence of coterminous female generations in print, of women who take their own work, and the work of other women at least as seriously as that of male poets. Those in my generation, not so many years ago, raised on the powerful voices of men, were made to think that we were exceptions, and felt ourselves, as writers and thinkers, drawn away from the company of women.

Though to jump the literary gender bar was a bruising sport. Thirty years ago, during an interview for a Ph.D. program, I was told by a well-known critic at a leading university: "Here, in English, we don't like women." A friend interviewing with the Graduate Chair at another university was told: "Sit where I can see your legs." Every one of my contemporaries can offer variants on these stories. How very recent that time was, how soon forgotten.

A dangerous forgetting, really, since it remains necessary to be vigilant, to continue to consolidate a position only partially won, and of too short a duration to be very secure. Speaking in 1999 of her appointment as poetry consultant to the Library of Congress in 1981, Maxine Kumin said: "Between 1937 and 1981, there had been one African-American consultant. I was the fifth woman named to the consultancy, a post that is now called Poet Laureate. We don't count, the head librarian said to the press when this issue was raised at the luncheon announcing my appointment. We do, I replied. Alas, we are still counting."

In the generations behind us, and therefore within us, lives The Great Silence—whether of mothers, grandmothers, great-grandmothers, or those so deep in time we can scarcely dream the dimensions of the public silence so long inhabited. We are the inheritors, no matter what our other differences, of that Silence, its abyss an echo chamber that enlarges speech and its resonance—poetic speech in particular, because it is the figures and forms of imaginative language that best contain and express silence. The unsaid and unseen have always been poetry's driving necessity, its images corresponding not just to what hasn't yet been seen, but to what can't be seen or said or known another way. So we may suppose that it is the huge reservoir of unspoken inner life of the female past that drives and energizes the extraordinary tide of contemporary poetry by women.

The delights of this anthology are in its plurality, its collection of such a rich and varied sampling of that tide flooding American shores. As its editors, Erin Belieu and Susan Aizenberg, make clear in their statement of rationale for selection, there is no political or thematic agenda for this anthology, no aesthetic or prosodic unanimity to its styles or substance; only their desire, as teachers and poets, to have such a company gathered in a single volume, a record and source book of the remarkable accomplishment of the last few decades. Happily, there is now no need to search, even as there is no evidence, for an identifiable "woman's voice"; what unifies the work is not a style of utterance, but that ancestral silence as the very substrate of its being, and the remarkable variety of utterance that now rises out of that silence, and harbors it as well.

Elaine Scarry, in her essay "Counting at Dusk," speaking of the outburst of poetry during the last decade of a century, points to its equivocal nature: "heal decades . . . at once disempower and reinvigorate the human will." As she points out, though *fin de siècle* traditionally meant enervation and decadence, the record of writing during the final decades of centuries indicates revivification as well: "poems, for example, by Chaucer, Sidney, Shakespeare, Spenser, Blake, Coleridge, Wordsworth—suggest that the end of the century inspires inaugurating linguistic acts . . . that invigorate the language not just of the next century but of a period far into the future."

Perhaps, looking back at a volume like this one, that far future will say of us, like Scarry in her litany above, that we have invigorated the poetry of our time even unto theirs, and, though nothing can ever compensate for so great a loss, that we have at last ended that Great Silence, and with such voices as do it honor.

—*Eleanor Wilner*

Introduction ~

Deciding to edit an anthology is, in many ways, like deciding to marry or devote one's life to making poetry—impulses both grand and foolhardy, born in the bottle rocket flare of enthusiasm; commitments that kindle first in the heart with the head (one hopes) not too far behind. Arriving at the decision to edit an anthology requires a leap of faith in one's self and a willingness to put the entirely rational on hold long enough to allow something interesting to happen.

Our shared enthusiasms began in having been relentless students, teachers, readers, and editors of American poetry for most of our adult lives. We have spent contentedly obsessive hours poring through bookstores, libraries, and Web sites, culling the latest publications and making mental lists of our favorite work to be included in that imaginary anthology most serious readers carry about in their heads. As poets ourselves, constantly searching for new ideas and fresh inspiration, we have been particularly devoted to the work of our peers—specifically to the writing of American women poets.

Yet the realistic shape for this anthology truly began to capture our imaginations and provoke our sensibilities only when we realized what a fundamental and long overdue addition such an anthology would be to the current literature. Consider the fact that when we first told our colleagues (also teachers and editors of poetry) that we intended to edit an anthology of contemporary American women's poetry—one comprehensive enough to be used in classrooms and to introduce young readers and writers to a vast and underexplored landscape within contemporary poetry—many of them assured us that such an anthology already existed. And they remained convinced that such an important collection must already be in print—until they went to the shelves to look for it.

Theirs was an understandable reaction, since such a glaring gap in the literature of American poetry is hard to immediately comprehend. It is even more difficult to make good sense of this absence when we consider the sheer size and force of what Alicia Suskin Ostriker, in her book *Stealing the Language: The Emergence Of Women's Poetry In America*, has so aptly called "the extraordinary tide of poetry by American women in our time." Consequently, this anthology is our response to, and attempt to fill, that curious gap. And it is, more importantly, our celebration of this extraordinary tide.

In what is the most comprehensive collection of American women's poetry ever published, we have attempted to gather and reveal the varied shapes and voices of American poetry written by women in the last ten years, poetry written in the spirit of an ever growing aesthetic and political freedom and understanding, poetry that leaves the visible and invisible walls of women's identity ghettoes behind. As editors, we have been guided by the belief that it is now possible to celebrate poetry written by women without such poetry being relegated to the perfumed category known as "women's poetry." Of course, not all will agree (and it is worth mentioning here that one, and only one, poet objected to the anthology's gender identification and declined our request to reprint her poems), but we hope this anthology will renew a fresh and useful debate around the subject.

In gathering this work together our approach has not been "canonical"— it could not have been, as no single volume could include the great number of poets whose work had a claim to be considered for this anthology. Rather we have worked to bring together a representative spectrum of the best and most widely recognized writing being done today by women around the country without privileging any particular theme or political agenda.

What then have been our more specific criteria for selection? Because we wished to focus on newer work, we decided to limit contributors to those who have published at least one full-length collection in the last ten years. Space considerations, and the large number of "emerging poet" anthologies, decided our choice to focus on those poets who had published two or more collections at the time we were assembling the anthology. We also chose, with two exceptions, to include only the work of living poets. Those exceptions, Lynda Hull and Jane Kenyon, have been important figures in recent American poetry and we felt that their early and untimely deaths should not exclude them from this collection.

We confined our choices to those writers who are primarily identified as poets, eliminating writers who, while having written fine poems, are more often engaged in writing fiction or essays. We strove for a balanced representation of poets in terms of geography, race, age, ethnicity, sexual preference, and aesthetic identification. Both writers of free verse and those working in traditional forms are well represented. Lovers of avant-garde poetry may be disappointed that even more of this verse is not represented here, but again, we consoled ourselves on this point by discovering several recent anthologies specifically devoted to such work.

Our central guiding criteria have been our own notions of excellence— indeed, a slippery concept and matter of taste. But here, we believe our collective twenty years experience as editors, our wide-ranging and differing tastes, the credentials of our contributors, and, most especially, the power and the beauty of the poems speak for themselves. And, as we have indicated, if it were not for the practical limitations of space and money, this collection might be twice as large.

There are many admirable poets whose work does not appear here. It is our hope that as the interest in poetry written by American women continues to flourish (as it no doubt will, given that women buy the majority of literary books in this country and constitute more than half of the people entering poetry M.F.A. programs), this book will be just the first of many interesting collections.

What then do these poets have in common other than gender? Though we can cite certain figures, tropes, and characters that seem to engage the imaginations of these writers, we would argue that the very reason for such a book as this is to illustrate and celebrate the great diversity of writing among women poets. As Ellen Bryant Voigt points out in her essay "Poetry and Gender," "If female experience—whether deriving from some inherent feminine nature or in response to cultural bias—is to be the primary given, then one will better understand the poetry it informs by examining the differences. . . . If truly little difference is to be found, if contemporary women's poems do sound alike, treating the same themes with the same tone, . . . then we must be writing very poorly indeed."

We agree, and believe that the variety of poems presented in this collection signifies a triumph of women poets, who speak in many ways and many voices (against what Eleanor Wilner so eloquently terms "the immense silence at our backs"), and demonstrates the excellence and vitality of women's poetry today.

Finally, our heartfelt thanks to the many friends and colleagues who so unselfishly gave of their time and talents as we worked on this project, especially: Maryrose Flannigan and Roxanne Thornhill at Associated Writing Programs (AWP); Neil Azevedo; Angela Ball; Michelle Boisseau; Copper Canyon Press; the English departments and writing programs of Creighton University, Kenyon College, Ohio University, and the University of Nebraska/Omaha; Lynn Emanuel, Candice Favilla, Jane Hirshfield, James Kimbrell, Carol-Lynn Marrazzo, Ross Martin and the folks at Nerve.com, Alicia Suskin Ostriker, Marie Ponsot, Hilda Raz, Brent Spencer, and Belle Waring.

Special thanks, also, to assistant editor Jeremy Countryman and to Elinor Wilner for their invaluable contributions; to our families, for their constant support; and to the poets who have so generously agreed to appear in this collection, and whose work continues to enrich us all.

—Susan Aizenberg and Erin Belieu
January 2001

Extraordinary Tide

Marjorie Agosin ∼

The Obedient Girl

The obedient girl
with the patent-leather shoes
and starched white dress.
The obedient girl
greets the general
who sliced the fingernails
of her younger brother
and burned the breasts
of her older sister.

The obedient girl
smiles, makes the appropriate
curtsies
and moans completely flustered
when the soldier
tells her she is beautiful
and rubs his hand of war between
her lifeless legs.

The obedient girl lives
because in a country of obedient children
young ghosts appear
on days of savage light
to kidnap disobedient girls,
gypsies lost in the forests
of light and shadow.

The obedient girl
approaches the soldier
and kisses him with fear
he is the soldier who burned
the books of her house,
who slashed the crimson dresses
and played with the candlesticks of
silver and blood.

The obedient girl
doesn't speak
she is a sleepy doll
who surrenders herself
as if her body were a country
of obscure travelers.

Fear

Fear
nested
like a murmur
lost in
parched throats.
We said nothing,
we were like decayed harps,
little moans
in the proximity
of all these perverse
distances.

Fear II

Fear was no longer that continuous presence that took pleasure in appropri-
ating our surroundings, our gazes that searched in the meager transparency
of the air. Fear was kept in the deep chrysalis of memory; it was a flickering
of eyes that peered menacingly without space or precise time. Sometimes I
thought that we were no longer a country of poets but a country of cowards
who after a long time of deceitful insomnia, after a time of dead words,
came out of oblivion. We wanted to remember the soaring utopia of our
dreams but were afraid; we feared ourselves, feared unusual fraternal gestures, feared the open embrace like a sigh of happiness. But it wasn't the
general with his long white summer capes that we feared. We feared what
we ourselves were becoming: a nation deaf before memory, a fearful and

lost nation amid the mute cordilleras, amid the mute forests. Everything around us insinuating a great silence, a time of lies and idleness.

Night

I
Beyond the night,
among the crystalline thresholds of dream,
the women travellers
with feet spouting rivers
wanderers through the erroneous wells of death,
search, inquire,
sing, weep
and ask the rosaries
about the day of the homecoming,
return in the secret dream of night
to the pitch-black house,
to the house without words,
to the beds populated by the dead
and their violet garlands.

II
Beyond the day,
the women travellers prepare themselves,
search, inquire and weep.
In the town, everyone knows them
but runs away
and they insist upon that sweet, peaceful
question:
Have you seen my son?

III
They search, sing, weep
and ask the rosaries
and the witches of the district,
who offer herbs for forgetting,
and return to the secret pitch-black house,
to the bed populated by the dead,

to the home without a voice,
to the austere language of absence.

Ai ~

Chance

written on learning of nuclear tests on unsuspecting civilians by the U.S. Government

An ill wind with a Samsonite suitcase
was passing through White Sands, New Mexico,
in February, 1952,
when Mama, Daddy, my little sister and I
were en route to Tucson
from Fort Riley, Kansas.
We were on a vacation
no one knew would take Daddy to the cancer ward.
The hard facts can't be taken back,
or rearranged like Scrabble pieces
to form another word that is not terminal.
"Open the windows," said Daddy.
"Let in some fresh air. Don't tell me
you girls have to use the bathroom again.
We'll stop when we see a gas station
and please, Stella,
don't take any towels, or soap.
We don't want to look bad being Negroes.
It won't be good for the race."
"They'll just say we stole anyway," said Mama,
as we drove through the gray afternoon.
The sand was as white as the dress of a bride.
The sky was a groom, pressing down on her.
Their union was doomed to disaster, but who knew,
as we pulled to a stop and Mama got out
and scooped up some sand
she planned to store with the other souvenirs
she bore home in triumph?

I had on my red Roy Rogers cowboy hat,
my western shirt, cowboy boots, and Levi's
and I pulled my cap gun from its holster and fired
at the dim outline of the sun,
as the wind blew up the highway
to the next defenseless, unsuspecting town.

The other day, I found a mirror
Mama appropriated so long ago
and when I looked in it,
I saw us in our old Ford
with one door held closed by chicken wire.
Back then, Daddy had faith in Jesus and democracy.
He didn't fear what he couldn't see, taste, or feel,
as he laid his hands on the steering wheel
and drove into his own nuclear winter.

Charisma

A Fiction

I didn't just read the Bible, I lived it.
I told my people, this is revolution.
I said, I interpret this attack
on my constitutional rights
with a gun and a guitar
to mean we are in trouble.
I held up a hand grenade, pulled the pin
and told them, "This one's for Jesus."
I prayed, "Lord, take me to heaven, take me today
and I won't falter on the way."
Did my people desert me,
did they say this man is crazy?
No, they didn't.
They prayed with me.
They lay facedown in Waco, Texas,
to await death and resurrection,
as it came from all directions, all in flames.
I never claimed to be the Jesus, who cured the sick

and caused the lame to walk.
I knew the sins of the flesh, I knew the shame
and I confessed my weakness.
I let my people be witness to it
and through it came my power
and the empty talk of changing sinful ways
that haunt a man,
until he betrays himself no longer
and gives in to the stronger urge
to fornicate and multiply dissolved.
I absolved myself between a woman's thighs
and I arose like Lazarus,
raised up from the dead
on the tip of his penis.
We had no life and death between us anymore,
we had rounds of ammunition
and all of you to listen to us burn
and in that burning learn
how to give your life for freedom
in Christian hunting season.
The AFT used child abuse as the excuse
to assault us in our home.
They had no proof
and if we had been left alone,
we might have shown the world
that God is like desire you cannot satisfy.
You must give in to Him, or die.
The Apocalypse cometh like a firestorm,
leaving some of us reborn,
others to smolder in the ruins
of New Jerusalem,
which will not come again,
until the war against the innocent is over.

The Paparazzi

I'm on the ledge
outside your hotel bedroom,
when I glimpse your current lover,

as he bends over you on the bed
and deposits a cherry
he holds between his teeth
atop the mound of your very dark brown hair.
You're blonde to your adoring fans,
but I know where you're not.
For a second, I feel hot,
as I watch him, but I should be cold,
get the shot,
and go trespass on some other private property.
Come on baby, come.
I've got to pursue another asshole,
who thinks a TV role
makes him too good to be exposed warts and all
to those insatiable public coconspirators,
who want to know
all his dirty, little secrets,
or just his brand of soap.
The alcohol, miscarriages, divorces
marriages, face-lifts, coke binges,
homosexual, hetero and lesbian affairs.
I've been there through it all
and I am there for you,
a friend, not an enemy,
stalkerazzi, or a tabloid Nazi,
storm-trooping onto your yacht
to photograph you
in your latest embarrassing situation.
Think of me as a station of your cross
and the camera as your confessor,
who absolves you,
as you admit to lesser crimes
than I know you are guilty of.
You media whore, I didn't ask you for excuses,
I asked you for more
and I know you'll give it to me
before the public moves on
to the next shooting star,
but even then, occasionally I'll still
ambush you in rehab
and send the message
from the land of the fading career

that you are tumbling
through the stratosphere
just like you used to,
but now the only sound you hear
as you hit bottom once again
is the click of the shutter
and not applause and cheers.
I don't want the truth,
I want the lies,
so look this way,
say something nasty.
Don't be shy.

Susan Aizenberg ⁓

Meeting the Angel

Not as a bird with twelve black wings and an eye
and a tongue for each of us. (Someone dies
each time he blinks.) And not shrouded in celestial
light, a fair-haired castrato. Not as Samael,
angel of poison, his venomous sword quivering
above the parched, open mouths of the dying.
He did not come as Azrael, *whom God helps,*
bearing apples so sweet their fragrance kills
our fear of leaving this known world. What did we
know of death, of suffering? Each day for weeks
we drove the autumn highway to the clinic,
where the angel's rough map ablated J.'s skin
with the blue tattoos of radiology, black
dissolve of surgical stitches. And like, or unlike
God, he was always with us, among the lush,
ongoing trees, the small mercies of fresh
air and afternoon light leavening the cracked
glass, our hearts' stutter, as we reached the exit.

Kiss

And when the moment,
   like an overdue train bearing to us
     someone loved and too long

        gone, a train we've waited days
     and nights for, pacing the platform,
   our pulses thrumming *when, when,*

arrives—the camera close up, lush
   sweep of strings, *adagio*, the light high key,
     resplendent as the dew-rinsed,

     saturated, dizzyingly green panoramas
   the cinematographer's mapped as Camelot—
     the moment

we have waited for, with the lovers,
   since their first meeting, Guinevere crouched
     among damp reeds, unafraid, despite

her torn dress, smiling as she watches—
   he's young, all muscle and wit, a man's
     easy grace—smiling, too, despite the chain

   and mail-clad villains, the honed,
 bloody swords, knight of girlhood's promise,
     you remember—that moment

     when the camera frames the kiss
 she's asked him, finally, for. They are not tender,
but open their mouths wide, so we think

       of eating, their heads working,
         a kind of fever, love's other face—
           we recognize it, don't we?   Lancelot,

the man, the archetypal *only, always,*
   we dreamt of as girls those rainy childhood
     afternoons, Kens and Barbies moving

stiffly in our small hands, our mothers'
stolen stilettos gorgeously tripping us up.
It's that kiss you want for so long

that when you take it you take it
greedy as a thief, and always with as much payment
due. And we want them to go on,

though we know the ending, that the camera
must pan to a three-shot, Arthur's ragged
face. We want them to go past

what they, and we, can bear, to follow
his head gentle down her neck, her mouth
against his bare shoulder. We want the music

to swell, lavish, hokey, romance
engulfing us like some over-sweet perfume,

so wholly our lives
become epic, a kiss worth whatever it costs.

Art

. . . ordinary isn't possible anymore
ADAM ZAGAJEWSKI

In the teachers' lounge, the tall, pretty
Irish woman tells me her anorexic
daughter's been hospitalized two years.
She's fifteen. Their debts are something she can
only laugh about. I sip tepid coffee,
tell her about the afternoon I watched
deputies cuff my son, pat him down
against a black and white while he invited
them to *suck his cock, fuck him in the ass,*
and cried. Today, I teach figurative
constructions to high school juniors signed up
for creative writing in hope of an easy grade.

I quote Wallace Stevens, wonder
what metaphor I can use to find the unities
in this: what was he *like* raging by that car?
Was the sun *fiery*? The police faces
stone? Soon, I'll speak to English teachers
from four schools about the value of "art
and imagination" to students whose twelve-step
stories of locked wards and halfway-house
failures I've listened to all week.
I don't know what to say about these stories,
how to explain that they come to me daily,
as if I wear some sign. And I don't know
what it means, as I watch them laughing
in school hallways, slamming their lockers,
tonguing each other in a sweet approximation
of love. When I call him at the hospital,
my son tells me a story: a friend
has died, the rumor is someone scotchgarded
his dope. Forgive me if this seems
extreme—I don't know how to make things
ordinary anymore, though I dress and go to work
each day as if the world were ordinary,
as if our lives might unfurl easily as some
well-mannered plot— carefully
rounded characters strolling bucolic paths,
safe beneath lucid trees, their steps
measured and graceful as the orderly
progression of their lives—a shapeliness
such as no one might imagine anymore.

Sandra Alcosser ~

My Number

I'm linked with the fate of the world's disasters and only have a little freedom to live or die
    VÎTESLAV NEZVAL

My number is small. A hundred pounds of water,
A quart of salt. Her digit is a garment.

I wear her like a shadow. We judge each other,
My number and I. She is the title. The license.

The cash drawer. My random number.
She protects me from myself. She desires me.

She says she's only one of thirty million species.
She wishes she were more than anecdotal evidence.

Being human she can erect elaborate scaffolding
To protect her emotions, can make an excuse of obvious

Dramatic proportions. My number is inconsequential
With dreams of glory. She spends three or four days each year

Just opening her mail. Do you know how many animals
Will be given lethal injections while you read this poem.

Five billion people = half a billion empty bellies.
If there is a god, why can't that god be smaller than my number,

Tiny, soft-spoken so she'd have to pay attention.
My number is a female impersonator (she has multiple meanings).

Her shape is misleading. The further she is from unity, the more deeply
Involved with the world. Like the winds and the grasses, she wears herself
    down.

She lies under hot flags of lilies, sings like a bee.
She gets so lonely she recites for her cat. She makes her face up

Like a death mask. She hangs her dresses on the clothesline outside.
Together we dance—my number and her best dresses.

Dancing the Tarantella at the County Farm

Our teachers prepared us years ahead
so that when I laze in bed past noon
twenty years later, ignoring my late father's
imperative-voice command—
get up and blow the stink off—
the poorhouse floats back to me
through its allée of hardwood trees.
It resembles a Georgian estate
surrounded by plate-flat farmland
and rumor that the basement
housed a torture chamber.
Our dogpatch class of nine-year-olds
grows suddenly grave as we approach.
Inside brick walls and flowered wallpaper
inmates have just finished lunch,
something like dried oatmeal
pasted to their trays, something difficult
to scrape away. Their faces have that same texture.
Our caretakers resemble each other—
same desire for order, same steel-arched shoes.
Each year they march us to the community room
to share each other's shame. My invitation—
to dance for the lady in a wheelchair, to display
long muscular legs. *You're all she has,* says the teacher
as she straightens my homemade costume.
But I am third grade. A nothing. I think
I'll never escape. Stronger than a father's voice,
the whisper of my teacher. *Bow deeply*
from stage left, her breath fused with the face
of the paralyzed woman, *and when the music begins*
get out there fast. I spin, I split, I do back flips.

I become St. Vitus again. I dance the spider bite
as hard as I can. See, I smile. Good girl.
My body becomes a wet rag. I wring it tighter and tighter.
Like a dervish. Like a top. It wants to fall over.
It wants to give up. If love were water
not a drop would be left.

By the Nape

Though sun rubbed honey slow
down rose hips, the world lost
its tenderness. Nipple-haired, joint-swollen,
the grasses waved for attention.
I wanted a watery demonstration for love,
more than wingpaper, twisted stalk of heartleaf.
Squalls rushed over pearling the world,
enlarging the smallest gesture, as I waited
for a drake in first winter plumage
to stretch his neck, utter a grunt whistle,
begin his ritualized display.
I'd held a wild mallard in my palm,
hoodlum heart whooping like a blood balloon.
I'd watched a woman suck coins
between her thighs and up inside her body.
How long she must have trained to let the cold world
enter so. The old man said his neighbor asked him
to milk her breasts, spray the walls, bathe in it.
That was his idea of paradise.
Sometimes I don't know who I am—
my age, my sex, my species—
only that I am an animal who will love
and die, and the soft plumage of another body
gives me pleasure, as I listen for the bubbling
and drumming, the exaggerated drinking
of a lover rising vertically from the sedges
to expose the violet streaks inside his body,
the vulnerable question of a nape.

Elizabeth Alexander ～

Apollo

We pull off
to a road shack
in Massachusetts
to watch men walk

on the moon. We did
the same thing
for three two one
blast off, and now

we watch the same men
bounce in and out
of craters. I want
a Coke and a hamburger.

Because the men
are walking on the moon
which is now irrefutably
not green, not cheese,

not a shiny dime floating
in a cold blue,
the way I'd thought,
the road shack people don't

notice we are a black
family not from there,
the way it mostly goes.
This talking through

static, bouncing in space-
boots, tethered
to cords is much
stranger, stranger

even than we are.

Affirmative Action Blues (1993)

Right now two black people sit in a jury room
in Southern California trying to persuade
nine white people that what they saw when four white
police officers brought batons back like
they were smashing a beautiful piñata was
"a violation of Rodney King's civil rights,"
just as I am trying to convince my boss not ever
to use the word "niggardly" in my presence again.
He's a bit embarrassed, then asks, but don't you know
the word's etymology? as if that makes it
somehow not the word, as if a word can't batter.
Never again for as long as you live, I tell him,
and righteously. Then I dream of a meeting
with my colleagues where I scream so loud the inside
of my skull bleeds, and my face erupts in scabs.
In the dream I use an office which is overrun
with mice, rats, and round-headed baby otters
who peer at me from exposed water pipes (and somehow
I know these otters are Negroes), and my boss says,
Be grateful, your office is bigger than anyone
else's, and maybe if you kept it clean you wouldn't
have those rats. And meanwhile, black people are dying,
beautiful black men my age, from AIDS. It was amazing
when I learned the root of "venereal disease"
was "Venus," that there was such a thing as a disease
of love. And meanwhile, poor Rodney King can't think straight;
what was knocked into his head was some addled notion
of love his own people make fun of, "Can we all
get along? Please?" You can't hit a lick with a crooked
stick; a straight stick made Rodney King believe he was
not a piñata, that amor vincit omnia.
I know I have been changed by love.
I know that love is not a political agenda, it lacks sustained
analysis, and we can't dance our way out of our constrictions.
I know that the word "niggardly" is "of obscure etymology" but probably
　　derived from the French Norman, and that Chaucer and Milton and
　　Shakespeare used it. It means "stingy," and the root is not the same as
　　"nigger," which derives from "negar," meaning black, but they are per-
　　haps, perhaps, etymologically related. The two "g"s are two teeth gnaw-

ing; rodent is from the Latin "rodere" which means "to gnaw," as I have
said elsewhere.
I know so many things, including the people who love me and the people
who do not.
In Tourette's syndrome you say the very thing that you are thinking, and
then a word is real.
These are words I have heard in the last 24 hours which fascinate me:
"vermin," "screed," "carmine," and "niggardly."
I am not a piñata, Rodney King insists. Now can't we all get along?

Equinox

Now is the time of year when bees are wild
and eccentric. They fly fast and in cramped
loop-de-loops, dive-bomb clusters of conversants
in the bright, late-September out-of-doors.
I have found their dried husks in my clothes.

They are dervishes because they are dying,
one last sting, a warm place to squeeze
a drop of venom or of honey.
After the stroke we thought would be her last
my grandmother came back, reared back and slapped

a nurse across the face. Then she stood up,
walked outside, and lay down in the snow.
Two years later there is no other way
to say, we are waiting. She is silent, light
as an empty hive, and she is breathing.

Pamela Alexander ～

Manners

Sit, she said. The wolf sat. Shake, she said.
He held his face and tail still
and shook everything in between. His fur
stood out in all directions. Sparks flew.
Dear sister, she wrote. His yellow eyes
followed the words discreetly. I have imagined
a wolf. He smells bad. He pants, and his long tongue
drips onto the rug, my favorite rug. It has arrows
and urns and diamonds in it. The wolf sits
where I've stared all morning hoping
for a heron: statuesque, aloof,
enigmatic. Be that way, the wolf said.
There are other poets.

Understory

i
The hay scented. The cinnamon, the horsetail,
The interrupted; maiden-hair, royal, ostrich, marsh!
The sensitive. The walking. The
resurrection! Ferns.

ii
In the big claw-footed tub,
washing each other for the first time.
You said, Don't let me forget
it can be like this.

iii
We looked down for a minute, at most.
What was it? Some wildflower
or moss, or one of those fluorescent orange newts

we'd startled with every step. When I stood up
a spider's web glistened
between the straps of your binoculars.
How long have we been here?

Look Here

Next time you walk by my place
in your bearcoat and mooseboots,
your hair all sticks and leaves
like an osprey's nest on a piling,
the next time you walk across my shadow
with those swamp-stumping galoshes
below that grizzly coat and your own whiskers
that look rumpled as if something's
been in them already this morning
mussing and growling and kissing,
the next time you pole the raft of you downriver
down River Street past my place
you could say *hello,* you canoe-footed fur-faced
musk ox, pockets full of cheese and acorns
and live fish and four-headed winds and sky, *hello*
is what human beings say when they meet each other
—if you can't say hello like a human don't
come down this street again and when you do don't
bring that she-bear and if you do I'll know
even if I'm not on the steps putting my shadow
down like a welcome mat, I'll know.

Soon

The mansion is full of spiders. Pick up
a large one—it stands in your palm and weighs
some amount muscles recognize. Less
than a lemon. More than a letter. The smallest
look like dust, but when you blow them

off the mantel they don't fall far (dust
can't save itself). The spiders slide
up and down, measuring tall windows for drapes
and then sketching them in.
The village is hours away but the land flat,
so that matins and vespers reach our inner ears.
Studying the intersection of attachment
and freedom, the spiders tremble like the hands of
Trappists—not from the work of the heart
(a spider's is unchambered) but of the spinneret,
which fibrillates, beams out
viscous geometries.   On the landing,
in its tub the size of a baby grand,
the philodendron stirs. It taps woody rhizomes
against the treads going downstairs,
the risers going up. The spiders
take in light and give off, at night,
a high and wiry hum. You will hear it
soon. The only rule is you must
walk from room to room, floor to floor.
You must not lie down on the parquet.
The mansion has many flights; we will not see
each other again. The only rule is you must not
touch anything. You must not sing back.

Julia Alvarez ⌐

Bilingual Sestina

Some things I have to say aren't getting said
in this snowy, blond, blue-eyed, gum-chewing English:
dawn's early light sifting through *persianas* closed
the night before by dark-skinned girls whose words
evoke *cama, aposento, sueños* in *nombres*
from that first world I can't translate from Spanish.

Gladys, Rosario, Altagracia—the sounds of Spanish
wash over me like warm island waters as I say
your soothing names: a child again learning the *nombres*
of things you point to in the world before English
turned *sol, tierra, cielo, luna* to vocabulary words—
sun, earth, sky, moon. Language closed

like the touch-sensitive *morivivi* whose leaves closed
when we kids poked them, astonished. Even Spanish
failed us back then when we saw how frail a word is
when faced with the thing it names. How saying
its name won't always summon up in Spanish or English
the full blown genie from the bottled *nombre.*

Gladys, I summon you back by saying your *nombre.*
Open up again the house of slatted windows closed
since childhood, where *palabras* left behind for English
stand dusty and awkward in neglected Spanish.
Rosario, muse of *el patio,* sing in me and through me say
that world again, begin first with those first words

you put in my mouth as you pointed to the world—
not Adam, not God, but a country girl numbering
the stars, the blades of grass, warming the sun by saying
¡Qué calor! as you opened up the morning closed
inside the night until you sang in Spanish,
Estas son las mañanitas, and listening in bed, no English

yet in my head to confuse me with translations, no English
doubling the world with synonyms, no dizzying array of words
—the world was simple and intact in Spanish—
luna, sol, casa, luz, flor, as if the *nombres*
were the outer skin of things, as if the words were so close
one left a mist of breath on things by saying

their names, an intimacy I now yearn for in English—
words so close to what I mean that I almost hear my Spanish
heart beating, beating inside what I say *en inglés.*

Estel

Your name, *Esther,* in your mother's shy *campesino* voice
sounded like *Estel,* though even then, unsure
whether I had misheard, I wrote it out,
and she nodded, yes, that looked like your name.
So that now at El Instituto Sordo Mudo
your white jumpers are all mislabeled
with the name you cannot hear, Estel,
learning to form those vowels in your mouth,
to read my lips explaining why you are here.
In the village, you were the errand girl,
carrying water up from the river; your head
cocked at an angle with the heavy loads
as if you were hearing, far off,
the sound of your new name being called.
La muda, the villagers shrugged when I asked
why you weren't in school, why you
were the little carrying horse, why you
didn't tell me your name along with the others,
flocking around me, begging for alms.
It was then I took an interest in you,
out there beyond the reach of the words I love.
Each time I came to the village, I lured you away
and wrote down words on the blank pages
I had meant to fill with poems after years
of my own silence; wrote down your name,
signed *you,* wrote *fishing boat, orange,*
whatever you pointed at I'd spell
until the paper darkened with your new words.
We walked the rocky coast looking for things
to name, I taking this opportunity
away from the watchful eyes of the villagers
to clean your cuts, feed you the oranges
you love, kill the lice in your hair
with a cream your mother couldn't afford to buy.
Once or twice I checked to see
if the words had taken, cutting the paper
in strips, pointing to something, asking you
to pick the name out from the pile in my skirt.
You seldom hit, the gulls were *waves,*

the palms were *fishing boats,* the seashells
tennis shoes, the world misunderstood—
but your name that wasn't really your name,
you always picked when I pointed to you!

Estel, at El Instituto Sordo Mudo,
they have fancier ways to teach you what I've tried,
but this is the gist of it: the world
expressed in words is yours, Estel.
You stand on the eight-year-old line, your pigtails
tied with white ribbons, dressed in white,
a blank intelligence about to be filled
with your new life. But child of my silence,
listen, there will always be this sheerest gap
between the world and the word, *Estel*
for *Esther,* poems instead of the touch
I wish I could give you, now, so far
beyond my reach, deep in the mute heart.

Angela Ball ～

The Dance Pianist

Last night I talked to a woman—
she approached where I sat
resting at the keyboard and we talked
a long time—my eyes went, I remember,
between her blue eyes and a wonderful arrangement
of velvet roses on a shelf
behind her—until someone
drew her aside and said, in a loud
whisper, "He's the dance pianist!"
Her face flushed, turned away
and I knew our conversation
for what it was: a lie's interval.
Poor woman—she's been discovered in public

talking to an object
or the wall. So this
is my lovable body!
I'd rather be Andrei Yefimich, straitjacketed,
guarding my view of the bone-charring factory
off in the distance, than here
with my animate music, my hands
silent, swift, eloquent
plastered with invisible banknotes,
performing an act of exchange.
Naked weeping overtook me.

The Man in a Shell

One day I went walking and
boom—there was Varenka,
the young lady
I'd planned to marry,
madly pedaling a bicycle
as if she were ten years old!

When I tried to warn her brother
about such behavior
he shoved me downstairs,

tumbling out of control, dignity flying away
forever, and there was Varenka:
"Ha-ha-ha."

How be a schoolmaster anymore?
How will pupils pay attention
to a man who has tumbled downstairs?
Sonorous Greek lost in roars.

Tuck in my blankets.
Things must be kept within bounds.
Draw the bed curtains.

A man should get married.
Ha-ha-ha.

The Kiss

I open the wrong door
at the Lieutenant General's
party, into a completely dark room,
only a chink of light
from the door, the fragrance
of violets, the far-off sound
of a mazurka. Then there's the rustle
of a dress, a woman's voice, "At Last!"
her arms around my neck
and the sound of a kiss. The woman screams
lightly and jumps away, and I rush headlong
out of the room. Then there's the party
again, and the May evening, and me—
shy, nondescript. How can I recognize
someone I've never seen, a woman waiting to kiss
someone entirely different? I can only
compose her from my favorite parts:
the arms and shoulders of this one, this blonde hair,
high forehead, slight smile. It's impossible
even to know exactly what kiss
I stumbled into, what her lips meant.
She must have been desperate
to make him happy, but instead, me!
And how much more. If only she knew
what men say among men about their eager
lovers. If only I could have
a minute with her in the light
instead of going back
to my gray tent, pale lamp,
some cardboard sleep.

The kiss spreads itself over everything,
ordinary camp life, the regiment's

hats, legs, horses. Often I wake up
full of my secret, needing to rush somewhere
and do something right away—
leap back into the dark room,
but it's impossible, like love
from beyond death or between people
who don't exist.

Finally the regiment returns
to the General's town, and I ride
by myself up to the house—see the garden's
flowers, and the long windows—
and suddenly it's all silly, the world
nothing but jokes—and me
the most pitiful.
When I get back to camp
and find a note inviting me
to the General's party
I stifle the flare of joy
and go to bed.

Dorothy Barresi ～

When I Think About America Sometimes (I Think of Ralph Kramden)

raising that truncheon of an arm
to shake it, ham-handed and heavy
for what he was always about to say: *to the moon, Alice!*
in the dingy quarters

by the sea of human toil and information we called
The Honeymooners
on television in the fifties.

But why did we think it was so funny?
Alice was his wife and lover, and though it is hard, admittedly,
to picture their lovemaking—
the sweat he heaved into her with a fat man's
slog and fury, not

grace, don't call it grace,

until their headboard,
scrolled with grapes and angels in the old manner,
must have quaked like rails underground, years like that,
layered in concrete, deep,
absorbing the shock and just taking it
because someone said
Cleave Unto Him
and she cleaved, O she cleaved,
smirking—

I can't help it. I do.
Now my Sanitation-working neighbor with a
wife and kid and back rent hanging over their collective heads
like the ghost of Christmas future

fights solidly, drunkenly this week
for two impressive hours,
at the end of which time
they spill onto the matrimonial sidewalk,

dishing it out like this for love:

Leave goddamn you.
Leave.
Just take the baby seat and go. Leave.
I'm not your psychiatrist,
I can't help you with your problems and I'm sick
and you're sick
and I'm sick of you. Meanwhile

nothing in this scene is unequivocal.
The wife weeps and curses, throwing sucker punches.
The baby on the lawn

weeps and howls,
butting his head against a geranium.
And the baby's car seat, for god's sake,

lofted like the very torch of liberty itself
in the husband's arms,
to light the trees—then all of Bakman Avenue if he could.
A mighty conflagration to end
and start things
over again,

back before the high school prom ball spins too many mirrors
over their dopey, lovestruck heads;

before their nosey neighbor
(a stock character in these situation comedies)
puts her finger to the dial
and calls the cops.

*

Wait. Let me start again.
My father was a sociologist.
My mother a housewife stranded in the desert
without a canteen
if you take my meaning—

five babies in eleven years, very little money.

Not that happiness didn't exist for us sometimes
the way it did for the Petries
in black and white,
                    Rob, Laura, their son,
Little-Pretty-What's-His-Name. No,
we had our moments,

our birthday parties and bocci on the lawn.
Our trip to Disneyland.
Our trip to Gettysburg.

But when Laura (Rob's due
home any minute. Quick, Milly, help . . .)

gave rise to a self-inflating life raft, huge, forbidden to her
    in her front hall closet
in New Rochelle,
in a place that was also a time and a lack, a pressing need,

we called it an *episode.*
We knew for her there would be
no real rancor,
and no fists raised

beyond the sweet vulgarity of working things out for laughs
until next week
on TV.

*

Or never.
Look, it's no one's fault; I can buy that.
Our noses flagged,
we were neither charming nor photogenic by the 1970s—
my prolix, super unsubtle American family
pushing against itself like a live birth in the canal, cramped, uncertain,

angry, dropping down and down without a camera crew
or a script in sight.
What did Walter Cronkite say
when the war I grew up with
ended?
No end at the light of the tunnel?

Something like that.
And there wasn't a light or a life raft for years.

No wonder we'd long since
grown bored with television.
Petulant or high on sleazy
Moroccan hash, my brothers and I had spun from sitcom to soap opera,

from game show host to moon shot
to assassination
and back again, but O the moon shots!
Those men weren't heroes; they were straight-arrow, uxorious types,

frolicking in their magic lunar vehicles
as though at some deluxe
country club—segregated, of course.
No wives or children allowed! And in that context

doesn't playing golf up there
make a lot of sense?

Low gravity, high density:

no need to plant our flag too deeply. Who'd want
to claim such a creepy place?
Let alone kill to breathe there.

      And the golf ball
hung like a word yet unspoken
for how many years?

  *

Don't look at me like that.
Violence, I have asked myself these questions
as a member of what family, what country,
what honor of blood to blame it on?

My father was a sociologist,
my mother an *agent provacateur* with a nervous habit of M&M peanuts
and staying up late all hours
in her splendid isolation,
for the purpose of taking notes, i.e., What
Jack Parr said.
Why Ed McMahon's teeth looked better
when he was wearing plaids,
why a certain starlet seemed despondent. Personally,

I was sleeping
vouchsafed in the heart of it all,
more abstract than any sleeping child.
Twenty-five years later,
I still can't find my face
in these two-way mirrors I've watched
like a burned out, brainlocked Saint Teresa, waiting for a sign.

*

Here's a scene
from a movie I never saw on the all night
cable movie classics station:

Barbara Stanwyck
learning she's been framed, or at least suspicious,

reaches for a hankie but this time
gets a good idea, a hand grenade! instead. Catch this, she says.
America,
don't look at me like that.
The dust may never settle.

Robin Becker ～

A History of Sexual Preference

We are walking our very public attraction
through eighteenth-century Philadelphia.
I am simultaneously butch girlfriend
and suburban child on a school trip,
Independence Hall, 1775, home
to the Second Continental Congress.
Although she is wearing her leather jacket,
although we have made love for the first time
in a hotel room on Rittenhouse Square,
I am preparing my teenage escape from Philadelphia,
from Elfreth's Alley, the oldest continuously occupied
residential street in the nation,
from Carpenters' Hall, from Congress Hall,
from Graff House where the young Thomas
Jefferson lived, summer of 1776. In my starched shirt
and waistcoat, in my leggings and buckled shoes,
in postmodern drag, as a young eighteenth-century statesman,
I am seventeen and tired of fighting for freedom

and the rights of men. I am already dreaming of Boston—
city of women, demonstrations, and revolution
on a grand and personal scale.
                          Then the maître d'
is pulling out our chairs for brunch, we have the
surprised look of people who have been kissing
and now find themselves dressed and dining
in a Locust Street townhouse turned café,
who do not know one another very well, who continue
with optimism to pursue relationship. *Eternity*
may simply be our mortal default mechanism
set on *hope* despite all evidence. In this mood,
I roll up my shirtsleeves and she touches my elbow.
I refuse the seedy view from the hotel window.
I picture instead their silver inkstands,
the hoopskirt factory on Arch Street,
the Wireworks, their eighteenth-century herb gardens,
their nineteenth-century row houses restored
with period door knockers.
Step outside.
We have been deeded the largest landscaped space
within a city anywhere in the world. In Fairmount Park,
on horseback, among the ancient ginkgoes, oaks, persimmons,
and magnolias, we are seventeen and imperishable, cutting classes
May of our senior year. And I am happy as the young
Tom Jefferson, unbuttoning my collar, imagining his power,
considering my healthy body, how I might use it in the service
of the country of my pleasure.

The Crypto-Jews

This summer, reading the history of the Jews of Spain,
I learned Fra Alfonso listed "holding philosophical discussions"
as a Jewish crime. I think of the loud fights
between me and my father when he would scream that only a Jew
could love another Jew. I love the sad proud history
of expulsion and wandering, the Moorish synagogue walled
in the Venetian ghetto, persistence of study and text.
If we are the old Christ-killers on the handles of walking sticks,

we've walked the earth as calves, owls, and scorpions.
In New Mexico, the descendants of Spanish *conversos* come forth
to confess: tombstones in the yard carved with Stars of David,
no milk with meat, generations raised without pork.
What could it mean, this Hebrew script,
in grandmother's Catholic hand? Oh, New World, we drift
from eviction to eviction, go underground,
emerge in a bark on a canal, minister to kings, adapt to extreme
weather, peddle our goods and die into the future.

Late Words for My Sister

You did not want to remember
    with me how he raged up the stairs
        unbuckling the black leather

strap we called *the belt*.
    How our four thin legs danced
        up and down on the bed like

the jointed limbs of marionettes
    while the burning lariat of his anger
        seared our legs; how his face blazed and his eyes

glowed as he took the whip back in a tight
    circle to strike again. And again. We begged him to stop.
        Remember? And when he relented, panting like an animal

that has run a great distance, he paused, and we could see
    the sweat on his lip and under his arms. He hung there,
        his bulk suspended from his shoulders

by a power greater than he, and as we crept past him
    he slapped me, hard across the face, sparing you
        that humiliation

because you were weak and the youngest
    and had only followed my example into evildoing.
        I tried to make myself small, to pass him, or no,

I'm remembering wrong. Maybe I sneered. Maybe
    I had not yet learned to cower before the bully,
        to bare my neck, to admit when I had lost.

How surprised you would be to see him now,
    an old man checking the price
        of milk at the supermarket against

the price in his head. The difference
    is a conundrum, a fracture in continuity,
        the way his daughters broke from his plan.

Dog-God

To the railroad tracks at the bottom of summer
where weeds flourished, I return.

Flat-chested girl in a soiled T-shirt, I liked
the gully's privacy and the rank smell there

where I found dimes flattened by trains and milky
marbles, and once a rusty knife.

I must have reached for a trinket
in the grass when the collie's narrow muzzle

came close, the tricolored wedge of her head a foreign flag.
My first thought—*I have to return her*—I pushed aside

and stood still so she would stay and I could touch
the rich black hair that shone on her. She didn't run away.

To test her, I jogged up the hill and she followed, friendly,
like the TV dog, and when she sat, I sat, flushed with my amazing

luck, and wondering how long it might last, the whole
summer, maybe. I stroked her white breast and said *Scotland* out loud.

She cocked her head as if I'd conjured, with a charm, her name
or home, or a place we'd visit that afternoon. At a stream,

she drank, and the sound of her lapping excited a new desire
to master what is beautiful and guileless and mute.

Erin Belieu ～

Erections

When first described imperfectly
by my shy mother, I tried to leap

from the moving
car. A response,

I suspect, of not
just terror (although

a kind of terror continues to play
its part), but also a mimetic gesture,

the expression equal
to a body's system of absurd

jokes and dirty stories.
With cockeyed breasts

peculiar as distant cousins,
and already the butt of the body's

frat-boy humor,
I'd begun to pack

a bag, would set off
soon for my separate

country. Now, sometimes,
I admire the surprised engineering:

how a man's body can rise,
squaring off with the weight

of gravity, single-minded,
exposed as the blind

in traffic. It's the body leaping
that I praise, vulnerable

in empty space.
It's mapping the empty

space; a man's life driving
down a foreign road.

Your Character Is Your Destiny

      but I'm driving:
to where the prairie sulks
like an ex-husband, pissing
away his downtime in a day-old
shave, the permanent arrangement
this sky moved out on years ago.

You're in my jurisdiction,
the territory that makes old men
look older than their unpolished boots;
where only truckers get by, cranked
on speedballs and shooting up what passes
for an incline; where dead-eyed ranch
dogs drink oil from a roadside pool,

sick in the kind of viscous heat that will
fuck you without asking, and
whenever it feels the need.
You're straight out of my town's

post office, not the face on
the flyer but the blank propped up
behind him. You're the new stoplight,

the red direction from nowhere,
the signal I want to run.

Choose Your Garden

When we decided on the Japanese,
forgoing the Victorian, its Hester
Prynne-ish air of hardly mastered urges,

I thought it would be peaceful.
I thought it would relax my nerves,

which these days curl like cheap gift wrap:
my hands spelling their obsessions, a nervous
tic, to wring the unspeakable from
a silent alphabet.

I thought it would be like heaven: stern,
very clean, virtuous and a little dull—

but we had to cross the bridge to enter
and in the crossing came upon a slaughter
of camellias, a velvet mass-decapitation
floating on the artificial lake,

where, beneath its placid surface, a school
of bloated goldfish frenzied, O-ing
their weightless urgency
with mouths too exact to bear:
    O My Beloved,
they said to the snowy
petals and to the pink petals soft as
wet fingers,
    O Benevolent Master,

they said, looking straight up at us
where we stood near the entrance, near
the teahouse half-hidden in a copse of ginkgo,

where even now, discreetly and behind
its paper windows, a woman sinks down
on all fours, having loosened the knot
at the waist of her robe.

Lovely

Not the epithet
for an aging man,

like this man,

now climbing a staircase
into December light,
the sun lapsing

through him like a curator's
X ray unearthing
a recycled canvas,

the early figure loosened from
his body's ruined fresco—

but he is: Lovely,

sobriquet given for certain
girls sleepwalking their foggy
cusp, dozing the wet rim
of beauty's unconsciousness;

madrigal of contraries
containing both the clean bell
of birdsong and the bow's

dry tongue dragging
low along the cello's hip.

It's there in the join, where
a man's thigh meets
the ass's curve, raw as the rose's

puckered labia, his private
a cappella unfurling.

Linda Bierds ~

Vespertilio

Julia Margaret Cameron

Like winter fog, the coal dust climbs her stockings,
although the coal itself has long departed, tumbled
barrow by barrow to an alternate shelter.
She scrubs the floor, sets across the gaping boards
square vats of rank collodion, of alcohol
and pyrogallol. Still the coal dust blooms,
until her apron darkens and her hem-strokes
brush to the path's pale stones

a soft hieroglyphics. She has walked
to the glass henhouse and bundles the hens
to their new roost, one wing at her breast, one wing
in her hand, the stiff legs riding her forearm.
Their livingness, she says, touching
a wattle and ruby comb, the tepid feet that stretch,
then curl, like something from the sea.

So the coalshed becomes her darkroom
and the henhouse welcomes the bent Carlyle,
Darwin and Tennyson, Browning, Longfellow,

each posed near a curtained backdrop, each
sharp in his livingness: a glaze on amber earwax,
a leaf of tobacco like ash on the beard.
But the portraits . . . Unfocussed, critics say. The lens
stepping down into fog. Aberrant. Distorted. Although
she prefers Undefined, as in Not yet captured

by the language of this world. They are rich
with the inner, she answers, with a glimpse of the soul
flapping up through collodion baths,

darkly transparent, like the great bats
that flap near the henhouse windows. She watches them
break at dusk past the tree line
then flash at the windows and flash, as if
they are seeking their lost counterparts—although
they are not birds, of course, but dense with wings,
so dense the sleek, half-opened wings

would cover a wattle, a comb, and opening, easily
cover the back, the breast,
and easily opening cover the tail,
the yellow, tepid, stretching feet: like
a dark sea spreads over its garden.

Lawrence and Edison in New Jersey: 1923

"Like a plum!" Lawrence says. "Frieda in anger
is a burst plum. Taut skin, the mouth's lolling gash.
Her face. And the simpering rains of Mexico."
But Edison, deaf, hears "heckles so," and "Isn't that true,"
he replies, "the public, the heckling swarms."

They are walking past blossoms of lupine and aster,
the aquatic stray of a weathered stump.
It is sunset, their shadows edemic
on the pathway before them. "That stump,"
Lawrence says, "its snout-crust of barnacle lichen
holds the backward grin of the blue whale."

"Yes the platinum spin of the fuel," sings the elder—
"the current's coil—then a carboned thread
glowing for hours." And so they continue, man
of the flesh, man of the mind: luster and circuit,
ripple and system. Past cattle, grain troughs,

then out toward a withered pond, Lawrence bobbing
near Edison's ear, its unwavering tangent of lobe crease.
At the water's frayed edge, they sit, Lawrence
lost to the ponds of his childhood—black mouths
in the fields like mineworks—Edison courting
the consummate marriage—motion and sound—

That the cantering profile of Muybridge's dobbin, he thinks,
might snortle and whinney! He smiles, leisurely
stabs at his dead ear. *Phono. Graph.* A little wax
gleams in the whorls of his thumb tip.
The head in deafness is a black pond, some occasional
wash-strokes of fin. He straightens, then:

"You might talk on my knee with the Morse code."
But Lawrence, distracted, hears "harsh cold"
and quickly the pond gels, the bodies of skaters stroke
in unison, as their scarves in unison
lift with their scarf-shaped breath. "We would circle
together as one," he says. "Round and around."

"Yes, round and around it spins, the disc
with its captured world. And the stylus—Lawrence!—
it glides on the wax like a blade."

Depth of Field

Specula. Gauze in a halo of disinfectant.
We sit in the small room, dimmed
by the x-ray of my father's chest
and the screen's anemic light. Because on film
the spots are dark, my mother asks
if, in the lung, they might be white: some

hopeless sense of the benign. My father smiles.
Outside the window, a winter storm
continues. Across the park, the bronze-cast generals
spur their anguished horses, each posture
fierce with rearing. Nostrils, lips, the lidless eyes.
Now all the flung-back heads have filled with snow.

After-Image

Three weeks past my father's death
his surgeons, in pond-green smocks, linger,
trail after me from dream to porch, down
the bark and needle pathway toward the river.
One nudges me, explains, as he did weeks ago,
the eye's propensity for opposites, why green
displaced their bleached-white coats. "Looking up
from the tablet of a patient's blood," he says,
"the red-filled retina will cast a green
on every white it crosses." A phantom wash
on a neighboring sleeve. "It startles us,"
he tells me. And: "Green absorbs the ghosting."
                                    Then he is gone, the path
returning to boot brush and the squirrel ratchets
my father loved. It is noon, the sky
through the tree limbs a sunless white.
I have come to watch the spawning salmon
stalled in the shallow pools. Age
has burned them a smoky red, though
their heads are silver, like helmets. Just over
the mossy floor, they float unsupported,
or supported by air their gills have winnowed.
I think I will gather them soon, deep
in the eye, red and red and red,
then turn to the canopy of sky and cedars.
It will support them soon, the green.

Chana Bloch ∼

Act One

Hedda Gabler is lighting the lamps in a fury.
From the front row center
we see the makeup streaking her neck
little tassels of sweat
that stain her bodice. She says *Yes* to Tesman
and it's like spitting.

We are just-married,
feeling lucky. Between the acts
we stop to admire ourselves in the lobby mirror.

But Hedda—how misery
curdles her face!
She opens the letters with a knife
and her husband stands there
shuffling, the obliging child
waiting to be loved.

Yes, she says, fluffing the pillows
on the sofa, *yes dear,* stoking
the fire. And Tesman smiles. A shudder
jolts through her body to
lodge in mine, and
     oh yes, I can feel that
blurt of knowledge
no bride should know.

How the Last Act Begins

*The trouble with you is you're not
loving enough.* A drastic

summons, a trumpet of
hard last words.

I'm dry as a biscuit
but somehow a breast of mine
stiffens, unbuttons
and offers itself. Is that
what you want?

Now your body's in bed again, crying
that it can't fall asleep.
I forget what to feel, but I'll do
what I'm trained to do:
go barefoot, make the children
take off their shoes. You require
absolute silence.

The mind thinks "lemon" and the tongue
puckers. But what about the woman
who painted a tiger on the wall so real
it scared her out of the house?

I'm not making this up:
the three of us on tiptoe, the shades
down, the house darkened, and you
center-stage, wearing
that shiny black satin eye-mask.

Puzzle Pieces

1

Sunlight in the alleys. There is always a window
to look out of. Barefoot,
in a half-slip, hair uncombed,
I stare at the buildings of red and brown brick,
the scaffolds abandoned for the weekend.

Before spring conceals them
the twig-ends of the tree are
knobby as grapestalks, fibrous, tensile.

And I never told you that—
was the way he started.
Then he looked away.

The seep of sunlight through the dusty blinds
is also a mooring.

2

I am threading silver filigree
through the squint of an earlobe.

Tickets, blue suitcase, phone number
scrawled on an envelope,
and through the window, two ladders
facing away from each other,
each casting a shadow on the sunlit wall.

If we'd gotten to the movies that night and if
his mother hadn't died and if the children
would only pipe down—

Stuck in the doorway, he waits,
a head on a stick of metal
on a block of stone.

Michelle Boisseau ～

Fog

Here begin dreams of flight, the wallpaper
coasting past with the watery plains
of woodwork, the terrain of rug beneath you

like a gone planet. Here the land
of giants begins, our hands a waterfall
of touch, our bodies looming in fog

the trees launch into the nursery windows.
Licking at our heels, the fog follows us
down the stairs, sallies through the screen door

then rolls into the creek like a hedgehog.
5 a.m., you're flying in our arms,
your gaze fixed on the architecture

that is face, stanchion and roof,
portals you stare into: What are you?
Where have you come from?

—while all about us float the gritty
sands of dawn, a flecked light
like wild rice drifting in a pot,

nothing more and nothing less, and the work
of sorting it out—light and dark,
first and last. But the only baptism

we can give you is hardly ours
to give, the fog loosed from the hillsides
and dampening the whole still house.

—Cassiopeia at Noon

The gaze is no longer leveled
at me. Just another aspect
of landscape, I am round and bluff
as the antediluvian hills
across the lake, anonymous
as this water maple, our compass
of shade and dry towels.

Now I see how I have hurried
from doorway to doorway
like someone caught in a downpour.
Since I was 12 it was duck and cover,
Chica, Chica, Catholic girl
hugging books across her chest.
Under surveillance.

It's easy here in obscurity,
room to stretch my sand-smeared legs,
let my suit gape where it will,
unwind the generic gray hairs
like roads out of town:
so long, so long.
Soon, I shall be invisible—

Sleeplessness:

These sibilants aren't the right sound
for it, nor the loosening sonorants

of *insomnia*. The body
doesn't relinquish the day, hissing

as it gives itself over, breath
by deeper breath. Though you wander

the weird factory for hours,
you don't get lost, drop off somewhere

so you can find yourself at dawn
floating back into your bed

like a scarf. Without sleep, morning
is no surprise. You've watched it assemble,

the day already old when you kick
the blanket off. You're the same except

giving the drapery a jerk, how skittery you are.
Awake all night means, once again,

you left everything wide open.
Look around your feet. Marbles clacking

in a box, the room has filled with grackles.
Their tin feet scritch across the floor.

Because you would not sleep, you asked for it.
They fix you with yellow eyes.

Their whir and chack make sense to you.

Catherine Bowman ~

Demographics

They don't want to stop. They can't stop.
    They've been going at it for days now,
for hours, for months, for years. He's on top
    of her. She's on top of him. He's licking
her between the legs. Her fingers
    are in his mouth. It's November.
It's March. It's July and there are palms.
    Palms and humidity. It's the same man.
It's a different man. It's August and slabs
    of heat waves wallow on tarred lots.
Tornadoes sprawl across open plains.
    Temperatures rise. Rains accumulate.
Somewhere a thunderstorm dies. Somewhere
    a snow falls, colored by the red dust
of a desert. She spreads her legs. His lips
    suck her nipples. She smells his neck.
It's morning. It's night. It's noon.
    It's this year. It's last year. It's 4 A.M.
It started when the city shifted growth

to the north, over the underground
water supply. Now the back roads are gone
   where they would drive, the deer glaring into
the headlights, Wetmore and Thousand Oaks,
   the ranch roads that led to the hill country
and to a trio of deep moving rivers.
   There were low water crossings. Flood gauges.
Signs for falling rock. There were deer blinds
   for sale. There was cedar in the air.
Her hands are on his hips. He's pushing
   her up and down. There are so many things
she's forgotten. The names of trees. Wars.
   Recipes. The trench graves filled with hundreds.
Was it Bolivia? Argentina? Chile?
   Was it white gladioli that decorated the altar
where wedding vows were said? There was
   a dance floor. Tejano classics.
A motel. A shattered mirror. Flies.
   A Sunbelt sixteen-wheeler. Dairy Queens.
Gas stations. The smell of piss and cement.
   There was a field of corn, or was it cotton?
There were yellow trains and silver silos.
   They can't stop. They don't want to stop.
It's Spring, and five billion inhale
   and exhale across two hemispheres. Oceans
form currents and counter currents.
   There was grassland. There was sugarcane.
There were oxen. Metallic ores.
   There was timber. Fur-bearing animals.
Rice lands. Industry. Tundra. Winds
   cool the earth's surface. Thighs press
against thighs. Levels of water fluctuate.
   And yesterday a lightning bolt reached
a temperature hotter than the sun.

From The El Paso Times "World of Women"

The bride wore a gown
of ivory satin.

On the figurine bodice
an appliquéd yoke
of imported lace.
The bouffant skirt extended
into a cathedral train.
The veil caught
to a petal-point crown.

The bridal attendants were in jewel-toned
waltz-length gowns of taffeta.
Their tiny hats matched.

The mother of the bride
chose a bronze sheath
and one gold orchid.
Her hat was of black feathers
with black accessories.

The mother of the groom
wore a peacock blue frock.
Her accessories were white,
her corsage—gardenias.

Heart

Old fang in the boot trick. Five chambered
asp. Pit organ and puff
adder. Can live in any medium
save ice. The stuff of sin and legend.
Charmed by Dolphy's flute or the first thunderstorm
in Spring, drowsy, it stirs from the cistern, the hibernaculum,
the wintering den of roots and stars. Smells
like the cucumber
Aunt Doris served chilled with Saltines
on chipped Blue Willow.
She grew clings, sugars, snaps, and strings
and had chiffon breasts
we called pillows
and bird legs and itty-bitty fat fingers

covered with diamonds from the mines in South Africa.
The smell of cucumber. Her mystery roses.

Light of all stars.
Heading out Old Bandera to picnic and pick corn
the light so expert that for miles
you can tell a turkey vulture
from a hawk by the quiver in the wing.
Uncle Pete born on April Fools, died on Ground Hogs,
pulls over not to piss but to blow away
any King or Diamondback unlucky enough to be
on the road between San Antonio and Cotulla.

Some men can't stand mystery, know what I mean?

Squinting from the back of the pick-up
into chrome and sun and shotgun confection,
my five boy cousins who love me more
than all of Texas and drink my spit
from a bottle of Big Red on a regular basis, know
what old Pete and his bejeweled bride
and the maid Carmen, the only adult
in the house not drunk after sunset,
have long since forgotten.

And that is. Snakes don't die.
They just play dead. That the heart
exposed to so many scrapes,
bruises, burns, and bites sheds its skin,
sprouts wings and flies, becomes the two-
for-one sparkler on the 4th of July,
becomes what's slung between
azure and cornfield: the horizon.
If you don't believe it
place your right hand on it
for the Pledge
like you've been taught.

Feel the hearing so deep.
Limbless and near limbless.
Prefers the ambush to the hunt.
Sets a trap, picks a spot, begins the vigil.

Resorts at times to bluff and temper.
Swallows vicitims whole.
Tastes like hope, forgiveness, and memory.
Tastes like chicken.

Lucie Brock-Broido ～

Her Habit

February

Master—

Because I was in the habit of you & because I have an ardor for the lie, *I cannot speak until I know.*

I have watched for you up & down the long clay path, demi-daily. Sometimes I think I hear you in the solemn bark of birds, or the cantering of dogs as they bring home their quarry—gently—in their mouths, no pierced skin, no feathers askew, only the unbruised slant of a neck broken by fear, limp now & perfect in the fluidity of damaged Form.

Have I told you I have quit taking any meats whatsoever? A mortal signal, a deference to form, it is to me a form of Prayer. *I got a bad whim.*

In truth, I have innumerable habits; I was a-Bed today. My world is as ordered as if—as if I had stacked the stars in the nightsky's orchard, senseless as crates of fish stacked glimmering, one-eyed & blank, one atop the other of them, cold as Rome apples or a new moon.

To all except great dread, the heart adjusts.

I do not let go it, because it is—
Mine

Prescient

Master—you were having your veins cleaned out of Me—
A burred spike down the artery's shaft, thistling.

You have the catchweed of quiet on your tongue, I have
The power of speech. Parts of the body will always live

By the lair—by November the pine boughs will corrugate my
Yard. A shock of Needles shook loose from their limb & I live

In a burgeon of nettles, in an emergency of old leaves from
The absurd magnolia which grew so hard to bloom

Twice this year & Failed, sterile
As a divination based on wish & wish & wish.

Forecast—Nothing ever felt like This.
Forecast—Hound Dog.

Forecast—The Incidents may presage war.
Forecast—I am my love—*a Lucky girl.*

Housekeeping

After the Zhivago of it all, the terrible sleeve
Of ice, cataracted, relentless am I now to weave

You through a season of small thaw, am I to hire
The grappling hooks to fish the winter's

Missing implements from the river's whipstitched
Seams, my self a beckoned pharos as I light the switch

In your corridor of kitchen dark. You have been outside
The body now. And the sled cuts the snow one half

A world away, here—burden beasts are dead of it.
The hoary load, metalled spoons on leather strops, the cleft

Of blade—forgive me for how long it takes to mend
The tear in the body's tailored skin

Like the Siberian boy in autopsy
Stitched shut at last, & asymmetrically.

Olga Broumas ~

Lumens

There are no secrets
It's just we thought that they said dead
When they said bread
    JOHN CAGE

OH LORD
I love when you take over
Her eyes and pierce me with your sky

THE KNIFE
Love of life
I promise to remember you

Each time we meet is the last

THE BIRD
To make poetry's possible
At home even briefly in the human wild

EACH LOVE
Parallel
Infinite
Unequal

NIRVANA STAIR
I come from small seas littered with
Playful islands

Feel how my heart is shaped
By that sheltering

CUSP
When you touched me
taking all that time
an ancient
and consecrated city
in orbit for centuries
found its dome

TATTOO
A child is a lonely thing to put in prison
Without a lover lonely in its parents' care

BRIDGE
A song unhinges bitterness easy enough from sorrow
Some vowel litany with stops to pass until
The most ordinary is not

AFTER YES
To build the chair
To build the chair
To build the chair
To sit
To sit
Witness the mystery
World

PRIVACY
Finally
    the only one I want
        to caress is you

You watch the changing
    light across the sky
        I watch your eyes

TEACUP

Flared at the lip like clematis
One swallow
Raised bottom where the sugar sleeps

FLORIDIAN

It's not just that you're wet but that you're swollen
Ocean where for me you dip

THE SEPARATION

Where desert boulders cleave: two stars
Small in the V, large up above

Where last I slept with you the tide
Eases the mark

DEVOTEE

I am grooming the body and rays of the sun
That will rise on the day you return

THE RETURN

As when setting a candle
In the molten wax of the one burnt low
In the hot candelabra

THE CROWNING

Baby, I call you, you
In me as if

INTERVAL

Two months since I sucked your nipple first
Eggplant purple then fig blue the taste
Drawn from your inner body lingers

CHASTE

Asleep
Mouth to mouth
For an hour

EVE TO GOD'S BACK

Leave me the snake
It is the you before the screen while you are gone

SELFISH
It's true musicians please
The public with their pleasure, but we
Eschew the stage

NIGHT AND LIGHT
Because your hand is my hand and my eye
And taste and smell and spirit I am I

THE PEACEFUL FIST
I said inside the small
Cathedral of my cunt eleven years before
That awning
Rose round the folded altar of your palm

PERPETUA
As the seed of a mole for
Generations carried across
Time on a woman's belly
Flowers one morning blackly
Exposed to poison and poison
Itself is not
Disease but mutation is one
Understanding the strong
Shaft of your clitoris I kiss
As the exposed tip of your
Heart is another

Photo Genic

I AM SINGLE AND I AM JUST

GODS TOUCH ME

I STAND IN THE WINDOW A LONG TIME

NO ONE CLOSES IT

MOTHER BREAKS THE GERANIUMS ALL DAY

THEN SHE SETS THEM IN WATER

UNDER THEIR TABLE IT'S NIGHT

ONLY GOD TOUCHED ME

I DON'T MOVE BUT I'M SWIMMING

I AM INVISIBLE BY THE EMPTY SILL

WHERE GOD'S SUNLIGHT ADORES ME

MOTHER UNDRESSES MY SHADOW

ITS ARMS ARE LONG

THEN ITS LEGS LEAVE MY FEET AND FOLLOW

I STAND IN GOD'S ARMS FOREVER

SHE SHUTS THE DOOR TO MY BEDROOM

I CRAWL OUT THE WINDOW

JULY

Teresa Cader ~

Spirit Papers

While her husband spent his afternoons napping
on the terrace, or vomiting into a spittoon,
Madame Chung visited the paper shops.

A lavender lotus blossom tea set,
two white horses pulling a red chariot,
black robes with gold fire-dragons,

how hard she worked to find them.
Was her husband not worth hours on foot
and the last of her marriage gold?

At the shop of the famous Tien Chi
she ordered an effigy of her husband's dog
and a likeness of herself, smiling.

She ministered to her husband
as spring rains closed the paper shops.
Then his breath became a dried leaf.

"Please serve my husband's tea hot,"
she wrote on the paper tea tray
she placed in front of his coffin.

She lit a torch beneath the dog's jowl.
The dog burst into flame, its head popped.
Smoke circled in black saucers.

Madame Chung watched the white horses
gallop into the sky to meet her husband,
who rose from his chair to greet them.

Empress Shōtoku Invents Printing in 770

Smallpox, insurrection. Was her kingdom not ravaged enough already?
Had the gods of disfigurement not been appeased?

She would not abide, she would not acknowledge impediment.

The priests' advice to order prayer in all the village temples
was enough to excite her mind to invention:

She would construct a million tiny pagodas,
commission architects of the written word

to print dhāranī for each of them
to ward off the demons of disease and war.

Amplified, repeated, the prayers would reach
the ears of Buddha in unison,

so that the loneliness of one priest praying,
the vulnerability of one prayer floating in black ink,

the unpredictability of a scrap of paper against a universe
of rain and wind and wayward candle flame,

might be fashioned into mystical choruses
rising into the air with simultaneous intention.

She would pray for her invention, she would give her priests the vision
to see multiplicity, to make a stone, a block, a metal sheet

empowered to copy whole prayers in rapid succession
like the singing of the stars, the flutter of bamboo leaves.

Were a million dhāranī not a million times more powerful?

And her private prayer, her wish for immortality,
would it not ascend on a million whispering tongues?

Marilyn Chin ⌒

Composed Near the Bay Bridge

(after a wild party)

1)
Amerigo has his finger on the pulse of China.
He, Amerigo, is dressed profoundly punk:
Mohawk-pate, spiked dog collar, black leather thighs.
She, China, freshly hennaed and boaed, is intrigued
with the new diaspora and the sexual freedom
called *bondage.* "Isn't *bondage,* therefore,
a *kind* of freedom?" she asks, wanly.

2)
Thank God there was no war tonight.
Headbent, Amerigo plucks his bad guitar.
The Sleeping Giant snores with her mouth agape,
while a lone nightingale trills on a tree.

Through the picture window, I watch the traffic
hone down to a quiver. Loneliness. Dawn.
A few geese winging south; minor officials return home.

Beijing Spring

Love, if I could give you the eternal summer sun
or China back her early ideological splendor, I would.
If I could hoist the dead horses back
and retrieve the wisdom charred by the pyres of Ch'in.
If I could give Mother the Hong Kong of her mulberry youth
and Father the answers that the ox desired,
they would still be together now and not
blame their sadness on the unyieldy earth.
If I had separated goose from gander, goose from gander,
the question of monogamy and breeding for life, the question
of the pure yellow seed would not enter.

This courtyard, this fortress,
this alluvium where the dead leave their faces—
each step I take erases the remnants of another,
each song I sing obfuscates the song of Changan,
ripples washing sand ripples washing sand ripples . . .
each poem I write conjures the dead washing-women of Loyang.

Lover, on Tiananmen Square, near the Avenue of Eternal Peace,
I believe in the passions of youth,
I believe in eternal spring.
As the white blossoms, sweet harbingers,
pull a wreath around the city,
as heaven spreads its blue indifference over
the bloodied quay, I want to hold you
against the soft silhouettes of my people.

Let me place my mouth over your mouth,
let me breathe life into your life,
let me summon the paired connubial geese
from the far reaches of the galaxy
to soar over the red spokes of the sun's slow chariot
and begin again.

Autumn Leaves

The dead piled up, thick, fragrant, on the fire escape.
My mother ordered me again, and again, to sweep it clean.
All that blooms must fall. I learned this not from the Tao,
    but from high school biology.

Oh, the contradictions of having a broom and not a dustpan!
I swept the leaves down, down through the iron grille
and let the dead rain over the Wong family's patio.

And it was Achilles Wong who completed the task.
    We called her:
The-one-who-cleared-away-another-family's-autumn.
She blossomed, tall, benevolent, notwithstanding.

Lucille Clifton ～

hag riding

why
is what i ask myself
maybe it is the afrikan in me
still trying to get home
after all these years
but when i wake to the heat of morning
galloping down the highway of my life

something hopeful rises in me
rises and runs me out into the road
and i lob my fierce thigh high
over the rump of the day and honey
i ride   i ride

blake

saw them glittering in the trees,
their quills erect among the leaves,
angels everywhere. we need new words
for what this is, this hunger entering our
loneliness like birds, stunning our eyes into rays
of hope. we need the flutter that can save
us, something that will swirl across the face
of what we have become and bring us grace.
back north, i sit again in my own home
dreaming of blake, searching the branches
for just one poem.

to michal

*Michal . . . looked through a window and saw
King David leaping and dancing before the
Lord; and she despised him in her heart.*
      II SAMUEL 6:16

moving and moaning
under our coverings
i could only guess
what women know
but wife
in the open arms of God
i became man and woman
filling and emptying
all at once

and oh the astonishment
of seed
dancing on the ground
as i leaped and turned
surrendering
not what i had withheld from you
but michal from myself.

what did she know, when did she know it

in the evenings
what it was the soft tap tap
into the room   the cold curve
of the sheet arced off
the fingers sliding in
and the hard clench against the wall
before and after
all the cold air   cold edges
why the little girl never smiled
they are supposed to know everything
our mothers   what did she know
when did she know it

Judith Ortiz Cofer ~

Photographs of My Father

On my walls there are three
photographs of my father.
In one he is a young recruit
standing *at ease,*
third from the left
with his platoon.
In another he has rank

on his cap—a formal
pose in a studio,
intended for his mother.
In the last, a blowup
from my mother's wallet
taken by a machine
in a foreign port, he is
a melancholy petty officer
in navy blues. Hazy
like a ghost sighting,
creased from her handling,
it is my favorite.

These are the survivors
from a day of fury. One morning
in my childhood, on his way
out to sea, he had sat
alone in the living room,
and without hurry, with care,
cut himself out of our family.
Book after book.
I watched him work
from my room, knowing
his actions were prelude
or aftermath to family strife.
My mother in the kitchen
holding her coffee cup
with both hands, also waited.

On the floor
my father's image lay
like peelings from an apple.
In his hands the scissors glinted
at the eye and snapped
like a live thing.

Nothing more. Just picture albums
shameful as a vandalized church,
never seen by me again. And years
after his death, my need to find
his face revealed in innocence,
unguarded, as I never knew it.

This vulnerable young man, this face
that fills me with grief and longing.
I am trying to believe in this boy.

Letter from Home in Spanish

She writes to me as if we still shared
the same language. The page
a laden sky, filled with flying letters
suspended just above the lines
like blackbirds on the horizon;
the accents—something smaller
they are pursuing.

     She says:
"after a lifetime of tending to people,
our vieja is obsessed
with useless endeavors—raising fat hens
she refuses to eat, letting them live
until their feathers droop and drag
on the dirt, like the hems
of slovenly women.

   "Listen,"
she writes, forgetting that the words
cannot pull me by the elbow, "she will not pick
the roses she grows, so that walking
through her garden is like following a prostitute—
the smell chokes you; makes you
want to loosen your dress.

    "She fills her house with old things:
baby pictures she misnames, mistaking me
for you; undoing the generations; yellowed ads
for beauty products and clothes; headlines
from the War; her last child's obituary—
the one who never tasted sugar,
then died of something simple.

"She has no use now
for those of us who survived. The other women
and I take turns at her side, but if we burn
a light in the dark rooms she prefers,
she covers her face as if ashamed.
If we dust the picture frames, she claims
we are trying to erase the past.

"But, basta. Enough for now."

I read her letter aloud, for the sound
of Spanish, and it becomes a kyrie,
a litany in a mass for the dead.
I take each vowel on my tongue.
La vieja brings tears to my eyes
like incense; *la muerte*
sticks in my throat like ashes.

Her blessing is a row of black crosses
on a white field.

from *Three Poems in Memory of Mamá (Grandmother)*

Cold as Heaven

Before there is a breeze again
before the cooling days of Lent, she may be gone.
My grandmother asks me to tell her
again about the snow.
We sit on her white bed
in this white room, while outside
the Caribbean sun winds up the world
like an old alarm clock. I tell her
about the enveloping blizzard I lived through

that made everything and everyone the same;
how we lost ourselves in drifts so tall
we fell through our own footprints;
how wrapped like mummies in layers of wool
that almost immobilized us, we could only
take hesitant steps like toddlers
toward food, warmth, shelter.
I talk winter real for her,
as she would once conjure for me to dream
at sweltering siesta time,
cool stone castles in lands far north.
Her eyes wander to the window,
to the teeming scene of children
pouring out of a yellow bus, then to the bottle
dripping minutes through a tube
into her veins. When her eyes return to me,
I can see she's waiting to hear more
about the purifying nature of ice,
how snow makes way for a body,
how you can make yourself an angel
by just lying down and waving your arms
as you do when you say
good-bye.

Martha Collins ～

The Border

Hasta luego and over you go and it's not
serapes, the big sombreros, not even coyotes,
rivers and hills, though that's more like it, towers
with guards, Stop! or we shoot and they do but you don't
need a border for that, a fence will do, a black
boy stuck to its wire like a leaf, a happy gun
in the thick pink hand that wags from the sleeve, even
a street, the other side, a door, a skin, give

me a hand, and she gives him a hand, she gives him both
her hands, the bones of her back are cracking, the string
has snapped, she's falling, she's pleated paper, paper
is spreading and there you are again, over
the edge, you open your hands and what have you got
but confetti and what can you do with confetti, our
side won, a celebration, shaken hands, it matters
now, whatever it is, but how close
you are, your street, the fence behind your house
is the zero border where minus begins, roots
turn branches, cellar is house, you close your busy
mouth to speak, an anti-lamp darkens
the day, and you love that street, its crazy traffic,
you climb that fence, you wave across, there's a rock
in your hand but it's not your fault, you like to travel,
the colorful people, but what if you fell, your house,
your children, the work that gets you up in the morning,
the language gone, the grammar, the rules, the family
talent, those searching eyes, but think of the absence
of eye, a higher tower, a little more wire—
Border? You crossed the border hours ago.

Lies

Anyone can get it wrong, laying low
when she ought to lie, but is it a lie
for her to say she laid him when we know
he wouldn't lie still long enough to let
her do it? A good lay is not a song,
not anymore; a good lie is something
else: lyrics, lines, what if you say *dear sister*
when you have no sister, what if you say *guns*
when you saw no guns, though you know
they're there? *She laid down her arms; she lay
down, her arms by her sides.* If we don't know,
do we lie if we say? If we don't say, do we lie
down on the job? To arms! in any case,
dear friends. If we must lie, let's not lie around.

Out of My Own Pocket

Light drifts from the stalled
Aegean ships to the bare table
where pages rise in a brief
breeze, then fall, opened
palms after a prayer.

What is required this time?
Paid my dues. Pain was referred
to another place. Point by point.
Settled in by the leaded window.
Wind out of my sails.

Then I considered the shape
I was in. Out of my own
pocket, I said, offering
pure air, all done with tiny
mirrors, sewn into the cloth.

Nothing now but to turn
the page, and then I hear *In my
book,* the voice not mine but
mine the slipping down
again, slope, shaft, strip, old

bones preserved, pressed
into the coal. Not the girl,
not even the wailing mother,
harbored rage trailing
the shimmering ships, and not

the ships or the whispering
sea, but a woman turning away
from the crowd, taking her keys
from her pocket, a woman
on her way, on her way home.

Like Her Body The World

hit and hit and hit and hit and fallen

getting up and trying to get up

now one part is hitting another part wounding its flesh

slicing its own veins breaking its bones

but wait we are coming help is on the way

now we are hitting the part that is hitting the part

now someone else is helping the part we hit

now it is arm against arm hand against hand

now it is eye against eye no one can see

now it is ear against ear there is no mouth

where is the up to get up to where is the body

where are the parts have the parts all fallen apart

we are part of the body we forgot

we thought we lived outside like a brain in a jar

we thought we were pure like thought with nothing to lose

but we are losing too we are losing parts

besides we were never that brain we were only a part

we thought we would never fall but we are falling

falling and falling and falling hitting the air

falling hitting ourself our own body

meanwhile the body the world will try to get up

or else the body the world will lie down will lie down

Jane Cooper ～

My Mother in Three Acts

At the top of the hill you were Muriel,
pale but still powerful as a Sumo wrestler,
generous, mother of mysteries held in reserve.
You were already dead then; I knew I couldn't save you.
In the nursery school room I began to rearrange
brightly colored clay figures: *la Sagrada Familia.*

Tripping down the hill you were Betty,
blond and still fashionable but too thin,
needling me, cosseting me. Dying of cancer
only sharpened your wit. I knew I couldn't save you—
I could barely even keep up! Mother of the quick retort,
of the enchanting story, mother of gifts and dissatisfactions.

At the bottom of the hill just as we reached the
house I had rented, I glimpsed a fugitive girl,
face turned aside toward the woods, slipping away
in a seagreen Japanese kimono; her hair was brown.
Was it you, mother of boyishness, mother of
deception, who saved me once, the one who evades me still?

Estrangement

You dream someone is leaving you, though he says kindly, *It's not
that you're cold*
or *After all you're an affectionate person.*

You can't explain how hard it is to explain or even to write this poem
so you blurt, *I was ashamed, they put me in the class for remedial speech.*

The doctor leans forward: *Do you feel you have failed me recently?*
The dream answers through you: *I am locked in a struggle with the*
   truth.

(I was ashamed, I couldn't speak, they voted me out of the shelter.
Like Rousseau's Sleeping Gypsy I lay exposed to the nuclear night
till a dog found my throat.)

You watch your own back growing smaller up the beach.

Hotel de Dream

Justice-keepers! justice-keepers!
   FOR MURIEL RUKEYSER AND JAMES WRIGHT

Suppose we could telephone the dead.
Muriel, I'd say, can you hear me?
Jim, can you talk again?

And I'd begin to tell them the stories they loved to hear:
how my father, as a young boy, watched Cora Crane
parade through the streets of Jacksonville with her girls
in an open barouche with silver fittings;
how the bay haunches gleamed as they twitched off flies,
polished hooves fetched down smartly into the dust,
ostrich feathers tickled the palates of passers-by.

Muriel, I'd say, shall we swing along Hudson Street
underneath the highway and walk out together on the docks?

. . . the river would be glittering, my grandmother
would be bargaining

with a black man on a dock in Jacksonville;
grapefruit and oranges would be piled up like cannonballs
at the fort in Old St. Augustine . . .

I'll never put you in a nursing home, you said early that year,
I promise, Jane, I'll never put you in a nursing home.

Later Cora Crane showed her dogs right next to my aunt's.
They had a good conversation about bloodlines
amidst the clean smells of kennel shavings and well-brushed dog
but never, of course, met socially
although she had dined with Henry James.

Jim, I'd say, remember that old poem "The Faithful"
you helped me by caring for? how what we owe to the dead
is to go on living? More than ever
I want to go on living.

But now you have become part of it, friends of my choosing years,
friends whose magnificent voices
will reverberate always, if only through machines,
tell me how to redress the past,
how to relish yet redress
my sensuous, precious, upper-class,
unjust white child's past.

Childhood in Jacksonville, Florida

What is happening to me now that loved faces
are beginning to float free of their names
like a tide of balloons, while a dark street
wide enough only for carriages, in a familiar city,
loses itself
to become South America?

Oh I am the last member of the nineteenth century!
And my excitement about sex, which was not of today,
is diffusing itself in generosity of mind.

For my mind is relaxing its grip, and a fume
of antique telephones, keys, fountain pens, torn roadmaps,
old stories of the way Nan Powell died
(*poor girl!*) rises in the air
detached but accurate—
almost as accurate
as if I'd invented them.

Welcome then, poverty!
flights of strings above the orange trees!

Kate Daniels ⁓

Prayer to the Muse of Ordinary Life

I seek it in the steamy odor
of the iron pressing cotton shirts
in the heat of a summer afternoon,
in my daughter's ear, the warm pink
cone, curling inward. I seek it
in the dusty circles of the ceiling fan,
the kitchen counter with its painted shells
from Hilton Head, the creaking boards
in the bedroom floor, the coconut
cookies in the blue glass jar.
The hard brown knob of nutmeg nestled
in the silver grater and the lemon
yogurt that awaits. I seek it not
in books but in my life inscribed
in two brief words—*mother, wife*
—the life I live as mistress of an unkempt
manse, volunteer at firstborn's
school, alternate Wednesdays'
aide at youngest's nursery, billpayer,
laundress, cook, shrewd purchaser of mid-
priced minivan. I seek it

in the strophes of a life
like this, wondering what
it could be like, its narratives
drawn from the nursery and playpen,
its images besmirched with vomitus
and shit. The prayer I pray is this:

If you are here,
where are you?
If you exist,
what are you?
I beg you
to reveal yourself.
I will not judge,
I am not fancy.
My days are filled
with wiping noses
and bathing bottoms,
with boiling pots
of cheese-filled pasta
for toothless mouths
while reading Rilke,
weeping.

My life is broken
into broken pieces.
The fabric is rent.
Daily, I roll
the stone away
but all is dark
inside, unchanged.
The miracle has not
happened yet.

If you are anywhere
nearby, show me
anything at all
to prove you do exist:
a poem in a small, soiled
nightie, a lyric
in the sandbox voices
raised in woe.

Release a stanza
from the sink's hot suds
where dirty dishes glow.
Seal a message inside:
encourage me
to hold on.
Inform me
in detail
exactly how to do it.

After Reading Reznikoff

When I think of those mothers giving up
their children at the gates of the camps,
or choosing one over the other, or accompanying
their youngsters to the showers of gas,
when I think of that wrenching, that
wailing, the force of those feelings,
the terrible potency, the fear breaking
their bodies in sweat and hives,
the vomiting and shitting, the mindless
lunging for their infants and toddlers,
their sons and their daughters, when I think of
that universe of last images, the eyes, the unspeakable
eyes of mothers comprehending, the backs
of the children waddling away, being led
away, being pulled away, recalcitrant curls,
fallen hems, toys dropped on the gravel paths,
the little waves, the dipped heads, the incessant
weeping, when I think of the bleeding wombs
of dying mothers, pleading mothers, the bellies
of mothers with unborn babies, the breasts bursting
with unsucked milk, when I think of the various
ways the weather must have been—the cold
crunch of snow, the flowery delight of early spring
—when I think of the camps and the deaths of the Jews,
the millions of Jews, I think of the mothers,
the bodies of the mothers, their bodies bearing

their children to death, I think of the noise
of transport trains, the terror of trains,
the engines cooling into inert steel,
the clatter and steam, the scenes enacted
in the railroad yards, and the trains remind me
to think of the men, at last I remember
those armies of men, their greatcoats and weapons,
no children inhabiting their rational bodies, the mystery
of murder, the bodies of the women so alive
with emotion, the bodies of the men so dead
to it all, I think not of God, desperately I try
to not think of God, my good, great God, neither
woman nor man, circling above in heartbroken panic,
the beating of wings, the cacophonous
suffering, the pungent cloud rising
of dark, dark feeling that silenced even Him.

Madeline DeFrees ～

In the Locker Room

                    I surprise the women
dressed in their bodies: in breasts,
knees, eyebrows, pubic
hair. Excitable children appear
to accept them. Pitted and fat, dazzling
and golden, the women
drowse under the shower, a preview of
bodies the children try on
with their eyes.

            At 65, I am less than
a child, whose mother walked
fearfully clothed, afraid of the water.
My grip on the towel gives me away. I move

into the pool suitably over my head
past my mother's responsible
daughter. Later, wild to learn, I practice
standing alone—only my underpants on—
under the gun
of the hair dryer.

           A queen-sized woman
sweetly accosts me, recommends
more clothes. Someone has pointed out
a peekaboo crack in the men's
locker room. "What a shame," she intones,
"such a nice clean
club." I loiter in my underwear
worn out with surveillance.
What we don't know
won't hurt us.

           Oh, but it does deprive us!
These ravenous mermaids
stripped to their scales, swim from
the framed reproductions, pale and diaphanous
planes engineered for unmistakable
languor. Something has changed
in the changing room where we step out of
lingerie meant for the fainting couch
and bring on the body in person.

In the middle of Priest Lake

           Sister Margaret Clare
ships the oars and takes off her veil,
her coif. Not long ago I was her high school student.
Her starched bandeau comes off, wind
riffles her hair. She runs her fingers through
a modified crew cut while I hesitate, eyes
half-closed, unwilling

                    to stare or look away.
"Take yours off," she says. "It feels great!" and
before I know it, I've unpinned the veil, loosened
the coif-strings, lifted the white band
for a sail. I salute the black and white headdress
blown from the mast
of my upraised arm, the freedom

                              I love unfurled
without warning. I'm a lifer committed to sunshine,
to ambient air
as suddenly knowing incurable need
I savor the small pleasure
given up—now given back—in the middle of this lake
miles from the difficult shore
Mother Superior holds fast.

Blueprints

From a long way off I can see the cross-
hatching. This anonymous man of the Plain
People of Lancaster County laid out

more than 100 barns, not depending on blueprints: *It's just a talent the Lord gave me.*
I can close my eyes and see the whole

structure sitting there. Sitting there,
alert for the whole structure, I count
33 question-mark forms under wide-brimmed hats

bent to a common task against the Prussian blue
blank of sky. My fingers trace a slow X
of suspenders, the unknown articles of risk

and faith in a landscape of minor mercies. *This*
one touched my heart, says the planner, asking
that his name be forgotten. The barn

belonged to a burned-out widow. People came from
miles around. The barn was raised again, clean
grain of the wood stood vertical, all knots

wrestled into a pattern. Translating this morning
the visual text into words, I ask that my name
be remembered, that the legend over my grave

be the planner's. *This one touched my heart.*

Toi Derricotte ～

Bookstore

I ask the clerk to show me children's books. I say,
"I'm buying something for my nephew, *Goodnight Moon.*
Are there others you can recommend?" She pulls down
six or seven and I stop her, "Any written by or for black folks?"
She looks as if she doesn't understand. Maybe she has never
heard the words *black folks* before. Maybe she thinks
I'm white and mean it as a put-down. Since I'm white-
looking, I better make it clear. "It's for my brother's son.
'black folks,' black people . . . you know . . . like *me!*"
As quickly as she can, she pulls books from the lower
shelves and loads my arms until the books are falling on the floor.
She wants me to know she's helpful. That her store has so many
to choose from, we couldn't load them in a van. "Thank you, thank you,
that's plenty!" For a moment, history shifts its burden
to *her* shoulders, and the names of the missing are clear.

Black Boys Play the Classics

The most popular "act" in
Penn Station

is the three black kids in ratty
sneakers & T-shirts playing
two violins and a cello—Brahms.
White men in business suits
have already dug into their pockets
as they pass and they toss in
a dollar or two without stopping.
Brown men in work-soiled khakis
stand with their mouths open,
arms crossed on their bellies
as if they themselves have always
wanted to attempt those bars.
One white boy, three, sits
cross-legged in front of his
idols—in ecstasy—
their slick, dark faces,
their thin, wiry arms,
who must begin to look
like angels!
Why does this trembling
pull us?
A: *Beneath the surface we are one.*
B: *Amazing! I did not think that they could speak this tongue.*

For Black Women Who Are Afraid

A black woman comes up to me at break in the writing
workshop and reads me her poem, but she says she
can't read it out loud because
there's a woman in a car on her way
to work and her hair is blowing in the breeze
and, since her hair is blowing, the woman must be
white, and she shouldn't write about a white woman
whose hair is blowing, because
maybe the black poets will think she wants to be
that woman and be mad at her and say she hates herself,
and maybe they won't let her explain
that she grew up in a white neighborhood
and it's not her fault, it's just what she sees.

But she has to be so careful. I tell her to write
the poem about being afraid to write,
and we stand for a long time like that,
respecting each other's silence.

For Sister Sue Ellen and Her Special Messenger

I thought you were without genitals, that nothing cracked you open and
    made you insatiable.
I thought the blood ran clear out of you like out of the side of Christ—
your body chalk dust, flaking ash,
burning in a yellow godlight;
your brain a seamless garment buried beneath your eyes.

Maybe it was God who taught you cruelty:
the black boy you made sit in his shit until it dried
had to stand up and say *pardon me sister pardon me class*
for the rest of eternity.

You could make a child stutter at her book.
You could make a child recognize his rot.
Perhaps you did it by ignoring, by letting be what had already happened.
A girl carried your words on paper.
Walking down the long corridor under huge stone statues,

what was she but a poor Irish factory worker's daughter
disappearing inside
the harrowing cleanliness and bright light?

Deborah Digges ～

Rough Music

This is how it's done.
The villagers surround the house,

beat pots and pans, beat shovels to drain spouts,
crowbars to shutters, rakes
raining rake tines on corrugated washtubs, or wire
whips, or pitchforks, or horseshoes.
At first they keep their distance
as if to wake you like blackbirds, though the birds
have long since fled, flown deep into the field.
And for a while you lie still, you stand it,
even smile up at your crimes
accompanying, each one, the sunrise stuttering across the ceiling
like the sounds within the sounds,
like lightning inside thrum-tink, woman-in-wood-shoes-fall-
down-wooden-stairs, like wrong-wrong inside rung-rung,
brick-smacking-brick housing ice-breaking-ice-
breaking-glass . . .
I mention this since this is what my dreams
are lately, rough music,
as if all the boys to women I have been, the muses, ghost-
girls and the shadows of the ancestors
circled my bed in their cheap accoutrements
and banged my silver spoons on iron skillets, moor
rock on moor rock, thrust yardsticks into the fans.
Though I wake and dress and try
to go about my day,
room to room to room they follow me.
By evening, believe me, I'd give back everything,
throw open my closets, pull out my drawers spilling my hoard
of dance cards, full for the afterlife,
but my ears are bleeding.
I'm trapped in the bell tower during wind,
or I'm the wind itself against the furious, unmetered,
anarchical applause of leaves late autumns
in the topmost branches.
Now the orchestra at once throws down its instruments.
The doors in the house of God tear off their hinges—
I'm the child's fist drumming its mother's back,
rock that hits the skull that silences the martyr,
or I'm the martyr's tongue cut out, fire inside fire,
clapper back to ore, ore into the mountain.
I'm gone, glad, empty, good
riddance, some shoulder to the sea, the likeness
of a wing, or the horizon, merely, that weird mirage, stone-

skipping moon, the night filled up with crows.
I clap my hands.
They scatter, scatter, fistful after
fistful of sand on water, desert for desert, far from here.

Akhmatova

So it had to be—
she doused the muse in kerosene, set her afire,
burned down the house of poetry.

It was a common kitchen stove.

She may have taken comfort in the warmth.

As for the cries of agony,
they would hereafter ghost the margins,
howl on in each cyrillic character omitted by decree—
"Dear Stalin, I have seen your way . . ."
"Dear Master, my poems belong to you now, to the state . . ."

since women are the most dispensable to tyrants.
Children can serve so beautifully as ransom.
They learn, besides, to carry any flag.
And men will die into a tortured beauty,
their broken arms laid straight against their sides,
their privates, even by their enemies, napkin-covered.

But women? Women are nothing.
They create the beast to know the depth of their desire.

They are like sparrows,
the battered coming closest for the grain,
or the part in the song where the oboe
breaks your heart like time itself,
then sneers to laughing.

If poetry is fire, it can't be written in the fire,
but sometime after, written in ashes

along the frozen road
if it be written down at all.

Yes, one can kill the thing not yet language,
feel one's mouth fill up with stones.

Better we all let go of the lie
that art can save a life, except perhaps its maker's,
and even then, one might argue
this is deception,

a false sun to fix the years
toward the day that one might simply see one's child again.

Surely inside her a vast Caina, a crown fire.
Oh, the lovers have given what they can
only to remain men.

They would say, "Something's gone out of her
and nothing offered in its place."

After the boy is taken a third time back to prison,
she would admit there's little left.
Life is a wild undoing!—

And when the poem she once burned down, burned
to the ground in the other life, reconstitutes itself inside her,
it is like someone else's shadow cursing,
figures approaching on the road.

It is a stone tied to a rope hurled round and round,
and the whistling,
and the terror of the blow.

At worst, it's just a door, the one that closes on us now,
and this lamp through the window.

See, they sit apart—old mother, aging son.
Oh, much, too much is lost.

Still, they begin.

Too much is lost—twenty-one years!
In fact they'll never come to like each other.
She cannot find the child's face in the man's.

Five Smooth Stones

The man who wants no children
is like five smooth stones.
His is the face that haunts the orphans,
proctors their dreams.
In the waking hours they wonder
who it is such sympathy arrives in.
So he is used this way.
He's given birth to something.
The man who wants no children dreams of children.
He would give his clothes away,
his overcoat and boots.
He walks the streets opening gates for the yard dogs
and the vagrants who live in boxes.
He washes with them in the public fountains,
and when he is alone he thinks of them,
and at the founding of the great museums.
He is beloved of his landlord.
Who wants no children loves women
who forget to lock their doors
while the weeds destroy the garden.
He is lucky.
There are many such women fat with faith,
fat with atavistic ritual beliefs,
beautiful women who smell of talc, semen, lilacs.
He has loved our children after all,
has on his shoulders carried little ones
across tide pools
as if each child were the world's store,
or a lamp and he the fire bearer.
Oh yes, he is a lighthouse.
He protects his seed, or spills it in secret
by the wayside.

Call him both brilliant, then, and lucky.
When he dies he dies with his heart intact,
and his soul becomes a cloud whose shadow
dissipates above the desert.
For the first stone is the lode stone
and the second is his headstone, and the third
one parts the waters,
and the fourth is buried with him,
and the fifth is never found.
The man who wants no children
is like five smooth stones.

Rita Dove ～

Rosa

How she sat there,
the time right inside a place
so wrong it was ready.

That trim name with
its dream of a bench
to rest on. Her sensible coat.

Doing nothing was the doing:
the clean flame of her gaze
carved by a camera flash.

How she stood up
when they bent down to retrieve
her purse. That courtesy.

History

Everything's a metaphor, some wise
guy said, and his woman nodded, wisely.
Why was this such a discovery
to him? Why did history
happen only on the outside?
She'd watched an embryo track an arc
across her swollen belly from the inside
and knew she'd best
think *knee*, not *tumor* or *burrowing mole*, lest
it emerge a monster. Each craving marks
the soul: splashed white upon a temple the dish
of ice cream, coveted, broken in a wink,
or the pickle duplicated just behind the ear. *Every wish*
will find its symbol, the woman thinks.

Exit

Just when hope withers, a reprieve is granted.
The door opens onto a street like in the movies,
clean of people, of cats; except it is *your* street
you are leaving. Reprieve has been granted,
"provisionally"—a fretful word.

The windows you have closed behind
you are turning pink, doing what they do
every dawn. Here it's gray; the door
to the taxicab waits. This suitcase,
the saddest object in the world.

Well, the world's open. And now through
the windshield the sky begins to blush,
as you did when your mother told you
what it took to be a woman in this life.

Blue Days

Under pressure Mick tells me one
of the jokes truckers pass among themselves: *Why
do women have legs?* I can't imagine;
the day is too halcyon, beyond the patio too Arizonan
blue, sparrows drunk on figs and the season's first corn
stacked steaming on the wicker table. . . . *I
give up; why do they?* As if I weren't one
of "them." Nothing surpasses these
kernels, taut-to-bursting sweet,
tiny rows translucent as baby teeth.
*Remember, you asked for it:
to keep them from tracking slime over the floor.*

Demeter, here's another one for your basket
of mysteries.

Götterdämmerung

A straw reed climbs the car antenna.

Beyond the tinted glass, golden waves
of grain. *Golly!* I can't help
exclaiming, and he smirks—
my born-again naturalist son
with his souped-up laptop,
dear prodigy who insists
on driving the two hours
to the jet he insists I take.
(No turboprops for this

old lady.) On good days
I feel a little meaty; on bad,
a few degrees from rancid.
(Damn knee: I used it this morning
to retrieve a spilled colander;
now every cell's blowing whistles.)

At least it's still a body.
He'd never believe it, son of mine,
but I remember what it's like
to walk the world
with no help from strangers,
not even a personal trainer
to make you feel the burn.

(Most of the time, it's flutter-heart
and Her Royal Celestial Mustache.
Most of the time I'm broth
instead of honey in the bag.)

So I wear cosmetics maliciously
now. And I like my bracelets,
even though they sound ridiculous,
clinking as I skulk through the mall,
store to store like some ancient
iron-clawed griffin—but I've never

stopped wanting to cross
the equator, or touch an elk's
horns, or sing *Tosca* or screw
James Dean in a field of wheat.
To hell with wisdom. They're all wrong:
I'll never be through with my life.

Nancy Eimers ~

Morbid

Neither the mailboxes nor the windows would tell me
how much love was mine
as the houses walked me home from school.

Gold and silver numbers nailed to the houses
were practical stars but did anyone care?

I wasted a lot of time and lust back then
on thoughts of Jesus, stars, dead birds, the back of the head
and the cinderblock shoulders of Marty DiPrimo

one desk away from my fingertips if I should dare

but sold and gone by sooty afterschool autumn dusk
and moody afternoon TV.

I used to scribble assassination haiku in study hall.

Friday night was rumors, car keys, seat belts, bra straps slipping down.
Egg and tomato splatted on fence boards,
toilet paper pennants strung from trees.

Lips and shadow, tampon holders, orchids pining, tongue on tongue.

But Friday night Jo Ellen Donatelli, black-haired greaser girl
who *had* a boyfriend, Carl,
swallowed a bottle of sleeping pills and did it, really, died—

all week in school, thoughts of armholes
of her sleeveless sweater spooling under her arms

gave camera shots: white bra, sculptured armpit. Almost home

my house pinned aimlessly to its *1720*
was already hunkering down in shame at what would be

the used up flame of Friday night.
I'd watch the TV late shows, midnight, three A.M., beyond all curfews,
taste of kiss in my throat

and lungs and down the muscle fibers to my fingertips

where God was microscopic cells and I was afraid
of the numberless houses
I could find in the dark.

A Night Without Stars

And the lake was a dark spot
                on a lung.
Some part of its peace was dead; the rest was temporary. Sleeping ducks
    and geese,
goose shit underfoot
                and wet gray blades of grass.
The fingerlings like sleeping bullets
                hung deep in the troughs of the hatchery
and cold traveled each one end to end,
such cold,
        such distances.

We lay down in the grass on our backs—
beyond the hatchery the streetlights were mired in fog and so
there were no stars,
            or stars would say there was no earth.

Just a single homesick firefly lit on a grass blade.
Just our fingers
            curled and clutching grass,
this dark our outmost hide, and under it
                            true skin.

No Moon

Now it's a way of remembering, dark by dark, the rows.
To think my way back to that rising full harvest moon

is to set in more winter firewood, for it will be cold.

To look at that moon is secretly to make a purchase
for no good reason, of old watch faces in bulk,

is to trace the trajectory of a mayfly on its slow crawl

across the splotched ephemeris of a tablecloth
from points *everlasting to dead at the end of a day.*

To look at the moon is to open up little bottles and boxes,

beach glass, blue jay feather, clearies, cat's eyes,
heart of a hummingbird, snowdrift, fingernails, rain,

until it breaks, it drips, it melts, it rots, it stinks of camphor,

it lies, it doesn't tell.
At dusk, the moon is low in the south

and nearing the Teapot in the constellation Sagittarius

as we travel eastward against the stars.
Each night this week the moon will wax in cosmic reverie. Not yet.

A crow flying cleanly over the houses

has the hardness of trees, or is it the houses
drawing near like trees in the sooty light

that keeps the very thought of us alive?

Down a road outside town I remember *silhouette trees*
and every silhouette giving in.

The moon rose over dinosaurial waddlings

of Canada geese between the cornstalk rows
as if the almanac had told it just what to do:

corn carried, let such as be poor go and glean.

Lynn Emanuel ∼

The Corpses,

hunched like poker players at my kitchen table,
under a seething stratum of cigarette smoke,
are unhappy

with the rewrites of the afterlife.
At their backs,
even the wallpaper

has a story to tell
about a few stout houses
in a bower.

Is bad taste catching? They want to know,
What's happening in this story?
Is the sea kissing up
to the shore? Are the whipped
egg whites of the clouds packed in the sky's refrigerator?

They are tired of being on artificial art support;
the corpses are tired of being used to prop open the plot.

A searchlight opens a sky.
This is the police, bellow the police,
and the corpses stumble forward into a

dowsing of bullets.
They cannot escape me.
Even in death they have a faintly greasy,
slippery look. And even a corpse can be a disguise.

Halfway Through the Book I'm Writing

This is the wonderful thing about art,
it can bring back the dead . . .

My father dies and is buried in his Brooks Brothers suit.
But I can't seem to keep him underground.
Suddenly, I turn around and there he is just
as I'm getting a handle on the train-pulls-

into-the-station poem. "What gives?"
I ask him. "I'm alone and dead," he says,
and I say, "Father, there's nothing I can do about
all that. Get your mind off it. Help me with the poem

about the train." "I hate the poem about the train,"
he says. But since he's dead and I'm a patient woman
I turn back to the poem in which the crowds have gone home
and the janitor pushes the big mustache of his broom across the floor,
and I ask, "Dad, is that you in there?"

"No, it's not."

A black cloud in the shape of Magritte's bowler,
plump and sleek and stark, hanging over the train station, says,
"I want to go to a museum; put one in the poem beside the station."

where it's morning and the ticket window is selling
tickets to a man in a hat and an enormous
trench coat, wrinkled and jowly, a woman

in white looks as cool as a martini in a chrome
shaker, a woman in red seethes in a doorway,
eager to become one of Those Beginning the Journey
and from the horizon's molten light the trains crawl out.

"And when I get to the museum I want to see
Soutine, Miró, Picasso, or Dali, I want eyes in my armpits
and my fingers, eyes in the air, the trees, the dirt."

"Father," I say, "you already are an eye-in-the-dirt."

It's early morning. In the pine tree I hear the phoebe's stressed
squeak, *fee-bee, fee-bay,* like the creak of the old guard at the museum
snoozing in his rocker before Soutine's still life of the butchered cows.

"Father," I say, "do you see them?"
And the phoebe says, Yes-squeak-
yes-squeak-yes-squeak-yes-squeak.

In English in a Poem

I am giving a lecture on poetry
to the painters who creak like saddles
in their black leather jackets; in the studio,
where a fire is burning like a painting of
a fire, I am explaining my current work
on the erotics of narrative. It is night.
Overhead the moon's naked heel dents
the sky, the crickets ignite themselves
into a snore, and the painters yawn
lavishly waiting for me to say Something
About Painting, the way your dog, when
you are talking, listens for the words Good Dog.

"Your indifference draws me like horses draw flies,"
I say while noticing in the window the peonies
throbbing with pulses, the cindery crows seething
over the lawn. "Nevertheless," I continue, "I call
your attention to the fact that, in this poem, what was
once just a pronoun is now a pronoun talking about
a peony while you sit in a room somewhere unmoved
by this. And that's okay. Gertrude Stein said America
was *a space filled with moving,* but I hate being moving.
If you want to *feel,* go to the movies, because poetry
has no intention of being moving; it is perhaps one
of the few things left in America that is not moving.

And yet, I am a fatalist when it comes to art
and orgasm in English, because in English
even a simile is a story and there is no trip

so predictable that some poem won't take it."
And just as I am finishing my lecture, here
is the snowy hem of the end of the page
and one of the painters says to me, "Actually,
I found that very moving. Get in the car.
I'll drive you home."

Angie Estes ～

Now and Again: An Autobiography of Basket

for Gertrude Stein

Comets are like scythes, they do not hold
your coat, although they may look
as if they are going to, just rounding
the corner into the century, but perhaps she was
speaking of commas, celestial bodies trailing
bright hair every seventy some years,
once through a lifetime if you're lucky
you see them, two women and a poodle
curved into hummocks, asleep
and slung between sheets, still now
and again her mouth would open,
grin, and then bear down
on something it looked like dahlias
she carried in her teeth and time
and time again it was my name,
so sometimes we danced, my paws
on her shoulders in the garden of Bilignin
while she sang *I am I because my little dog
knows me* to the tune of "On the Trail
of the Lonesome Pine," *each part needing its own
place to make its own balancing*
as in a sentence she said, there is a mirror
of that and another photo, too,
where we sit as we were told to

on the sofa in front of the portrait
she painted me on the wall behind, when time
and time again she told me to sit
because she loves me in that painting
she says there I am God's dog, ASCOB,
who barks all the time but is impossible
to hear, that *my* epitaph, too, should declare
Any Solid Color Other than Black
when the time comes to call
everything back to where it belongs,
to its place in some long sentence
where I was going to say we are
the commas, tipped like hammocks
in the wind, but then again now
I think, rather, we are the hammocks
in which the commas swing.

Annunciation in an Initial R

But whose initial? Left here, illuminated
    but abandoned by its text. Surely *R* stands
for religion, *religare*, something to bind us
    back, to remind that—whether reading, kneeling,
or waving goodbye—a word can enter
    our womb in a breath. Bordered with heads,
each open mouth tongued orange or blue
    with the tip of a pen, the letter *R* could be
autumn, all parchment and loss, each leaf
    embedded with flame.

More like *enunciation*, I should think,
    with the lungs a heavy butterfly heaving
its cocoon, and the conception some act
    of ventriloquism, immaculate and marooned.
Perhaps *R* is for rental—as in the villa
    where they sit, Mary and Gabriel tilting
their heads. And the goldleaf rolling in
    wherever space remains is nothing
but time, in which everything floats. Is this the way

rooms imagine us to be: round-shouldered
and arched, all presence and tense, waiting
   for words to arrive in our ear? Space
now fulfilled, place where bulbs are forced
   to bloom—like skulls without thoughts, are they empty
without us? Initials can begin

or put an end to a name, tell stories,
   train vines, and use the bodies of others
to form their own shape; jungle gyms
   of intention, designed to mean
this one and not another, initials took the place
   of people, already replaced
by words, until they finally took over
   the page and made everything
in their image. Anthropomorphic, historiated, foliate:
   they became, like us, inhabited.

If *R* is for annunciation, then *T* can signal
   crucifixion: cross illuminated, tipped
on its side, cartwheeling to Golgotha,
   where *X* marks the spot. *Te igitur,* You therefore,
clementissime Pater, per Jesum Christum Filium tuum Dominum nostrum,
   supplices rogamus, ac petimus
the priest chants, arms and palms espaliered
   at his sides. Slowly lowered, the hands meet
again, cupping each other the way Adam and Eve
   hid from God their most private
parts, the parts he could not bear
   to see. Like flags waved by sailors
from decks of separate ships, their hands
   made the semaphore which means
      end of word.

Kathy Fagan ～

Moving & St Rage

—*billboard on Ohio State Route 36*

             Of course, something is missing,
which accounts for his sainthood, his legendary fury;
and while it would be false to say that Moving never dwelt
upon the source of that absence,
wondering what hand of god or man,
what rupture or obscuring force
might snatch a vowel from its rightful place,
                  shaping him thus, charting forever
the course of their merged destinies,
equally false would be to claim
she'd loved him any other way,
or that she was not drawn to Rage
as to the flame, and he to the sentiment
her name made: his lips mouthed roundly on her
                first syllable, his jaw clenched
shut as he uttered the last; nor was the paradox lost
on them, susceptible as they were to words,
and symbols, like the ampersand,
cousin to the treble clef,
whose plainer features also set
the pitch and tumble of mortal endeavor,
                and joined these two like ones before
who'd met on the grassy medians of myth
to pledge those troths the gods grow jealous of:
there are limits placed on endless love.

And that is why Rage came to travel, and walks
the foreign seacoast of an ancient city now,
anonymous among the crowds, and through a speech so vastly
                strange, it does not interrupt his reverie;
nothing can: not the whirl of birds and white
umbrellas in the sun of the *platia,* not the darkly pretty twinning couples
espaliering ocher walls—all's to Rage
a froth and sway he cannot comprehend;

and useless as it is to question
which of them felt banished first, or when
                          their hardening of hearts began
like the fortification of separate kingdoms,
question they must, Rage & Moving, cursed to live
beyond their primes, and one half-day and -world apart,
to ride a wheel of common failures
that is hope turning up
and regret coming down, and that makes a sound like
                    See Me   See Me,
spewing grit and salt and stars, grinding
on its dark axis—and while she knows that Earth
itself has blocked the moon she loves from sight,
Moving can't recall tonight the reason
bodies spin this way, or who first named the blank
moon New, believed an unlit promise with a faith
                          the there-not-there was whole,

and not a lost and gone forever, hugely missed and missing O.

Revisionary Instruments I

Sallie sits beside me as we wait for you and studies the painting of the hot-air balloon.

From brown hills cradling blue water it rises, toward a cropped, enormous yellow sun.

I have seen it for days, this bad painting. It is remarkable only for its size, the tenacity of its brightness, and the signatures of those patients to whom it is dedicated.

I had thought I'd committed each one of them to heart.

But today I notice, suspended in middle air between the sea's horizon and basket's base, identical surnames in childish hands. One boy, one girl, their Latin name written as high as their arms could reach.

I'll remember it, later, as *Esperanza*. I'll think it impossible even as I do.

What revisionary instruments our hearts are, I'll write; *how merciful our misremembrance,*

since, if truth were known, a family of headstones was what I thought of then, floating in that patch of sky, and not of hope, not of hope at all.

She Attempts to Tell the Truth About True Romance

Don't know a man or woman can do it, tell the truth about love.

Don't know a man or woman that knows it.

One look at the popularity o them books and magazines on the subject where the only place a woman sweats s'between her bosoms and even the saddest endin's meant to make us swoon shows that

ploppin real boys and girls down in the middle o that makes for a different story altogether and that's cause enough for their existin in the first place.

And while most grownups realize that, they ain't heartily resigned,

creatin swarms o young people ill prepared for disappointment and one mightily vicious circle I might add.

And Michael and I was afraid at the end of August.

It's only now I know how's afraid we were.

We'd heard a lot about love but nothin useful,

the usual jabber bout reputation when it's peace of mind advice was called for, tips on savin some of our sanity's opposed to virginity.

But since when's a parent done anythin right when it comes to the love of a child, and if they did Cupid's mama'd a slapped that bow and arrow right outa her son's hand when she had a chance and placed a .45 in his chubby fist instead.

Least that way we'd be sooner dead.

But I digress.

See I saw a boy on the bus just today toss the hair off his face like a bad memory,

with a quick lil jerk o his head to the right like Michael used to do,

or I mightn't a gotten on the topic at all.

Yes he'd the name o the archangel alright which made me happy at the time and disposed me toward him—

I was that kinda girl—

and he and I's fallin deep that August which is where the fright came from,

and it's a sick joke on us that the commonest occurrences such as this, birth, and death don't get related proper but I'll try my best which is more 'an most as I've already said.

Michael claimed he knew where the deer slept that summer and not half believin I followed him there,

just a giant nest o pine needles and dry leaves in a clearin in the woods of which he smelled,

and there was antler fuzz flyin everywhere from the teenagers scrapin their new horny growth off.

Saw it clingin myself to the treebark and boulders like milkweed or cottonwood or dandelions only velveter—

Michael filled my hands with it—

and I remarked how it must hurt though they's compelled to do it and
don't all livin creatures know a thing about that,

where's Michael said it more involved a markin as in territories: cat
glands, dog piss, creasin the corner of a book page down to find your
place,

just so much more o that here-I-am, remember-me, here-you-are, so-
once-was-I,

and then he pointed at a hole fresh-dug, some stones around it, and
told me he'd buried some split wood there, half-charred he'd found the
day we'd met,

and that in time the earth like a hidden furnace'd turn the wood to coal
and the coal to diamond which he'd be placin on the third finger of my
right hand in a life to come.

A life to come.

Had himself his spiritual side that boy even with both his hands down
my pants.

And when it comes to romance I've not met a man since to compare.

Rain and bicycles got married in my mind.

He'd had one that summer and i'd been a wet one, and my how he
sounded like rain when he came and rain when he rode away.

And when I told him so as I did each time he'd say "Then kiss the
drizzle of me, darlin" and laugh so's his gums showed and what could I
do?—

my body vibratin like a dozen violins backed into a corner.

We'd pile a stack o records on the phonograph and rock on the porch
swing til our backs held the rhythm of it,

even off the swing and parted—

why I swung in my sleep!—

and just about when the last record spun out sayin dusk dusk there'd
be suddenly sundown in earnest,

Michael's forearms blazin like the peaches he ate and my face lit up like
there was sunset in my own skull.

And I've related already his hair tossin gesture and the thing with his
gums and his two magic tricks—

did I tell you those?—

but mostly I loved how he'd look at me, that summer, like there wasn't
as much longin in the world as in his heart,

and it was just about when that look ended,

got inexplicably tossed off his face like his too-long hair, and the one
where I felt like a dull lesson in a schoolbook begun,

that I started wishin he'd just be shot clean through the chest one day
so's I could mourn beautiful like Maria,

and swear truthful I'd been loved right that one time,
and have done with it.

Course if wishes were horses we'd all ride to town.

And truth be known the Frenchman was right: "The heart changes
and that is our worst misfortune."

And askin why's bout as useful as askin why anythin does—slow and
sneaky-like so you don't take notice.

Guess any time that dyin takes is slow.

And when it comes to love it don't go pretty like autumn or the end of
a day. T'ain't a song that plays but regretful music nonetheless,

an aria o exclamation on out into eternity where the coal turns to
diamonds and the deer-down you hold in the round of your arms is so
light it's like the shape of a loneliness.

Grief so much everywhere you hardly notice anymore. Like that last
record left over-long on the phonograph, it's in people's hearts,

and it goes Tsk.
Tsk Tsk.
Tsk Tsk.
Tsk Tsk. . . .

Candice Favilla ～

West Texas Rain Journal

In Ojinaga-across-the-river
where I buy without prescription,

I hunch outside a farmacia
and swallow liquid codeine, slick

as the wide streets—no pavement and
the lawless tread of displacement—

lozenges of clay enamelling my sick throat
while the ocotillo and the creosote

plant throb into profound inaction.
Those branches, bombs of perfume and mosquitos,

resin of Vapo Rub. Ozone.
Bean fields. Melons. Opium.

Horse flies. Synthetic hormones.
Then returning north across the border

when a blackbird crashes off my door.
One dent. Another twist. Some disorder

in the gap-toothed streets of Presidio
where folks are driven back by rain, wings

of white mud clapping trucks, natives
diving under awnings and into muck

and baldly open fruits.
I'm here with myself.

And stuck because a creek is up.
The great sky snarls, pregnant

with the press of water. Buttes
piled like clay chicks I want to shoot

into where the desert gets serious.
Stopped again at a café like a gravel pit

to eat beans and rice and sip
(by now I'm chipping) more cough syrup.

I am the fountains of clay
which mark the heart's abeyance.

I'm waiting for an image
to destroy me, to explain:

the limestone mountains seem ageless,
comfortably meaningless, and unalive

as theme parks. As though the soul
had blistered open—acetylene stray, too much

the cutting of an illuminant—
as eyes baked by flash, split and peeling,

I reel from the seedy particularity
of objects; their dark contrivances

are suspect, a seduction
of correspondences. I knew a boy

who claimed that his father had cooked
his own hand in a microwave oven

to learn how it feels.
Imagine that. Months ago

near a ghost town I cannot
now cross the water to

I saw a black man walking
in the grinding desert. He seemed

to need nothing. He carried
only a sack of water. Now a buzzard

lifts from the splotchy tarmac.
Tell them back there

on the West Coast that I
am never coming home.

Red Clay

Of world without integument,
we build in huddling shade,
and are, ourselves, as shadows
over blueprint and balustrade,
sleepwalkers, having lost

what is vigorous and whole,
utterly whole. Wind pesters wind.
Flies invade the silences—a city
of shade that now manifests
and now fades as the body

of air blows about
and we stir, fitful,
our actions merely half-

conceived. Fugue.
What a word is this

that so congests the mind?
Under it another and
another we can
almost reach through
to our bodies. Who.

*

Once I met the beloved
in a glade of murmuring reeds.
O moth of accidental gestures,
come unto me. A bee put a ring
on my smallest finger, and I

voiced with the children,
faith. Or yet I am not
truthful. How dare I
confuse that fact and that
we met in the workplace yes

it must have been the workplace,
a room smashed with carbon
and my fingernail blackened
from cloying to the surface
of afternoon. Thus I entered

a thronging woods, a tangled woods,
the clarity but once only. We
wandering, dumb with too long
at it—almost as though
the names had made us foreign.

Carolyn Forché ⌁

Elegy

The page opens to snow on a field: boot-holed month, black hour
the bottle in your coat half vodka half winter light.
To what and to whom does one say *yes*?
If God were the uncertain, would you cling to him?

Beneath a tattoo of stars the gate opens, so silent so like a tomb.
This is the city you most loved, an empty stairwell
where the next rain lifts invisibly from the Seine.

With solitude, your coat open, you walk
steadily as if the railings were there and your hands weren't passing
    through them.

"When things were ready, they poured on fuel and touched off the fire.
They waited for a high wind. It was very fine, that powdered bone.
It was put into sacks, and when there were enough we went to a bridge on
    the Narew River."

And even less explicit phrases survived:
"To make charcoal.
For laundry irons."
And so we revolt against silence with a bit of speaking.
The page is a charred field where the dead would have written
We went on. And it was like living through something again one could not
    live through again.

The soul behind you no longer inhabits your life: the unlit house
with its breathless windows and a chimney of ruined wings
where wind becomes an aria, your name, voices from a field,
And you, smoke, dissonance, a psalm, a stairwell.

The Testimony of Light

Our life is a fire dampened, or a fire shut up in stone.
JACOB BOEHME, *DE INCARNATIONE VERBI*

Outside everything visible and invisible a blazing maple.
Daybreak: a seam at the curve of the world. The trousered legs of the women
    shimmered.
They held their arms in front of them like ghosts.

The coal bones of the house clinked in a kimono of smoke.
An attention hovered over the dream where the world had been.

For if Hiroshima in the morning, after the bomb has fallen,
    is like a dream, one must ask whose dream it is.

Must understand how not to speak would carry it with us.
With bones put into rice bowls.
While the baby crawled over its dead mother seeking milk.

Muga-muchu: without self, without center. Thrown up in the sky by a wind.

The way back is lost, the one obsession.
The worst is over.
The worst is yet to come.

The Garden Shukkei-en

By way of a vanished bridge we cross this river
as a cloud of lifted snow would ascend a mountain.

She has always been afraid to come here.

It is the river she most
remembers, the living
and the dead both crying for help.

A world that allowed neither tears nor lamentation.

The *matsu* trees brush her hair as she passes
beneath them, as do the shining strands of barbed wire.

Where this lake is, there was a lake,
where these black pine grow, there grew black pine.

Where there is no teahouse I see a wooden teahouse
and the corpses of those who slept in it.

On the opposite bank of the Ota, a weeping willow
etches its memory of their faces into the water.

Where light touches the face, the character for heart is written.

She strokes a burnt trunk wrapped in straw:
I was weak and my skin hung from my fingertips like cloth

Do you think for a moment we were human beings to them?

She comes to the stone angel holding paper cranes.
Not an angel, but a woman where she once had been,
who walks through the garden Shukkei-en
calling the carp to the surface by clapping her hands.

Do Americans think of us?

So she began as we squatted over the toilets:
If you want, I'll tell you, but nothing I say will be enough.

We tried to dress our burns with vegetable oil.

Her hair is the white froth of rice rising up kettlesides, her mind also.
In the postwar years she thought deeply about how to live.

The common greeting *dozo-yiroshku* is please take care of me.
All *hibakusha* still alive were children then.

A cemetery seen from the air is a child's city.

I don't like this particular red flower because
it reminds me of a woman's brain crushed under a roof.

Perhaps my language is too precise, and therefore difficult to understand?

We have not, all these years, felt what you call happiness.
But at times, with good fortune, we experience something close.
As our life resembles life, and this garden the garden.
And in the silence surrounding what happened to us

is the bell to awaken God that we've heard ringing.

Alice Fulton ⌢

== ==

It might mean immersion, that sign
      I've used as title, the sign I call a bride
after the recessive threads in lace = =
the stitches forming deferential
          space around the firm design.
            It's the unconsidered

mortar between the silo's bricks = = never admired
            when we admire
the holdfast of the tiles (their copper of a robin's
      breast abstracted into flat).

      It's a seam made to show,
the deckle edge = = constructivist touch.
      The double equal that's nowhere to be found
            in math. The dash
      to the second power = = dash to the max.

It might make visible the acoustic signals
of things about to flame. It might

            let thermal expansion be syntactical. Let it
add stretch

while staying reticent, unspoken
as a comma. Don't get angry = = protest = = but a

comma seems so natural, you don't see it
when you read: it's gone to pure
transparency. Yes but.
                    The natural is what

poetry contests. Why else the line = = why stanza = = why
        meter and the rest. Like wheels on snow

            that leave a wake = = that tread in white
                    without dilapidating
                    mystery = = hinging
            one phrase to the next = = the brides.

Thus wed = = the sentence cannot tell
whether it will end or melt or give

            way to the fabulous = = the snow that is
the mortar between winter's bricks = = the wick that is

            the white between the ink

Wonder Bread

*You asked me what my flowers said—then they
were disobedient—I gave them messages.*
EMILY DICKINSON, LETTER #187

What eucharist of air and bland

was this nation raised on? No one understood
my funny flowers—and Darwin—

Darwin was regarded as a charlatan.
Few viewers think

evolution is the truth.
My flowers *were* absurd.

Snips of sugar. Snails with spice.
Puppy dogs. Tales. Everything.

Nice!

But why did I admire nature so?
Was it that I liked

the absence of a Master
neuron in the brain—

the absence of a Master
cell in embryos—

the nothing in the way of
center that would hold?

What causes less comfort
than wonder?

What—does not console?

Take: A Roman Wedding

> ... She, hating the whitethorn wedding torch as if
> it were a thing of evil ...
> OVID'S METAMORPHOSES, BOOK I

It was lit at the bride's hearth while she played
    at resistance, clinging to her mother's arms
            in lovely terror: let me be chaste! Her part
            in the mock rape was to beg.

A parade formed to take her
                        to his house.
    What festive obscenities.
                    She listened.
    Pipes and timbrels.
                    Venereal hymns.

Thigh or breast?
                        What wild X is seized?

The groom tossed walnuts like a soiled confetti.
    A boy ran with the torch. A portent.
                            If it soared: children.
                            If it flickered: a jinx.
The orange veil hid the right of her glance.

                    It was a drastic enhancer, the fire
thrashing round the whitethorn core. It was hair
        grabbed by heaven, coronary-colored. Spires
        from Apollo's crown, it gored the night. Spermed

a tail like a comet's
                    and metastasized
to her new hearth.
                    Became
    a tossed bouquet.
                    Became
heavier on consummation,
        when the smoke was weighed.

The remnants, a negative
                    of baby's breath,
were divided by the guests.

Once upon a bride there was a time.
Between twelve and twenty. But a minor

    all her life. Once—no often, every war—
    she was taken by force, as spoils, as lifting
                    her over

the threshold remembers.
                        And the whitethorn still grows.
The organza branches

            of today's hybrids—though susceptible
                    to fireblight—
            are entirely free
of nettles.

Tess Gallagher ~

Trace, In Unison

Terrible, the rain. All night, rain
that I love. So the weight of his leg
falls again like a huge tender wing
across my hipbone. Its continuing—the rain,
as he does not. Except as that caress
most inhabited. Ellipsis of
eucalyptus. His arms, his beautiful
careless breathing. Inscription
contralto where his lips graze
the bow of my neck. Muslin half-light.
Musk of kerosene in the hall, fixative
to ceaselessly this rain, in which
there is nothing to do but be happy, be
free, as if someone sadly accused
came in with their coat soaked through
and said, "But I only wanted
to weep and love," and we rolled toward
the voice like one body and said
with our eyes closed, "Then weep, then
love." Buds of jasmine threaded through
her hair so they opened after dark,
brightening the room. That morning
rain as it would fall, still
falling, and where we had lain,
an arctic light steady
in the mind's releasing.

Fresh Stain

I don't know now if it was kindness—we do
and we do. But I wanted you with me
that day in the cool raspberry vines, before
I had loved anyone, when another girl and I

saw the owner's son coming to lift away
our heaped flats of berries. His
white shirt outside his jeans so
tempting. That whiteness, that quick side-glance
in our direction. We said nothing,
but quickly gathered all the berries we could, losing
some in our mirth and trampling them
like two black ponies who only want to keep their backs
free, who only want to be shaken with
the black night-in-day murmur of hemlocks
high above. Our slim waists, our buds
of breasts and red stain of raspberries cheapening
our lips. We were sudden, we were
two blurred dancers who didn't need paradise. His shirt,
his white shirt when the pelting ended, as if
we had kissed him until his own blood
opened. So we refused every plea and
were satisfied. And you didn't touch me then, just
listened to the cool silence after. Inside,
the ripe hidden berries as we took up our wicker baskets
and lost our hands past the wrists
in the trellised vines. Just girls with the arms of
their sweaters twisted across their hips, their laughter
high in sunlight and shadow, that girl
you can almost remember as she leans into the vine,
following with pure unanswerable desire, a boy
going into the house to change his shirt.

Valentine Delivered by a Raven

Its beak is red and it has a battlefield-look,
as if it's had its pickings and come away
of its own volition. Elsewhere the Emperor Frederick
sleeps on, guarded by ravens, and may yet rise
from deathly slumber and walk the earth.
Who knows what's long enough
when death's involved. I stand on my love's grave
and say aloud in a swoop of gulls over
the bay, "I kiss your lips, babe," and it's not

grotesque, even though the mind knows what it
knows, and mostly doesn't. Language,
that great concealer, is more than generous, gives
always what it doesn't have. I stare into the dazzling
impertinent eye of the messenger. He's
been tending the dead so long his eyes are garnets,
his wings cracked open to either side, two
fissures savage with light. I bend
in recognition and take up a holly bough left
as in the old adornment of doorways. The hard, red
berries glisten and tremble in their nest of
green, so when he speaks I hear him
with the attention of a red berry before a covetous
bright eye, and what I need I take
in empires before he flaps away on my love's errands
and I am cinnabar and fog in the doorway.

Un Extraño

Light begins. Snow begins.
A rose begins to unhinge
its petals. Sleep
begins. An apple lets go
of its branch. Someone tells
a secret like an echo
wrapped around a shadow,
a shadow soaked in love.
The secret begins to make
a difference. It travels
on the borrowed heat
of what the shadow
passes over. The lip
begins its mustache.
The heart begins its
savage journey
toward love and loss
of love. But you, you
don't begin. I stare
at your hand on my breast.

Their dialogue is the wingless
strength of the stem
bearing its flower
in rain, in sun.

Day begins. Night begins.
But you don't begin.
You know that one thing
the loveless lovers forget,
that to begin is to agree
to live among half-forces,
to shine only when the moon
shines and all is ready.

You make me ready
but you do not begin.
I let you never begin.
It's my gift to our most uncertain
always. I agree only to coincide
outside each death-enchanted
wave. What we are making
isn't a shroud or a halo.
It's a banished hive
stinging itself alive with
vast multiplications. We taunt love
as the bullfighter taunts
death, preparing the dangerous lunge
until it catches us unawares
that split second
in which love shudders
its starkest glimpse
into us. The magenta cape
swirls its silk across our lips
like a breath unraveled in the moment
the matador kneels to the bull.
My *adorno, el novillito.* Don't
begin. Don't ever begin.

Amy Gerstler ～

Siren

I have a fish's tail, so I'm not qualified to love you.
But I do. Pale as an August sky, pale as flour milled
a thousand times, pale as the icebergs I have never seen,
and twice as numb—my skin is such a contrast to the rough
rocks I lie on, that from far away it looks like I'm a baby
riding a dinosaur. The turn of the centuries or the turn
of a page mean the same to me, little or nothing.
I have teeth in places you'd never suspect. Come. Kiss me
and die soon. I slap my tail in the shallows—which is to say
I appreciate nature. You see my sisters and me perched
on rocks and tiny islands here and there for miles:
untangling our hair with our fingers, eating seaweed.

The Nature of Suffering

We know so little about what matters,
what lasts, what constitutes virtue,
what defiles logic by being steeped
in feeling. It's impossible to keep
oneself clean. Every thought
is lecherous and dispensable.
I know I'm not worth the gunpowder
it'd take to blow me to limbo.
You've said so, so often.
Still, I can't leave.
One couldn't trudge far through
this bone-chilling melancholy,
I don't care how impressive
or fur-lined your credentials.
Seclusion produces peculiar symptoms.
A slumbering priestess suffers convulsions.
She's you, trying to shake off
the world's grip, even in her sleep.

What am I to make of her glacial smile?
Outward evidence of voluptuous suffering?
The kiss that's been so long in coming,
rumbling up from her erotic depths?
I found her in a pitiable condition,
much disfigured, but she had already
chosen her road. Every step one takes
is a kind of violation. If I'm
permitted to continue, I must give up
everything. I must be bled white.

Saints

Miracle mongers. Bedwetters. Hair-shirted wonder workers. Shirkers of the
soggy soggy earth. A bit touched, or wholly untouched living among us?
They shrug their bodies off and waft with clouds of celestial perfume. No
smooching for this crew, except for hems, and pictures of their mothers . . .
their lips trespass only the very edges of succor. *Swarms of pious bees precede
her.* One young girl wakes up with a ring on her finger and a hole in her throat.
Another bled milk when her white thigh was punctured. All over the world,
a few humans are born each decade with a great talent for suffering. They
have gifts that enable them to sleep through their mistreatment: the sleep of
the uncomplaining just, the sleep of the incomplete. Our relationship to
them is the same as our relationship to trees: what they exhale, we breathe.

Housebound

When we fuck, stars don't peer down: they can't.
We fornicate indoors, under roofs, under wraps;
far from nature's prying eyes—from the trees'
slight green choreography, wrung from rigid trunks,
that leaves us unmoved. In full view of the shower
head and bookcases, we lick and tickle each other.
Every stick of furniture's a witness. We'd like
to believe our love's a private sentiment, yet
how many couches, cots, and benches have soaked up

some? Lust adheres to objects, becomes a prejudice
instilled in utensils by human use. How can I blind
these Peeping Toms—silence the libidinous whining
of these sipped-from paper cups and used toothbrushes?
I can't. I wait for the outspoken adolescent spoons
to rust and hold their tongues so we can be alone.

Patricia Goedicke ~

Lacrimae Rerum

Dogs yap, sirens wail through the city.
                              Air raid, ambulance:
        lone bobby pin like an insect crushed in a corner.
            And tea cups, abandoned hubcaps
              Or beer bottles, and the cracked lips that swigged them,
                              or the quick blurt
    and stutter of soldiers' feet.
                    But the lovers pay no attention, when does anyone listen
        to chairs, to the kitchen table with its mute
                        self-effacing surfaces?
            The back seats of cars sag
          beneath toys, cigarette butts, plastic
                          Dairy Queen cups and chewing gum.
    The egg timer sits on its shelf, one shoe
                curls inconsolably in the closet,
and then there's the doorknob, that once turned
                              easily in the hand, the cruel
            entrances and the exits, the keys
                  frozen now,
                        motionless in a foreign pocket

because metal has its own fatigues;
                stress cracks even steel girders, chipped plates
          and coffee cups touched by mouths
                that are closed now, sealed in the great silences

                    of childhood:
as the lungs of the world strain
            in the bellows of a giant accordion of rocks, trees, rivers
                    and hollow mailboxes, all lovers inhale
                only to exhale, like morning fog on a window
    where night's breath weeps for awhile
                            and then vanishes, finally even the sweetest
                sexual damps and dews slide away.

From the Boat

What is it, then   between us
                in the press of parties   stammering
            in packed elevators   not meeting
                            each other's eyes
                    the metal boxes slide
                up and then down

as the sea roars   and turns over
                        the land envelops us, out there
        rolling blankets   of trees
                        the sky lifts itself
                    into staggered blue
            distances

on the steel gray
                churning planks
                            of the ocean
        gulls ride,
                anxiously turning their heads

and crying to each other   mewing
                    shrill needles pierce the air
            into shredded mist over oiled
                                heaving green mountains
in the slick chop   In the long
                ponderous swells
            mates hidden   mothers

                    from their young

bob up   squawking
            teetering on top of one
                            wallowing wet sledge
            after another

who can see anything   From here
                a few small
                        damp fluffy dots
            on those vast   shifting plates
                        yammering

from the boat's exhilarating deck   rocking
            but confident   with binoculars
                            we look down on them
                    and try to name them,   who are they

all day we watch them
                strange beings,   feathered
            over each other's shoulders
                                    surging onto the crests
                        sliding into the troughs

The Ground Beneath Us

For the end of the story sucks. Not air
exactly. Or gravel either. Nothing

to sleep next to. It reams us out like the exhaust
of retreating armies.

But you are a retreating army.

The roof trembles,
and the floor.

The shell around us is cracked

and you're in my arms, shaking. Over the crumbling
excavations beneath us. Where I won't,

I will not drop you.

Our neighbor walks in front of her tottering
mother, leading her on a string. *But not you,*

never you.

My old baby, my balding
word lover, all throb

and fire in my bed, such
razzmatazz!

And we were always equal.

As you took care of me
let me take care of you.

Dear lizard, dear snake tongue,
companion among the dictionaries,

though we thought we could write our way up
out of the battlefields of our lives,

look where we were going.

With your head in the clouds you mutter
we'll never make it, never . . .

But in and out of the overcast,

snow covered peaks disappear
and reappear in seconds;

like the ghost eyes of portraits

the words you write precede
and follow us everywhere.

The ground beneath us is silent. But the dictionaries
and the libraries are still with us, towering

against the sky, Hellooooooooooooo
up there, yes you are the mountain,

the mountain the poem becomes.

And Yet

there are so many islands,   sep-
                               arated
            in the brain.
     Walk across the channels.   Follow
                   a sandpiper

            Will you be there?

Clearer and clearer, at the edge
                   where land and sea meet
    everywhere, windblown
             pebbles
      in all corners
               and

I see you in the water
             the veiled skin of it
    cloudy blooms of light
               you who disappeared
        so many years ago   scattered
  dispersed   vaporized
      still here

Beckian Fritz Goldberg ~

My Bomb

Better than a dream, it left gargantuan
roses in the Japanese garden, and the rabbits
heavy as children. We would crouch
in the classroom beneath our desks
and concentrate on being small, study
the whitecaps of our knees. Once

we went below the library,
the dark shelves stacked with cans
of creamed corn, green beans, mandarin oranges
we'd eat like the dead for five years
and rise again. Thus,

I learned the catechism: *proton, electron,
neutron.* I learned to contemplate
the Invisible. I went to sleep

in the fire-cloud folding like the brain
and dreamt about the power of my bomb,
girls flashing to the sidewalks, cities
filigreed, the bird-cinders,
light bright as the mirror on the shoe of God

and afterward, pink as phoenixes,
the American Beauties pressing their
mammoth lips to the charge of the sky.
This is how I loved the earth

with my life. With the pure nuclei of
my matter. How it fell into my hands.
Better than desire,
my bomb lit the face of my own

twentieth century. I had it
so no one could use it. I would have more
so no one could have enough.

Swallower

Open the cupboard, cherries rounded up in the darkness.
Sometimes the childhood mystery of the old woman's room.
Its scent bulging out from the polished wooden things,
    from the laciness over which the mirror threw
    back the room, scent wormholing

personal galaxy to personal galaxy. Space is the problem,
the whole
                weep of it. Most of the time. The cherries
themselves, swallowers. All that inked up redness.
As if the eye-mouth-nostril angel of orifices was
                the only guardian, only

loop into good time. Now

the self is a hundred vigils.
Some of them over bowls and silent bureaus,
some of them over blood-relations, over
that moon over *is this the right bus.*
Then.

Once. I was struck sick while climbing a hill—all
I looked for was a place to heave myself, kneel
and quiver. Even as I approached the feverish
    patinations of my wing-split I knew the trees
    flowering east were tasseling

sheer memory. Its marriages I hate.
The cherries take you
somewhere in you that's out of order: China

dogs lustery on the sill, fleur-de-lised
wallpaper, the rouged up faces of hand-tinted photographs.
Each face a pulp tightened around a single incident.
How shall I leave the room when I die?

Outside my house the fence wood swells after
rain, the air heavy as fruit. The error is in the equation,
fragrance was a gate upon the heart,

yet only one
        the responsible object.

Rebirth

One summer I saw the old wing
of the hospital where I was born—in the windows
stacked boxes of cleanser, disinfectant.
It stared at me like an old brick warehouse.
It stood in the middle of a field.
I was startled by the bored look of it
as a woman by the distant
expression of a lover. We slowed
past on the road as my mother told me
it had been snowing, a May blizzard that evening
and the very road
down which I had no memory—
this humid August and a day moth's
fibrillations over ragweed over sawgrass.
I said my first light
was on the cellar door open and the hammers
ringing: Father sawdust shadows brothers
and that echo wowing the spring air.
She said I came out dark-haired,
a good sleeper.
I said it was
the chickens walking under the lilac.
She said I first moved when the town band
played a concert in the park.
She did not say *the stars were clear and close*
as the lashes of the ecstatic . . .
And I did not say *the night moved in rings*
like blood fielding a trumpet.
The windows were dimming in rows
like schooldays. Or that part of our life
only someone else remembers. I said
my first love
was autumn sky lost in the empty
corn cribs and the cows steamy and lonely

without end. She said
I was born happy.

Jorie Graham ~

Thinking

I can't really remember now. The soundless foamed.
A crow hung like a cough to a wire above me. There was a chill.
It was a version of a crow, untitled as such, tightly feathered
in the chafing air. Rain was expected. All round him air
dilated, as if my steady glance on him, cindering at the glance-core where
it held him tightest, swelled and sucked,
while round that core, first a transition, granular—then remembrance of
thing being
seen—remembrance as it thins-out into matter, almost listless—then,
sorrow—if sorrow could be sterile—and the rest fraying off into all
the directions,
variegated amnesias—lawns, black panes, screens the daylight
thralls into in search of well-edged things. . . . If I squint, he glints.
The wire he's on wobbly and his grip not firm.
Lifting each forked clawgrip again and again.
Every bit of wind toying with his hive of black balance.
Every now and then a passing car underneath causing a quick rearrangement.
The phonelines from six houses, and the powerlines from three
grouped-up above me—some first-rung of sky—him not comfortable,
nature silted-in to this maximum habitat—*freedom*—
passers-by (woman, dog) vaguely relevant I'd guess though he doesn't
look down,
eyeing all round, disqualifying, disqualifying
all the bits within radius that hold no clue
to whatever is sought, urgent but without hurry,
me still by this hedge now, waiting for his black to blossom,
then wing-thrash where he falls at first against the powerline,
then updraft seized, gravity winnowed, the falling raggedly
reversed, depth suddenly pursued, its invisiblity ridged—bless him—
until he is off, hinge by hinge, built of tiny wingtucks, filaments

of flapped-back wind, until the thing (along whose spine
his sentence of black talk, thrashing, wrinkling, dissipates—the history,
                                                        the wiring,
shaking, with light—) is born.

The Guardian Angel of Not Feeling

As where a wind blows.
I can teach you that.
The form of despair we call "the world."
A theft, yes, but gossipy, full of fear.
In which the "I" is seen as merely a specimen,
incomplete as such, overendowed,
maneuvering to rid itself of biological
precipitates—hypotheses, humilities,
propensities. . . .
Do you wish to come with me?
You know how in a landscape you see distances?
We can blur that. We can dissolve it
altogether. You know the *previous age?*
How it lacks shape until it's cut away by
love? We gust that lingering, moody, raw affection
out, we peck and fret until it's
gone, the flimsy courage, the leaky luggage
in which you carry round
your drafty dreams—of form, of hinged
awareness, all interlocking-up—dream on—
the chain is rattling that you've cast,
yet it is made of air, of less, look, here
it mirrors, here it curves
in space, here it resembles—quick—for just a
nanosecond—*happiness*—incorruptible whole—
how soothing, so real, a ledge above the
waterfall—You know, in music,
how you hear—you strain to hear—
the isolation of the meager, the *you* alone,
an *interim* bristling with arguments, illusions—
they are lesions, they are spreading across a naked
skin, a rolling, planetary stretch of human skin,

not like the feeling of an unseen presence,
not like—oh wave demolishing,
we're waiting for the phone to ring,
we're busy—no?—we cling—the versions
of the desolation we clock-out in lists, in
miles—The wave, the wave appears
but then withdraws, it ruffles at its rim
as *whereabouts,* moonlight thrashes in its
curl, clatters as inventory in its curl,
the wave—wake up—the wave I'll give you
tiny bits of if you'll still—
Postpone the honeycombing day,
let the sandbar rise up beneath us here,
the bed will do,
the spattering of texture, shade—brocaded shirtsleeve on
the chair—the corridor of mysteries
you call your hair—the masonry of your
delays—pen, paper, ink—my friend,
look at the ink, dip fingers through its open neck,
bring hand to lip—there—do it again, again,
blazon the mouth, rub in, exaggerate—
the little halo forms, around the teeth,
the mirror on that wall shows you the thing,
furious, votive—
oh look, the tiny heart
mouthing and mouthing its crisp inaudible black zeros out.

Willow in Spring Wind: A Showing

Pointless homesickness. Pointless shudderings.
Wind now clockwise: surrendering this way.
Wind now counter: surrendering that.
Wide tree with its good throat up from the dark
flinging forth embroiderings of inaudibles,
limbs jerked like a *cough*—then like a credo, flung—
then *broken oars,* then oars not broken at all but thrumming in
                                        unison into
the open sea of my
watching.

Clasp me, trellis of glancings,
delicatest machine—
body of the absconding *god*—
replacing something (I know not what)—
undulating, muttering liquidly . . .
Is it my glance or is it the willow kneeling wildly now
as if looking for corpses,
dragging its alphabet of buds all along the gravelly walk—
scraping—ripping—along the seemingly insatiable
hardnesses of gravel? Also the limestone wall they slap. . . .
Where is the sharp edge that we seek? Where
                    the open mouth?—
the true roughness—halo distended—
glittering with exaggeration—
dazzling the still philosophies—

Of the Ever-Changing Agitation in the Air

The man held his hands to his heart as he danced.
He slacked and swirled.
The doorways of the little city
blurred. Something
leaked out,
kindling the doorframes up,
making each entranceway
less true.
And darkness gathered
although it does not fall. . . . And the little dance,
swinging this human all down the alleyway,
nervous little theme pushing itself along,
braiding, rehearsing,
constantly incomplete so turning and tacking—
oh what is there to finish?—his robes made rustic by the reddish swirl,
which grows darker towards the end of the avenue of course,
one hand on his chest,
one flung out to the side as he dances, taps, sings,
on his scuttling toes, now humming a little,
now closing his eyes as he twirls, growing smaller,
why does the sun rise? remember me always dear for I will

return—
liberty spooring in the evening air,
into which the lilacs open, the skirts uplift,
liberty and the blood-eye careening gently over the giant earth,
and the cat in the doorway who does not mistake the world,
eyeing the spots where the birds must eventually land—

Linda Gregerson ~

Saints' Logic

Love the drill, confound the dentist.
Love the fever that carries me home.
Meat of exile. Salt of grief.
This much, indifferent

affliction might yield. But how
when the table is God's own board
and grace must be said in company?
If hatred were honey, as even

the psalmist persuaded himself,
then Agatha might be holding
her breasts on the plate for reproach.
The plate is decidedly

ornamental, and who shall say that pity's
not, at this remove? Her gown
would be stiff with embroidery whatever
the shape of the body beneath.

Perhaps in heaven God can't hide
his face. So the wounded
are given these gowns to wear
and duties that teach them the leverage

of pain. Agatha listens with special
regard to the barren, the dry,
to those with tumors where milk
should be, to those who nurse

for hire. Let me swell,
let me not swell. Remember the child,
how its fingers go blind as it sucks.
Bartholomew, flayed, intervenes

for the tanners. Catherine for millers,
whose wheels are of stone. Sebastian
protects the arrowsmiths, and John
the chandlers, because he was boiled

in oil. We borrow our light
where we can, here's begging the pardon
of tallow and wick. And if, as we've tried
to extract from the prospect, we'll each

have a sign to be known by at last—
a knife, a floursack, a hammer, a pot—
the saints can stay,
the earth won't entirely have given us up.

Line Drive Caught by the Grace of God

Half of America doubtless has the whole
of the infield's peculiar heroics by heart,
this one's way with a fractured forearm,
that one with women and off-season brawls,

the ones who are down to business while their owner
goes to the press. You know them already, the quaint
tight pants, the heft
and repose and adroitness of men

who are kept for a while while they age
with the game. It's time

that parses the other fields too,
one time you squander, next time you hoard,

while around the diamond summer runs
its mortal stall, the torso that thickens,
the face that dismantles its uniform.
And sometimes pure felicity, the length

of a player suspended above the dirt
for a wholly deliberate, perfect catch
for nothing, for New York,
for a million-dollar contract which is nothing now,

for free, for the body
as it plays its deft decline and countless humbling,
deadly jokes, so the body
may once have flattered our purposes.

A man like you or me but for this moment's
delay and the grace of God. My neighbor
goes hungry when the Yankees lose,
his wife's too unhappy to cook,

but supper's a small enough price to pay,
he'd tell you himself, for odds
that make the weeks go by so personal,
so hand in glove.

Mother Ruin

One fall after another. The snow
will oblige. It lies on its back in the drainage
of streetlight. It opens its dress
for the rain. *Old friend. I knew*

we'd be meeting again. Old prompter.
It gives up the bushes, gives up the stairs,
gives up the semblance of order
we've made, the pathways

that signify neighborliness. I am not a learned
iconographer, but I've seen how the patches hold out
under soot. Live long, said my father,
It'll do your mean heart good. Which the rain,

infecting the airborne and earthbound alike
with its news from the yellow sky,
rehearses to obsession: You'll have
your way with your betters at last.

And how the mild hands loosen
their hold. The snow has a mind to simplify,
as I do, I hope, and a body of blessed
amnesia. But always the rain

insinuates, which is death to abide by,
and always the honey-mouthed wind,
till the fastness that made things all of a piece
dissolves.

Linda Gregg ～

The Limits of Desire

Love came along and said, "I know,
I know. Abandoned after all
those promises.
But I can't help. I traffic
in desire, passion, and lust.
Trade bread for more bread,
change blood into wine.
I take the heaviest things
and make them joyous."
We sit under the fig tree.
How fragrant she is, her hand
over the folds of her dress.

Head bowed, voice quiet
in the warm wind.

Stuff

High up there she saw what
survives in the violent sunlight.
And felt no particular emotion.
The sea below, stone.

    Circle that.

The wind in the bright heat
made a sound like winter.
The wind moving strongly
in the whitening wild wheat.

    Circle *whitening.*

Goat, poppies, dry creek bed.

    Circle all of it.

Parts of sentences: *bleached
in the thin far-away,
momentary, and.*
A veil in her mind moved,
momentarily uncovering
memory and *of.* She felt
dazed by *facts* and *cared-for.*

    Circle *facts.*

Fish Tea Rice

It is on the Earth that all things transpire,
and only on the Earth. On it, up out of it,

down into it. Wading and stepping, pulling
and lifting. The heft in the seasons.
Knowledge in the bare ankle under water
amid the rows of rice seedlings. The dialogue
of the silent back and forth, the people moving
together in flat fields of water with the patina
of the sky upon it, the green shoots rising up
from the mud, sticking up seamlessly above the water.
The water buffalo stepping through as they work,
carrying the weight of their bodies along the rows.
The wrists of the people wet under the water,
planting or pulling up. It is this Earth that all
meaning is. If love unfolds, it unfolds here.
Here where Heaven shows its face. Christ's agony
flowers into grace, spikes through the hands
holding the body in place, arms reaching wide.
It breaks our heart on Earth. Ignorance mixed
with longing, intelligence mixed with hunger.
The genius of night and sleep, being awake
and at work. The sacred in the planting, the wading
in mud. Eating what is here. Fish, bread, tea, rice.

The Tree Falling in a Vacant Forest

The window open. Hearing
the summer wind in the dark trees.
Offering up silence
to the given silence.
Farther up the mountain
are stone paths between
walls of piled-up rocks
protecting abandoned fields.
The church bells ring once
at one and nobody stirs.
Mute, alive and awake.
Stillness so much like prayer,
so much like death.
The dreadful distance
between one person

and another. Each one
listening to that single high note
in all the singing.
Each one hearing the same one.

The Unknowing

I lie in the palm of its hand. I wake in the quiet,
separate from the air that's moving the trees outside.
I walk on its path, fall asleep in its darkness.
Loud sounds produce this silence. One of the markers
of the unknown, a thing in itself. To say
When I was in love gives birth to something else.
I walk on its path. The food I put in my mouth.
The girl I was riding her horse is not a memory
of desire. It is the place where the unknown
was hovering. The shadow in the cleavage
where two mountains met. The dark trees
and the shade and moving shadows there
where the top of the mountain stops and meets
the light much bigger than it is.
Its weight against all the light. A birthplace
of the unknown, the quick, the invisible.
I would get off my horse and lie down there,
let the wind from the ocean blow the high grass over
my body, be hidden with it, be one of its secrets.

Marilyn Hacker ~

The Boy

Is it the boy in me who's looking out
the window, while someone across the street

mends a pillowcase, clouds shift, the gutterspout
pours rain, someone else lights a cigarette ?

(Because he flinched, because he didn't whirl
around, face them, because he didn't hurl
the challenge back—*"Fascists?"*—not *"Faggots."*—*"Swine!"*
he briefly wonders—if he were a girl . . .)
He writes a line. He crosses out a line.

I'll never be a man, but there's a boy
crossing out words: the rain, the linen-mender,
are all the homework he will do today.
The absence and the privilege of gender

confound in him, soprano, clumsy, frail.
Not neuter—neutral human, and unmarked,
the younger brother in the fairy tale
except, boys shouted *"Jew!"* across the park

at him when he was coming home from school.
The book that he just read, about the war,
the partisans, is less a terrible
and thrilling story, more a warning, more

a code, and he must puzzle out the code.
He has short hair, a red sweatshirt. They know
something about him—that he should be proud
of? That's shameful if it shows?

That got you killed in 1942.
In his story, do the partisans
have sons? Have grandparents? Is he a Jew
more than he is a boy, who'll be a man

someday? Someone who'll never be a man
looks out the window at the rain he thought
might stop. He reads the sentence he began.
He writes down something that he crosses out.

Twelfth Floor West

Brandy, who got it from a blood transfusion,
was in for MAC, with a decubitus
ulcer festering. Baffled and generous,
her Baptist sisters brought each day's illusion
that she'd look back at them, that her confusion
would focus into words. They swabbed the pus,
they cleaned the shit, they wiped away the crust
of morning on her lids. The new bruise on
her thigh was baffling. They left an armchair
facing the window: an unspoken goal.
They'd come next morning, find her sitting there
with juice and coffee and a buttered roll.
The day she was released to hospice care
they came to meet her. They held her thin cold
hands on the gurney in the corridor.
The ambulance stood in the bay downstairs.

Invocation

This is for Elsa, also known as Liz,
an ample-bodied gospel singer, five
discrete malignancies in one full breast.
This is for auburn Jacqueline, who is
celebrating fifty years alive,
one since she finished chemotherapy,
with fireworks on the fifteenth of July.
This is for June, whose words are lean and mean
as she is, elucidating our protest.
This is for Lucille, who shines a wide
beam for us with her dark cadences.
This is for long-limbed Maxine, astride
a horse like conscience. This is for Aline
who taught her lover to caress the scar.
This is for Eve, who thought of AZT
as hopeful poisons pumped into a vein.
This is for Nanette in the Midwest.

This is for Alicia, shaking back dark hair,
dancing one-breasted with the Sabbath bride.
This is for Judy on a mountainside,
plunging her gloved hands in a glistening hive.
Hilda, Patricia, Gaylord, Emilienne,
Tania, Eunice: this is for everyone
who marks the distance on a calendar
from what's less likely each year to "recur."
Our saved-for-now lives are life sentences
—which we prefer to the alternative.

Broceliande

for Marie-Geneviève Havel

Yes, there is a vault in the ruined castle.
Yes, there is a woman waking beside the
gleaming sword she drew from the stone of childhood:
hers, if she bore it.

She has found her way through the singing forest.
She has gotten lost in the maze of cobbled
streets in ancient towns, where no lovely stranger
spoke the right language.

Sometimes she inhabits the spiring cities
architects project out of science fiction
dreams, but she illuminates them with different
voyages, visions:

with tomato plants, with the cat who answers
when he's called, with music-hall lyrics, work-scarred
hands on a steering-wheel, the jeweled secret
name of a lover.

Here, the water plunges beneath the cliff face.
Here, the locomotive purrs in the station.
Here, beneath viridian skies, a window
glistens at midnight.

Rachel Hadas ~

Still Life in Garden

Speechless, considering, feet well apart:
exactly how my mother would take root
deep in the garden, so you stand. It's early;
a summer day spreads out.
Bushier by the hour, long wavering rows
form lines and paths and furrows as of thought
marking a brow.
It's a small garden; no
reason for amazement if you tread
neatly in the footsteps of the dead.
Stealthily day by day
tomatoes, beans, cucumbers take on gloss
and heft, and everything seems effortless,
except the digging, planting, weeding—plus
the same vague tenderness,
the deep and inexhaustible green brood
you now are lost in, standing where she stood.

Shells

Scalloped synecdoches of satin cloud,
breezes from the Gulf, the creak of wings
(pelicans, egrets, sandpipers), whole coast
portable, rinsable, set out to dry

on towel-draped stools in late-afternoon.
Or was the waxing moon already up?
The soft sky throbbed in one long single note
deepening till evening was sore.

Glimmering memento scribbled on a slate
held up between a finger and a thumb,

dry in a twinkling: apricot and pearl
or blurry madras; burgundy and cream,

distaff or wing shape, scoop or lobe or drill.
Listen. A tiny thread of siren song,
note of an unseen bird, or a child's call
to a grandparent (this last the sign

of an affection still reciprocal).
Turning away from the exchange, I drift
over to take a towel, to rinse . . . and then
immediately forget the feeble errand

and find myself drawn back to the warm water.
They cradle me, these fluent twists of color.
A pale pink shell's unspeaking guarantee
cups a kind of convoluted promise

not that the dead will visit—they are dead.
But while we living bathe in such mild air,
neither will I rinse them from my mind,
beloved bones dismantled into sand.

On That Mountain

Evidence everywhere: accumulation.
Leaves atremble and narratives of branches
ramifying, so ever more connections
stay unfinished nor ever to be finished.
Do we not all have separate destinations?
Not that it matters. Aching opalescence
held us all spellbound, motionless, atingle,
balanced like sun and rain before a rainbow,
thunder purring and lightning white as daylight.
After the storm passed, all the world was gleaming,
glossy, almost lubricious with potential,
each blade of grass a dagger in the morning,
each leaf a goblet, brimming, winking, ready

to repay some small measure of night's thunder.
Couples stood tiptoe, trembling at departure,
kissing, breathing *Oh, let me touch your wisdom;*
let me then taste reciprocally your beauty.
More than mere iridescence—transformation.
Recall the dark face, thunder cowled at midnight.
Recall the bright face, rinsed clean for separation
as we're making our several preparations,
so many roads diverging in the greenwood,
putting on the inevitable blinders—
I must keep to my path and my path only—
closing our ears to thunder and cicadas,
closing our eyes to all those trembling branches,
meekly turning our backs on opalescence,
on the jewels of potential transformation,
getting ready to go back down the mountain.

Falcon

Stumbling along a sidewalk clogged with snow,
I don't see him, then suddenly I do.
He pops from nowhere in the blizzard's wake,
gesticulates, guffaws, then turns to walk
the way I'm going, "so that we can talk."
He does all the talking—wants to tell
me of an apparition on his sill
that morning. "Talons! Wingspan of four feet!"
It seems some hefty bird of prey alit
and beat its wings across the windowpane—
not albatross, not eagle, but their kin.
I'm asking some vague question or other;
he interrupts. "The falcon was my mother.
Funny, huh." It's not a question; he
demands acknowledgement. And I agree;
I think the falcon was his mother too.
That's settled; his decoding must be true.
We smile, then turn and trudge our separate ways,
negotiating strata of mixed grays.

Metaphor and myth and déjà vu;
romantic notions of madness, too.
Wingstroke: the cruel diagonal, the slash
of entry into time, the gory gash
inflicted by a visionary claw
on winter's blankness. What was it he saw?
Wings agitated in their little storm,
a private blizzard in the public one,
swoosh of arrival or epiphany?
I don't dispute that some reality
alighted on his window sill. I see
his face light up: relief at recognition.
The vision came; he recognized the vision.
His wounds may still be throbbing. All the same,
he's like a person who retrieves a name
or crucial clue that he had thought was gone
from the fierce blizzard of oblivion.

Mutability

What is it that always rearranges
the scenery? Not lack of appetite.
We love the world as it is, and then it changes.

Like a massive door on silent hinges
swinging open to reveal some sight
our next blink abruptly rearranges,

each fresh glimpse first shows and then estranges.
Reality is this and then is that.
Stay just the way you are, world! But it changes.

Everything unknown at first entrances,
shimmering with dangers, clues, and doubt
experience organizes, rearranges.

Drab is familiar. Glamorous is strange.
We drink them in as time is running out,
loving the world as it is until they change,

laws of space or logic of romances.
Life lies ahead of us and then does not.
Something inexorable rearranges
the scene we thought we knew, and the world changes.

Kimiko Hahn ～

A Boat Down the River of Yellow Silt

The first box held tiny yellow apples
from the tree behind your home.
Now inside the vestibule
a brown box with *mochi, manju,*
and a persimmon
like the hearts of various creatures.
I will eat one sweet tonight, one tomorrow
and after the ripening
on the sill that corners the morning sun
as we leave for the world
I will eat the one you tended yourself:
slice it open and lick the dark halves
that nourish its oval pit—I will
suck out these plump tongues of fruit
that speak for you.

Radiator

i.
Any strong sensation is a welcome break
from oxygen—

ii.
horse manure outside the stable
cigar smoke saturating the train seats
steamed asparagus from the steamer

iii.

I am not sure what I want
except that he wants
much the same: coal, flint, radiator.
But is X more
of my heart than my heart?

iv.

Any sensation penetrates my skin.
The cold porcelain tub,
the splintered deck,—

v.

X could last into the first snowfall,
the predicted blizzard.
And no you don't, I think to tell him,
wish I was your girlfriend.

vi.

for the taste of his mouth:
the acid of coffee and tobacco, the acid
of any initial encounter—

Clippings

the mundane in between correspondence

i.

What I learned on this past trip:
Sexual tension is never disappointing.
There are black stingrays with white polka dots.
Coral is a type of anemone.
(Some somersault. Some move at a rate of four inches/hour.)
Lower one's expectations in men.
Some sexualize activities, some sublimate sexual energy.
$5/day parking behind The Art Institute.
Marxism is not dead.
We are not necessarily seeking sex so much as stimulation.
A can lead to B and then become B.

ii.

Note to myself:
Forgot to mention in my last letter
how a friend's bird
is in love with a paper towel tube.
It fluffs its crown and wings,
struts of course,
then rubs its brow
and attempts to stick its head in the tube.

iii.

What I noticed on this past trip:
when I am away from you I feel homesick—
that feeling of nausea and hunger,
empty and full. Bleeding and bled.
Of missing a part of the body—
have you seen it?

iv.

Save clipping:
The cuscuta in Bryant Park
strangle then suck
the ivy in the northwest corner.
Also known as hell bind
and devil's sewing thread,
if the parasite sprout
does not find a host immediately
it creeps along,
the tip growing, the rear dying off,
till it finds something
to coil around.
Horticulturists
advise gardeners to weed by hand
or spray MCPA or DCPA.

v.

Save clipping:
"Secret Life of Jupiter's Moons."
Their molten cores may allow
enough change
for life. We can see the cracks

on the bald surface
through the delighted telescope.

    vi.
What I noticed this past hour—
the spirit nestles in the mundane
not the fantastic. So
I look in my bowl of cereal.
My basin of water.
A tank of clown fish.

Annotation in Her Last Court Diary

The before-snow sky lasted like the perpetual twilight
of a day when drinking might begin early
and extend an arm over the shoulder of the afternoon.
And, because not at the office,
one could lie across the bed fully clothed
and come once, twice, whatever.
Then what?

Susan Hahn ～

For Beauty

The day the gardeners planted
the impatiens, the surgeon
marked my abdomen with his fine
blue pen—X's
where his knife would make
the delicate cuts. I left with his map
pressed into my skin—
before he'd suck to rid me

of the voluptuous fat. Outside,
the workers were making their own
minute incisions in the April dirt—
the ground pockmarked and waiting
for beauty to be put. Inside,

I scrubbed with a rag and soap
to cleanse myself
of the path his hand
would take if I'd let him level
my belly, make it less
earth shaped—the world one flat
bruise, like paper imprinted
with the late evening news.

The Fifth Amendment

I do not witness myself
lifting the sweater from the shelf,
placing it in my soft bag
and then at home slipping it out
onto the unmade bed, spreading it
over my head and breasts—
how you stole them
with your touch.
I am mute if They ask

if we made love
that autumn evening—the ground
a crumpled blaze of leaves,
the wind forcing the waves further
onto the closed-off
beach with its bold sign
DO NOT TRESPASS.
When they question me
I do not lie. I do not say

your name out loud,
it remains inside me like a gun,

going off—the silencer on. Constantly
I explode and press
my face against the pillow
when I rise
under another man, you always
on my tongue, and call

to you wholeheartedly only
behind shut doors, show you
my latest infractions—
out of my purse comes a fake
gold band, a stick pin, a pocket
knife. I do not tell them
this is my life.

January Ovaries

The bulbs do not winter well
beneath the bitter ground this year.
In the spring I'll have to plant plastic
flowers in the box below

my window. No man will come
with a real bouquet, nothing will rise
from this cold. My body
curls into a zero. Soon the world
will be minus

one female. My grandmother
lies ten miles west
of here and tonight I feel her
frozen pelvis, see her ovaries—
just stains on what was once
the silky insides of her plush
casket. She hid her change

for a decent burial and now I scream
out to this mean January evening.
I hate the wind that whirls

the girl out of our bodies, tosses
us aside like a lover on his way
to call on someone else,
hands so full of pink
peonies like the ones
that used to soar

on both sides of my yard—
burst open in June's midmonth heat—
when life was a blinding dazzle, ignorant
of the dangerous freeze of this
long and barren night.

Brenda Hillman ～

The Mysteries

Writing about the mysteries
you can't quite say what they were.
Sacrifices? fasting? walking below
or sprinkling drops of water near
the marriage bed where the celebrants lay
briefly with the sacred one before
the raising up of objects?
You, the writer separated from her
by centuries, know only that later she'll
reappear sometimes on vases . . .
Hell was invented about this time;
later sources aren't reliable.

Aristotle writes that you'll suffer
over the mysteries but will learn
nothing new. The past slips into you finally.
Generations kept these secrets.
Islands fell asleep looking at the sea.
The one who ruled you above will rule you
below, taking you down to show you

the cut part of the wheat.
Probably she was earth,
your hunger was beautiful,
her hunger was beautiful,
but what do you really know?

Much was enacted, much was shown,
the burning one is sought
as an emblem; just once you will lie down
between her legs. The ritual
goes on with its potions,
its implied promises; the priest goes on
with his combs, his animals,
the exhausted wheat held up—
you try in vain, and after your research
among the transcripts of the institution
what gives you immortal life turns out to be
the breath of another person . . .

Belief in the subterranean rooms
has haunted you. Not finding them
isn't it the same as if you had?
We know you through your writings
and your complaints. Of course
she found you, though you believed
she loved you less than she should have—
your short smile, your long tears,
your fingers exiting the page,
the chords of your mysteries
absolute and wild and brief—

The Arroyo

—The perspective of lines or

innocence—

I love other bodies.

They always seemed to know
the secret before I did . . .

My mother has come outside to hang up towels: Cannon.
      I'm in my nada body, I'm about ten
      dragging magnets through sand
      in the arroyo to collect garnets from iron filings . . .

For others, it's "the ditch" or "the wash" or "drainage ditch"—

she's the thin expert at hanging out daily life. Squinting, I see
she's either a 1
or a 0 who never makes a mistake outdoors . . . pink towels, shorts,
sock sock / sock sock . . . The sun is the mistake that works.

The dragging then the filings then picking out
      garnets with tweezers in the 100 degree
      heat of the arroyo—

She calls my name;
it brightens; it's years before my period: chrome
glint of the abandoned fender; the doll's head
softens near the jar. These garnets
have backward facets. The present tense saddens them. Before
the flash flood I can make it
to the end of the arroyo where the hollow
chalk couple has been shown having sex on a rock.

If knowing alternates with seeing,
      dragging magnets through the sand thinking of them
      is the place where I am not.

Childhood is one of our low points.

When I cough, the doves
      fly away . . .
She hangs up clothes
      her single, her nada humming, when she
      turns sideways she is gone. Pinch bird-beak
      clothespins. She uses my whole name to call me in—)

A power comes up, it's in between the voices, it says
       you can stop making sense . . .

The hollow chalk couple—
       oh when I see them   I will touch their penis;

it is the small blue tombstone turned sideways.

Touching it is the invention of the new. Touching
the signs next to them—FUCK DICK   (heart heart heart)
is the both invention. Sex and more
exciting than doing it without talking—

> *I looked for the one who sought me*
> *without measure and the waters broke away . . .*
> *Waited for one who called*
> *but she had gone in. I called*
> *my love much later   the same*
> *when I was not him.*

The doll has become soft when left
for about twenty minutes; white   *s   take over the eyes;
our garnets on wax paper like menstrual blood.

Floods will come over the earth
but the hollow's better; winds replace
the chalk couple with sand;
the hawk sweeps and is gone;   coyote; various
night viceroys with yellow eyes;
Hollow body fills later   (in legs
with)   specks of time,
boys with wandering and orderly hands; laughter; such as— oh D.
       oh P., oh L., oh P., and oh A.

I loved other bodies.   Even those
I did not love   (those of this generation, we all . . .)

Cruel lovers and kind, when stoned in the south
and beaches between . . . And the faceless

chalk couple haunts me now: taught: touch
language with the north hand, flesh
with the right;

even three decades later, in danger
of sort of, the new disease and terror
of backward,
convinced one self is not
the way to live because we are lived *through*—

not to fail what was left blank—

I gather the little jars of the elements,

to show her;

within pure joy exists
a kind of hollow,
the inverse river, the opposite of water—

Male Nipples

—not utter, not
useless, the uselessness of desire, the slight
depression around the center

.

—When the motorcycle boy would light
        his cigarette, I longed
for the flat nipples, the scars, the contralto 'when'

.

and after you saw that the flower
of hell is not hell,
        but a flower—

.

How the beautiful boys' nipples in the pool
in Arizona looked
"underwatery"—pennies which have been thrown in

.

—and after you saw
that the flower of hell
was not one bit hell, but a flower—

.

convinced him to take only
his shirt off. They were, well, one
was brown and one was like the inside of a story—

.

—the ones of divers,
how they point down under the wetsuits:

.

  when I first put
my tongue on his (having decided
  he is not my mother)—

.

Oh, the bodies I loved were very tired.
I liked their skin. And
I was no sad animal no graveyard—

.

—and after you saw that desire
is hell, that the flower of hell
is not hell but a flower, well,

.

—So I told the little hairs
around his nipple: lie flat! and they did,
like a campfire, without the stories—

.

those of soldiers in the desert war and often
his left one tastes metallic as in
childhood, when I licked my brother's BB gun

.

Kept not finishing
            people I loved.
I tried, —but.

.

The top lip of a Corona beer
is about the size
of one of his—

.

        And after you saw that the flower
        of hell is desire, the almost, well,
you still had desire—

.

—So the moon came up
        pink tonight
like one of what had been missed

Jane Hirshfield ~

The Lives of the Heart

Are ligneous, muscular, chemical.
Wear birch-colored feathers,
green tunnels of horse-tail reed.
Wear calcified spirals, Fibonaccian spheres.
Are edible; are glassy; are clay; blue schist.
Can be burned as tallow, as coal,
can be skinned for garnets, for shoes.
Cast shadows or light;
shuffle; snort; cry out in passion.
Are salt, are bitter,
tear sweet grass with their teeth.
Step silently into blue needle-fall at dawn.
Thrash in the net until hit.
Rise up as cities, as serpentined magma, as maples,
hiss lava-red into the sea.
Leave the strange kiss of their bodies
in Burgess Shale. Can be found, can be lost,
can be carried, broken, sung.
Lie dormant until they are opened by ice,
by drought. Go blind in the service of lace.
Are starving, are sated, indifferent, curious, mad.
Are stamped out in plastic, in tin.
Are stubborn, are careful, are slipshod,
are strung on the blue backs of flies
on the black backs of cows.
Wander the vacant whale-roads, the white thickets
heavy with slaughter.
Wander the fragrant carpets of alpine flowers.
Not one is not held in the arms of the rest, to blossom.
Not one is not given to ecstasy's lions.
Not one does not grieve.
Each of them opens and closes, closes and opens
the heavy gate—violent, serene, consenting, suffering it all.

On the Beach

Uncountable tiny pebbles
of many colors,

Broken seashells mixed in with whole ones.

Sand dollars, shattered and whole,
the half-gone wing of a gull.

Changed glass
that is like the heart after much pain.
The empty shell of a crab.

A child moves alone in the grey
that is half fog, half wind-blown ocean.

She lifts one pebble, another,
into her pocket.
From time to time takes them out again and looks.

These few and only these. How many? Why?

The waves continue their work of breaking
then rounding the edges.

I would speak to her if I could,
but across the distance, what would she hear?
Ocean and ocean. Cry of a fish.

Walk slowly now, small soul, by the edge
of the water. Choose carefully
all you are going to lose, though any of it would do.

Not-Yet

Morning of buttered toast;
of coffee, sweetened, with milk.

Out the window,
snow-spruces step from their cobwebs.
Flurry of chickadees, feeding then gone.
A single cardinal stipples an empty branch—
one maple leaf lifted back.

I turn my blessings like photographs into the light;
over my shoulder the god of Not-Yet looks on:

Not-yet-dead, not-yet-lost, not-yet-taken.
Not-yet-shattered, not-yet-sectioned,
not-yet-strewn.

Ample litany, sparing nothing I hate or love,
not-yet-silenced, not-yet-fractured, not-yet- .

Not-yet-not.

I move my ear a little closer to that humming figure,
I ask him only to stay.

Painting

There is a painting of it: an eighteenth-century miniature from the
Kangra School of India, of the lovers, Krishna and Radha. In other
paintings, they have sheltered together, stood under a canopy of
invisibility among cows and the village girls who tend them. His hand
has covered her breast. In other paintings, we have watched her prepare
for him, behind the screen of a bedcloth held up by her friends. She is
putting red dye on her nipples and the bottoms of her feet, while he
looks down from an upstairs window, smiling. His body is blue, his
flute's notes possess a god's effortless irresistibility. But here it is
different. Though her eyes and mouth turn toward him with undeniable
longing, she stops him with one raised hand. Inscribed on the page are
his words, "Hear me, hear what I ask," and hers—they are simple,
immediate—"I hear, my Lord." But still she is leaving, walking away.
Though her torso turns back, her feet are already rising a little out of
her slippers—the god, though not the viewer, can see the red dye as she

goes. Under the silk of a sari so fine it could pass through the hoop of
her earring, her nipples are standing.

Each Happiness Ringed by Lions

Sometimes when
I take you into my body
I can almost see them—patient, circling.
Almost glimpse the moving shadow of the tail,
almost hear the hushed pad of retracted claws.
It is the moment—of this I am certain—
when they themselves are least sure.
It is the moment they could almost let us go free.

Linda Hogan ～

Nothing

Nothing sings in our bodies
like breath in a flute.
It dwells in the drum.
I hear it now
that slow beat
like when a voice said to the dark,
let there be light,
let there be ocean
and blue fish
born of nothing
and they were there.
I turn back to bed.
The man there is breathing.
I touch him

with hands already owned by another world.
Look, they are desert,
they are rust. They have washed the dead.
They have washed the just born.
They are open.
They offer nothing.
Take it.
Take nothing from me.
There is still a little life
left inside this body,
a little wildness here
and mercy
and it is the emptiness
we love, touch, enter in one another
and try to fill.

Tear

It was the time before
I was born.
I was thin.
I was hungry. I was
only a restlessness inside a woman's body.

Above us, lightning split open the sky.
Below us, wagon wheels cut land in two.
Around us were the soldiers,
young and afraid,
who did not trust us
with scissors or knives
but with needles.

Tear dresses they were called
because settler cotton was torn
in straight lines
like the roads we had to follow
to Oklahoma.

But when the cloth was torn,
it was like tears,
impossible to hold back,
and so they were called
by this other name,
for our weeping.

I remember the women.
Tonight they walk
out from the shadows
with black dogs,
children, the dark heavy horses,
and worn-out men.

They walk inside me. This blood
is a map of the road between us.
I am why they survived.
The world behind them did not close.
The world before them is still open.
All around me are my ancestors,
my unborn children.
I am the tear between them
and both sides live.

Tear dresses are traditional Chickasaw women's clothing.

Map

This is the world
so vast and lonely
without end, with mountains
named for men
who brought hunger
from other lands,
and fear
of the thick, dark forest of trees
that held each other up,
knowing fire dreamed of swallowing them

and spoke an older tongue,
and the tongue of the nation of wolves
was the wind around them.
Even ice was not silent.
It cried its broken self
back to warmth.
But they called it
ice, wolf, forest of sticks,
as if words would make it something
they could hold in gloved hands,
open, plot a way
and follow.

This is the map of the forsaken world.
This is the world without end
where forests have been cut away from their trees.
These are the lines wolf could not pass over.
This is what I know from science:
that a grain of dust dwells at the center
of every flake of snow,
that ice can have its way with land,
that wolves live inside a circle
of their own beginning.
This is what I know from blood:
the first language is not our own.
There are names each thing has for itself,
and beneath us the other order already moves.
It is burning.
It is dreaming.
It is waking up.

Janet Holmes ～

Depressive Episode

It's funny, but I don't remember much.
By day a rhombus travels over walls

reputed to be white: when evening falls
the lot's halogen streetlight makes the switch
and keeps the pattern of that window etched
just opposite my bed. I want to sleep.
They give me drugs that promise some escape
but fail. I have a buzzing they can't touch.
I have a clarity that I can't reach.
Words will not come. The nurses will not talk
or care for me. The doctor tells me, later,
that this, regrettably, is normal. Such
is their perspective: Someone with the luck
of health has tried to take her life. They hate her.

Whistle

1.
says Come here, says
Hi, says Go Team,
one note or two:
you call the dog,
he comes wagging;
you call someone
(maybe a child)
and the child knows
to come when you
whistle for her—

At the ballpark,
at the concert,
use your fingers
and screech, you, on
the winning side,
high-pitched: better
than air horns. You
know what's good, and
she's a *good* child,
covering her
ears.

Greet. Command.
Urge—

     Here I am!
Across the square!
Get over here!
You! Now!
        Yes, you—

   2.
Hold the grassblade here,
between your thumbs. Now

cup your hands.

              Put your
lips to the small spout
of your knuckles: make
a flute of the grass.

When you breathe, the blade
trembles: you blow, it
sings for you.

        Easy.

   3.
And the puckery kind,
the melodic, carrying
its own tune: that's when you're
a musical instrument—
and you know what that's like,

being an instrument,
don't you? Everybody does
this one. You force the shape
of your mouth small, small, and make
the sounds, the tremolos,

the Whistle While You Work,
the Bridge Over the River
Kwai. It can be pretty.

It can keep you company
later, when you're alone.

    4.

Those two notes: every parrot,
every construction worker
knows them and can perform. You
are meant to remember: *you
are on display.* It's supposed
to make you feel good, that they
have labored to remind you.

    5.

This is least satisfactory,
but the only one I can do.
(And I can't wink with my left eye,
only with this one.)
               Part your teeth,
a little. Then send out your breath:
sounds like wind with a bit of pitch
attached. Can't hear it far away.
Useless for calling, for making
most tunes. It's only a little
puff
      of the breath you weren't holding—

Fantasie Metropolitan

A ways off, someone is singing as he walks
down West End Avenue after the opera's done,
and the neighborhood of open windows looks

like balconies now hushed for him: a tux
here, and, radiant, a stylish sequined ballgown
a ways off shimmers . . . Singing as he walks,

he outdoes Luciano, Placido; he shocks
an eavesdropping producer ("Perfect tone!");
a neighborhood of open windows looks

down upon him, beaming (a young boy mocks
his carriage; but that's what you get from children).
A ways off, someone is listening as he walks

towards her, singing, unaware; she shakes
her hair: *What's that?* Attention caught, the one
discerning neighbor among the windows looks

up from her sofa: a warm evening, her book's
half-finished. She'd like a glass of wine.
A ways off, someone is singing as he walks
her neighborhood. She opens the window. Looks.

Fanny Howe ～

Basic Science

One cadaver said to the other
cadaver, "You're my cadaver."

The conversation ended there
but not its effects.

Their souls had evaporated.

It was up to love to raise them
from their litters and let them

arrive as the living poor
at the surface of the earth. It did.

At first the maculate pair
poked and picked through refuse.

Denials were their daily breads.
Then they were sold to those

who found their fertility a bonus.
Owned then by the living with names

and fortunes, with lovers who say,
"Lover, I'm your lover,"

cadavers were still the majority.
They kept creation going and love

as well—like hands on a cold
or sunburned back—a weight

with properties that animate.

Bathroom

On certain days a sweat folds in over her, covering her as weather covers a little city. Ghosts of dogs still bark. A man stumbles, dodging a flake. Pink rubbish rises to meet him and burns his cheek. Snow she says is ash from the sun's fire. On the apophatic path being is having. It's where I move even though I can't.

Today she feels she is permanently everywhere she has been and must return to inhabit the same spaces before it's too late. But there is something between her and happiness even if she leaves a voice-recorder attached to a telephone in the room she has most recently vacated. It's like putting backbones in the fridge.

Tell me about it, people say to indicate that they know the story already.

Yesterday was like an ordinary run-of-the-mill comic book in black and white. I mean, one frame was alienated from the next. I never felt my denials more intensely. I went to church in a dirty train depot to wash away the sweat and think. In the public worship hole the meditation booths are often slimy, refuse litters the rim of the toilet bowl, and a stink floats between door and wall, making it impossible to get past the noxious to the pure. This is where the word "pew" was probably born.

I talk too much and prayed that God would help me practice silence. In the booth I remembered that Joseph speaks rarely in heaven, Mary even more rarely, and Jesus not at all. I remembered a realization that I once remembered after realizing the same thing several times and always forgetting that I had. It had to do with heaven being the Xian version of enlightenment. That's all I can recall.

Out in the fresh air I hurried down the streets, hearing my soul whisper: "No name. No passport. No money. No identification. No map. No home."

If you are the handmaiden of Zero, you will soon discover that Its manifestations of uncreated energy must be acknowledged whenever possible. Prayer is effective when it is directed towards the universe as a massive machine, and not towards an airy idea of Maker. After all, when Maker turns into Taker, you hate hate hate It. Better to recognize the materials as fixed, even when invisible to the naked eye. There is no escaping the universe.

Starlet

That terrible day my heart took a blow that nearly killed
it. While silver lilac shivered in the Hollywood Hills,
I packed and prepared to fly. My heart, once red as a
valentine, seemed to contract and blacken like a prune.

If you want to know the truth, I missed happiness by
inches. A meeting (planned for seven years) never took
place. The person lost me. I could not find him. As a
result, my personal pulse dropped the formula for
survival. I fled the city of colors, emptying, with each
mile, my will to go on.

On the night freeway my heart felt like a body in a pine
box, calling "Preacher, keep it short, for God's sake."

Every minute was a sort of monument in a mortuary.

1. To be lost is to be undiscovered.
2. To find is to discover what was already lost and waiting.

But where is the object of desire in fact?
Is it really out there, waiting?
How can it be there, when it requires time to find it?
And if the time required to get there doesn't yet exist, how
do I know it's there at all?

My Broken Heart

On the 85th night of 19__ there were 280 days left in the year.
The cure began. Just as Pascal carried the date of his revelation
in his breast pocket, I began to carry a dated hanky next to my heart.
Healing is a job that requires a mop.

This arm I am leaning on is perfectly suited to mine.
(I always wanted to say that.) Now cold winds have come
and the doctor has determined that my hope was full of holes.
"But holes in the universe are made of matter."

On the 305th night of 19__ there were 60 days left in the year.
The cure began. Beauty of style depends on similarity.
Snow for instance is a perfect show, because the sky
opens like a flower shaking out its secrets.

This time of year reminds me of the dot that completes my name.
The dot over the letter that pertains to the first person
singular is a symbol for me of my head.
I always put on my dot when I'm already out of the word.

At last I only have hope for heaven.
Like a person who has "come to" after fainting,
I now know the meaning of the question:
"Where in the world?"

Women should sit down like me—
wherever they are standing now—and refuse to move.
I always wanted to say that.
Whoa! Is someone here, or is this, like, a hat tossed in the air?

Am I really better at being crushed than I was before?

Marie Howe ～

The Attic

Praise to my older brother, the seventeen-year-old boy, who lived
in the attic with me an exiled prince grown hard in his confinement,

bitter, bent to his evening task building the imaginary building
on the drawing board they'd given him in school. His tools gleam

under the desk lamp. He is as hard as the pencil he holds,
drawing the line straight along the ruler.

Tower prince, young king, praise to the boy
who has willed his blood to cool and his heart to slow. He's building

a structure with so many doors it's finally quiet,
so that when our father climbs heavily up the attic stairs, he doesn't

at first hear him pass down the narrow hall. My brother is rebuilding
the foundation. He lifts the clear plastic of one page

to look more closely at the plumbing,
—he barely hears the springs of my bed when my father sits down—

he's imagining where the boiler might go, because
where it is now isn't working. Not until I've slammed the door behind

the man stumbling down the stairs again
does my brother look up from where he's working. I know it hurts him

to rise, to knock on my door and come in. And when he draws his
    skinny arm
around my shaking shoulders,

I don't know if he knows he's building a world where I can one day
love a man—he sits there without saying anything.

Praise him.
I know he can hardly bear to touch me.

How Some of It Happened

My brother was afraid, even as a boy, of going blind—so deeply
that he would turn the dinner knives away from, *looking at him,*

he said, as they lay on the kitchen table.
He would throw a sweatshirt over those knobs that lock the car door

from the inside, and once, he dismantled a chandelier in the middle
of the night when everyone was sleeping.

We found the pile of sharp and shining crystals in the upstairs hall.
So you understand, it was terrible

when they clamped his one eye open and put the needle in through
    his cheek
and up and into his eye from underneath

and left it there for a full minute before they drew it slowly out
once a week for many weeks. He learned to, *lean into it,*

to *settle down* he said, and still the eye went dead, ulcerated,
breaking up green in his head, as the other eye, still blue

and wide open, looked and looked at the clock.

My brother promised me he wouldn't die after our father died.
He shook my hand on a train going home one Christmas and gave me
    five years,

as clearly as he promised he'd be home for breakfast when I watched him
walk into that New York City autumn night. *By nine, I promise,*

and he was—he did come back. And five years later he promised five
    years more.
So much for the brave pride of premonition,

the worry that won't let it happen.
You know, he said, I always knew I would die young. And then I got sober

and I thought, OK, I'm not. I'm going to see thirty and live to be an old
    man.
And now it turns out that I am going to die. Isn't that funny?

—One day it happens: what you have feared all your life,
the unendurably specific, the exact thing. No matter what you say or do.

This is what my brother said: Here, sit closer to the bed
so I can see you.

The Kiss

When he finally put
his mouth on me—on

my shoulder—the world
shifted a little on the tilted

axis of itself. The minutes
since my brother died

stopped marching ahead like
dumb soldiers and

the stars rested.
His mouth on my shoulder and

then on my throat
and the world started up again

for me,
some machine deep inside it

recalibrating,
all the little wheels

slowly reeling and speeding up,
the massive dawn lifting on the other

side of the turning world.
And when his mouth

pressed against my
mouth, I

opened my mouth
and the world's chord

played at once:
a large, ordinary music rising

from a hand neither one of us could see.

What the Living Do

Johnny, the kitchen sink has been clogged for days, some utensil probably
    fell down there.
And the Drano won't work but smells dangerous, and the crusty dishes
    have piled up

waiting for the plumber I still haven't called. This is the everyday we
    spoke of.
It's winter again: the sky's a deep headstrong blue, and the sunlight
    pours through

the open living room windows because the heat's on too high in here, and
    I can't turn it off.
For weeks now, driving, or dropping a bag of groceries in the street,
    the bag breaking,

I've been thinking: This is what the living do. And yesterday, hurrying
    along those
wobbly bricks in the Cambridge sidewalk, spilling my coffee down my
    wrist and sleeve,

I thought it again, and again later, when buying a hairbrush: This is it.
Parking. Slamming the car door shut in the cold. What you called
    that yearning.

What you finally gave up. We want the spring to come and the winter to
    pass. We want
whoever to call or not call, a letter, a kiss—we want more and more and
    then more of it.

But there are moments, walking, when I catch a glimpse of myself in the
    window glass,
say, the window of the corner video store, and I'm gripped by a cherishing
    so deep

for my own blowing hair, chapped face, and unbuttoned coat that I'm
    speechless:
I am living, I remember you.

Lynda Hull ～

Red Velvet Jacket

It's almost Biblical driving this midnight burning highway
past South Bronx exits
with the names of streets once known, where torched cars
spiral columns
acetylene blue & white. We're in the universe of lost things
where the lights are out,
the lamp pawned & soon the record player, that enamelled table,
clothes, the rooms & faces,

air hissing soft through the rolled-down window like
silk velvet slipping hot
into my handbag, velvet fine as a fingerprint whorl,
maroon as the long dusty cars
that sharked these avenues, mildewed upholstery like
it was always raining night,
the insides ripped out of everything. But I was talking
about the red velvet jacket

that hangs even now in the mind flaring its slow veronicas
in recollection's wind that breathes
the mineral glamour of cornices & pilasters, districts
that burned years ago.
These days at the fringes even trains turn express,
the bombed-out blocks & clustered faces
blurred featureless. Out of sight, out of mind. Midnight's
burning highway, another charred strip-joint.

Recollection: gather back the gleaming fragments & Warsaw
    flashes
a museum model of the Ghetto—
the Jews immured, a system of catwalks and barricades,
the trams' blackened windows
so that citizens might blindly pass, might invent consoling
    fictions.
Columns of flame light now
this tangled graffiti to a kind of incantation.
Called back in wonder,

the strangeness, the story endlessly told any life unfurls,
causal chains of small decisions,
almost random, those accidents of grace or luck. That red velvet
'30s jacket. How it sleeked
over the hips, elaborate glass buttons, how it made me feel
a little dangerous, a sense
of stolen fortune or history, as if I'd been chosen
for extraordinary moments, as if

I'd walked untouched, fire parting smoothly before me, liquid
& blue, that refused to singe,
to mar the bearer with a scar to signify the event.
Red velvet the color
of that long car we'd cruise under the river through
    Alphabetown,
then the Bronx, Hunts Point
& its flooded streets awash with crates of rotting fruit,
streets that figure still

relentless in the endless anarchy of dreams—
the Puerto Rican dealer, Juan, his wife, the kid. (Shift the car

to 5th, don't stop,
don't slow down.) But the door splinters all over again.
The jump-the-dealer routine.
Red velvet sleeve rolled up, snake of blue vein, snake
of salsa rising from the streets,
the warmth sexual, turning me capable, the grain of the wood

on the floor flowering into the music, each fiber,
each splinter, until the tree
it came from greened in the mind. No, it's the watery
green of neon flickering
the boy's face by the window, the baby in his arms dangling
over the street, the mother screaming.
His face striped green & blue & the water of the neon
stutters turning Spanish

on my tongue. *Darme, darme el niño.* Accidental grace.
I just wanted the screaming to stop.
Someone muffles the mother, but he's watching me—sole white
     face,
blanched translucent—& across his face
all the complexity a gaze can be. Calculation at first, fear,
disdain, the crying child. And what
did he see? Some hopped-up 16 year old with police-colored
     skin.

God I was innocent then, clean as a beast in the streets.
At the fringes of Warsaw's Ghetto
stands a prison where they sorted Jews from politicals,
politicals from homosexuals,
where masses dispersed to nameless erasure. There's a tree
     there,
lopped & blackened, yet it shines,
enshrined in prayer scrolls, nailed icons. Oh, lucky life,
I didn't understand until tonight,

called back from the ruins in that jacket, dark stain blooming
through the sleeve, the child squalling
in my useless arms. I don't know what happened to the jacket
& all those people are lost to a diaspora,
the borough incinerated around them, nowhere in this night

I drive through. Silk velvet and its rich hiss
the shade of flame offering its drapery, its charm
against this world burning ruthless, crucial & exacting.

The Window

Streak of world blurred charcoal & scarlet, the El slows,
brakes at the platform, Little Chinatown,
& there's that window, peeling frame, screen split

to rippling raingusts. A curtain breathes
through busted glass, a glimpse of hallway
enamelled green, rows of numbered doors, nothing more,

and then the train lurches forward sparkling
its electric signature above slick, hissing rails.
Soon, soon, I'll stop there, the window's pull

irresistible as the force of a star collapsed
to black gravity. I'll step through the window,
take up again the key for the one room to which

I keep returning. Let me wait again there by the sill
as I wait still. Here's the steeple of the burnt church,
beloved of vandals, the sooty block of

old law tenements where chipped tubs rise
porcelain on their feet in cold-water kitchens,
unashamed, small gray animals, the startled

array of insects we lived with.
Where are you? In the hallways, bodies passing
smell like bodies, unwashed, ginsoaked, dopesick,

the musk & salt. Where are you?
Hear with me the slant beat of that orthopedic shoe
striking pavement a few stained facades away.

With each echoing step, feel again the raw acceleration,
hope, or is it fear looming, receding?
Steaming hellmouths in the asphalt. If each of us

contains, within, humankind's totality, each possibility
then I have been so fractured, so multiple & dazzling
stepping towards myself through the room where

the New Year's dragon lies in its camphored sleep.
In the days I lived here, a thousand rooms
like it, making love was a way of saying *yes,*

I am here, these are my borders, hold me down
a little while. Make me real to myself. One more shining
thing gone after in the night that disappeared

with morning. No substance. But I'd like you
to place your hands, cradling the neck's swanny
arch, stand here by the copper dormer window

that's like an endless gallery of such windows
with fire escapes burdened by doves' insatiable
mourning. Then let it happen, the desire to be out

in the world, more than in it, wholly of it,
trammelled, broken to neoned figments.
All it takes is a few adjustments—

purple those lids, the lips as we did then,
that old mirror clouded with vague continents. We're
ready to inhabit the sequinned gowns, martini glasses

pouring their potions over the street, the milky syringes
& oh, those ravening embraces, the ravished streets
& whispered intersections. Slick back

the hair, and then the wig. I could never face anything
without the wig. Transformed, the old vaudeville desire
struts & kicks its satiny legs, the desire to be

consumed by ruined marquees, these last drifting hotels,
to be riven, served up singing, arched & prismed
from a thousand damp boulevards. Those things which shine

in the night, but what vertigo to surrender, falling
through the elaborate winged buildings they only have
in neighborhoods like this anymore, January's bitten snow

cold about the ankles. Let me move again, a wraith,
past these windows—bridesmaids' gowns the color
of casket linings, flammable, green

as gasoline poured from the can to flame the alley
outside the Welfare's fluorescent offices,
police stations, the shabby public hospital's endless

waiting rooms. How exactly pinned-to-the-wall
love was in that harsh economy, the world, the world, the
    world.
What I remember is the astringent sting of air.

Living on nothing but injections & vodka, a little
sugar. The self, multiple, dazzling. What I remember
are the coral husks of lobsters broken clean

through restaurant windows, steaming. Through these
windows tumble fragments, the stories, lavish
vertical fountains of opera. Dressed as death's-heads,

crowds demonstrate against the new war
with placards before the marble stairs. Like a wraith
let me move again among them, through the rooms

of this building, home of my fondest nightmares, let me
stay the hand twisting in rage, let me crush
the white & violet petals of sleep, the black sticky heart

of sleep over the delicate eyelids, over the bodies'
soft geographies, over the sorrow, the grandeur
of columns & esplanades, the soot-shouldered graces

outside the museum. Rude armfuls of orchids
fill the florist's windows, these lunar ones
curved like music staffs above dissolving aspirins

I might bring back to the room for you. Oh phantoms.
Oh the many lives that have fountained through
my own. Soon, soon, I shall stop upon that platform

& you will meet me there, the world rosegray beyond
the scalloped tops of buildings & we shall seek
that thing which shines & doth so much torment us.

Barbara Jordan ⁓

Viper Light

Dampness, and things drift out of focus
in the hampering not-quite-dark:
a calla lily's 40-watt
softness downhill, elect over shadowy hosta.

Odd, as the light withdraws, how I grow
more distinctly incarnate:
an instrument of touch, vulnerable to the obstacles
that each step supposes—

branches hung low, the quarrels of roots.
Often I stop,
like a listener at a keyhole, feeling the wind
examine an ankle or wrist, sensing

the tiny exhalations I'm surrounded by.
Glints. The clicks of twigs.
I look up at a sky
that falls miraculously close, and step through

a casement of vines,
tapping the ground as I would going downstairs
in the dark, vertigo of unknowing
into the cluttered world and its subterfuge.

This Poem

Let the form be a garden in wild wilderness,
a hyacinth language, a turning in wind
                        when marginal influences
disrupt the flow.

Build thought as a bee does,
one concern at a time, a hexagonal symmetry
                        deep in the structure;
or explore the foundation

of a derelict house, its cellarhole cracked
by bracken and trees—with daffodils blooming
                        alongside the door,
and off in the woods, sometimes

a forsythia. And a carrion beetle to bury
the mouse, the skeletal memories of things
                        that are gone;
or hidden, like antlers, deep in the pines

where branches are tossed,
a path to the edge of recorded time, that stops
                        at a place
where the language is lost.

Peaceable Kingdom

Distance is at bay, and emptiness has gone
where emptiness goes:

into the arches of morning, wordlessly
back to its distillates
before myth, even before Adam
               named the serpent and the bee,
said *fox,* and *wood thrush,* and glimpsed
the fact of yes and no
in an elemental light—that knowledge
differentiates, requires separation

as a painting needs perspective,
else lion and lamb float beside the child
enlarged beyond proportion—
for each must reckon with a horizon
conceived as endpoint, a kind of teleology
                  of matter.
But by innocent distortion
memory will coincide the parts
into a whole—insubstantial, primitive
      as Eden—
everything equal, having been gathered
from some rib of thought
extending its imaginary line back
to what was, is, and not.

Allison Joseph ～

Soul Train

Oh how I wanted to be a dancer
those Saturday mornings in the
living room, neglecting chores

to gape at the whirling people
on our television: the shapely
and self-knowing brownskinned

women who dared stare straight
at the camera, the men strong,
athletically gifted as they

leaped, landed in full splits.
No black people I knew lived
like this—dressed in sequins,

make-up, men's hair slicked
back like 40's gangsters,
women in skin-tight, merciless

spandex, daring heels higher
than I could imagine walking in,
much less dancing. And that

dancing!—full of sex, swagger,
life—a communal rite where
everyone arched, swayed, shimmered

and shimmied, hands overhead
in celebration, bodies moving
to their own influences, lithe

under music pumping from studio
speakers, beneath the neon letters
that spelled out SOUL TRAIN—

the hippest trip in America.
I'd try to dance, to keep up,
moving like the figures on

the screen, hoping the rhythm
could hit me in that same
hard way, that same mission

of shake and groove, leaving
my dust rag behind, ignoring
the furniture and the polish

to step and turn as they did,
my approximation nowhere near
as clever or seductive, faking

it as best I knew how, shaking
my 12 year old self as if something
deep depended on the right move,

the righteous step, the insistent
groove I followed, yearning to get
it right, to move like those dancers—

blessed by funk, touched with rhythm,
confident in their motions, clothes,
their spinning and experienced bodies.

Wedding Party

I wanted to have a wedding
where a band called Sexual Chocolate
would play cover versions
of "Turn the Beat Around"
and "Got To Be Real", tunes
so disco everyone's forsaken them
in the oh-so-cynical '90's.
I wanted my bridesmaids
in orange tulle, groomsmen
in light green, their cummerbunds
so wide their waists became
some thick, enticing region,
regal as an alleyway.
I wanted folks to glide
onto the dance floor,
doing quaint, antiquated dances
like the funky chicken, Latin hustle,
polyester divas doing moves so fine
even Shaft himself would have
to stop, grin his approval.
I wanted finger foods

in snack sizes, a wedding cake
piled so high in gumdrops
and coconut that no one's
blood sugar level would be safe.
I wanted it crass, and big,
and ugly, bad enough
to make relatives shudder
whenever they remembered
my denim patchwork gown,
platform heels. Instead,
I'm here at the city clerk's office,
an ordinary woman in an
ordinary dress, marrying
an ordinary man in ordinary
shoes. Still, I know that party
is going on somewhere, if only
in the strange regions of my mind:
music and costumes
by Earth, Wind, and Fire,
catering by Momma and Company,
and the m.c., of course,
is a dapper black man
who wishes us *love, peace, and soul,*
our lives one everlasting ride
on the Soul Train bound
for Boogie Wonderland,
li'l Stevie's harmonica
blowin' us one last tune
in the key of life.

Brigit Pegeen Kelly ～

Song

Listen: there was a goat's head hanging by ropes in a tree.
All night it hung there and sang. And those who heard it
Felt a hurt in their hearts and thought they were hearing

The song of a night bird. They sat up in their beds, and then
They lay back down again. In the night wind, the goat's head
Swayed back and forth, and from far off it shone faintly
The way the moonlight shone on the train track miles away
Beside which the goat's headless body lay. Some boys
Had hacked its head off. It was harder work than they had imagined.
The goat cried like a man and struggled hard. But they
Finished the job. They hung the bleeding head by the school
And then ran off into the darkness that seems to hide everything.
The head hung in the tree. The body lay by the tracks.
The head called to the body. The body to the head.
They missed each other. The missing grew larger between them,
Until it pulled the heart right out of the body, until
The drawn heart flew toward the head, flew as a bird flies
Back to its cage and the familiar perch from which it trills.
Then the heart sang in the head, softly at first and then louder,
Sang long and low until the morning light came up over
The school and over the tree, and then the singing stopped. . . .
The goat had belonged to a small girl. She named
The goat Broken Thorn Sweet Blackberry, named it after
The night's bush of stars, because the goat's silky hair
Was dark as well water, because it had eyes like wild fruit.
The girl lived near a high railroad track. At night
She heard the trains passing, the sweet sound of the train's horn
Pouring softly over her bed, and each morning she woke
To give the bleating goat his pail of warm milk. She sang
Him songs about girls with ropes and cooks in boats.
She brushed him with a stiff brush. She dreamed daily
That he grew bigger, and he did. She thought her dreaming
Made it so. But one night the girl didn't hear the train's horn,
And the next morning she woke to an empty yard. The goat
Was gone. Everything looked strange. It was as if a storm
Had passed through while she slept, wind and stones, rain
Stripping the branches of fruit. She knew that someone
Had stolen the goat and that he had come to harm. She called
To him. All morning and into the afternoon, she called
And called. She walked and walked. In her chest a bad feeling
Like the feeling of the stones gouging the soft undersides
Of her bare feet. Then somebody found the goat's body
By the high tracks, the flies already filling their soft bottles
At the goat's torn neck. Then somebody found the head
Hanging in a tree by the school. They hurried to take

These things away so that the girl would not see them.
They hurried to raise money to buy the girl another goat.
They hurried to find the boys who had done this, to hear
Them say it was a joke, a joke, it was nothing but a joke. . . .
But listen. here is the point. The boys thought to have
Their fun and be done with it. It was harder work than they
Had imagined, this silly sacrifice, but they finished the job,
Whistling as they washed their large hands in the dark.
What they didn't know was that the goat's head was already
Singing behind them in the tree. What they didn't know
Was that the goat's head would go on singing, just for them,
Long after the ropes were down, and that they would learn to listen,
Pail after pail, stroke after patient stroke. They would
Wake in the night thinking they heard the wind in the trees
Or a night bird, but their hearts beating harder. There
Would be a whistle, a hum, a high murmur, and, at last, a song,
The low song a lost boy sings remembering his mother's call.
Not a cruel song, no, no, not cruel at all. This song
Is sweet. It is sweet. The heart dies of this sweetness.

Petition

These are the long weeks. The weeks
Of waiting. Let them be
Longer. Let the days smolder
Like the peat slung
In plastic sacks by the greenhouse
And let the seedlings not rush
Into growth but climb the air slowly
As if it were a ladder,
One small foot at a time.
Let the fetid smell of bone meal
Be the body unlocking
As the river does, slowing to a hazy laze
That pulls the boaters in
And makes the fish rise up. And
As the wide-wheeled yellow tractors
Roll along the highway,
Stalling traffic in their wakes,

And the dust from the playing fields
Settles over us like pollen,
Like the balls dropping softly
Into our mitts, let
The willow's love of water—
Its dark and beaded rain—
Be the only storm we long for.

Botticelli's St. Sebastian

I have seen a robin cock his head so,
Listening for the change in weather,
Feeling in the field's pale grass turning paler
The moment of his own departure.
I have seen the bird throw his whole body
In the air, and go, the small bird go,
And the bared ground at once lose heart,
As if taken by a sudden grippe.

And I have seen blond wood, fine-grained
As this stripped flesh, seen the long
Boards of strong wood—when bound fast
And bitten by the drill—spew up phrases
As curled and extravagant as Sebastian's gaze,
The way the lover does at consummation,
Lost to himself and to the world, but still
Safely shaded by the tree he rose from.

I have seen, I have seen the lake's heart
When the rain comes through, when the water's
Dark flesh is driven, *I have seen* the heart
Move like a doe through the woods, move
Like a stunned doe, deeper and deeper,
Through trees that turn and close behind her,
The way water closes over a dropped stone,
Or a torn limb, or a lasting wound. . . .

O, the forgotten traveller!

Wild Turkeys: The Dignity of the Damned

Because they *are* shame, and cannot flee from it,
And cannot hide it, they go slow,
One great variegated male and his harem of four wild hens

Halting our truck as they labor
To cross the road into the low fields they are indentured to.
They go slow, their hearts hardened to this;

Those laughing-stock, shriveled, lip-stick red hearts—
Swinging on throat and foreneck
Beneath the narrow heads that are the blue

Not of the sky but of convicts' shaved skulls—
Have been long indurated by rains and winds and filth
And the merciless exposures of the sun.

They do not look up, they do not fly—
Except at night when dark descends like shame,
When shame is lost to dark, and then,

Weak-winged, they heave themselves
Into the low tree roosts they drop from in the morning,
Crashing like swag-bellied bombers

Into the bare fields and stingy stands of trees
They peck their stones and seeds from.
Yesterday they were targets, but now they go slow,

As if this lacuna between winter and spring, still gray,
But full of the furred sumacs' pubescent probings,
And the faint oily scent of wild onion vials crushed open,

Gave hope to even them, or as if they knew
All seasons to be one, the going back,
The crossing over, the standing still, all the same,

When the state you defend is a lost state,
When lurching into an ungainly run
Only reminds you that there is nowhere to run to.

And this movement, this jerking
Of these heavy goffered carapaces forward,
This dumb parading that looks at first glance furtive,

Like skulking, the hunkered shoulders, the lowered heads,
Reveals, as we watch, the dignity that lines
Of pilgrim-sick possess as they halt toward some dark grotto—

A faith beyond the last desire to possess faith,
The soldier's resolve to march hump-backed straight into death
Until it breaks like oil over him

And over all that is lost.

Jane Kenyon ∿

Dutch Interiors

for Caroline

Christ has been done to death
in the cold reaches of northern Europe
a thousand thousand times.
                         Suddenly bread
and cheese appear on a plate
beside a gleaming pewter beaker of beer.

Now tell me that the Holy Ghost
does not reside in the play of light
on cutlery!

A woman makes lace,
with a moist-eyed spaniel lying
at her small shapely feet.
Even the maid with the chamber pot
is here; the naughty, red-cheeked girl. . . .

And the merchant's wife, still
in her yellow dressing gown

at noon, dips her quill into India ink
with an air of cautious pleasure.

Having It Out with Melancholy

If many remedies are prescribed for an illness,
you may be certain that the illness has no cure.
      A. P. CHEKHOV, THE CHERRY ORCHARD

1 From the Nursery

When I was born, you waited
behind a pile of linen in the nursery,
and when we were alone, you lay down
on top of me, pressing
the bile of desolation into every pore.

And from that day on
everything under the sun and moon
made me sad—even the yellow
wooden beads that slid and spun
along a spindle on my crib.

You taught me to exist without gratitude.
You ruined my manners toward God:
"We're here simply to wait for death;
the pleasures of earth are overrated."

I only appear to belong to my mother,
to live among blocks and cotton undershirts
with snaps; among red tin lunch boxes
and report cards in ugly brown slipcases.
I was already yours—the anti-urge,
the mutilator of souls.

2 Bottles

Elavil, Ludiomil, Doxepin,
Norpramin, Prozac, Lithium, Xanax,
Wellbutrin, Parnate, Nardil, Zoloft.
The coated ones smell sweet or have

no smell; the powdery ones smell
like the chemistry lab at school
that made me hold my breath.

3 Suggestion from a Friend

You wouldn't be so depressed
if you really believed in God.

4 Often

Often I go to bed as soon after dinner
as seems adult
(I mean I try to wait for dark)
in order to push away
from the massive pain in sleep's
frail wicker coracle.

5 Once There Was Light

Once, in my early thirties, I saw
that I was a speck of light in the great
river of light that undulates through time.

I was floating with the whole
human family. We were all colors—those
who are living now, those who have died,
those who are not yet born. For a few

moments I floated, completely calm,
and I no longer hated having to exist.

Like a crow who smells hot blood
you came flying to pull me out
of the glowing stream.
"I'll hold you up. I never let my dear
ones drown!" After that, I wept for days.

6 In and Out

The dog searches until he finds me
upstairs, lies down with a clatter
of elbows, puts his head on my foot.

Sometimes the sound of his breathing
saves my life—in and out, in
and out; a pause, a long sigh. . . .

7 Pardon

A piece of burned meat
wears my clothes, speaks
in my voice, dispatches obligations
haltingly, or not at all.
It is tired of trying
to be stouthearted, tired
beyond measure.

We move on to the monoamine
oxidase inhibitors. Day and night
I feel as if I had drunk six cups
of coffee, but the pain stops
abruptly. With the wonder
and bitterness of someone pardoned
for a crime she did not commit
I come back to marriage and friends,
to pink-fringed hollyhocks; come back
to my desk, books, and chair.

8 Credo

Pharmaceutical wonders are at work
but I believe only in this moment
of well-being. Unholy ghost,
you are certain to come again.

Coarse, mean, you'll put your feet
on the coffee table, lean back,
and turn me into someone who can't
take the trouble to speak; someone
who can't sleep, or who does nothing
but sleep; can't read, or call
for an appointment for help.

There is nothing I can do
against your coming.
When I awake, I am still with thee.

9 Wood Thrush

High on Nardil and June light
I wake at four,
waiting greedily for the first
notes of the wood thrush. Easeful air
presses through the screen
with the wild, complex song
of the bird, and I am overcome

by ordinary contentment.
What hurt me so terribly
all my life until this moment?
How I love the small, swiftly
beating heart of the bird
singing in the great maples;
its bright, unequivocal eye.

August Rain, After Haying

Through sere trees and beheaded
grasses the slow rain falls.
Hay fills the barn; only the rake
and one empty wagon are left
in the field. In the ditches
goldenrod bends to the ground.

Even at noon the house is dark.
In my room under the eaves
I hear the steady benevolence
of water washing dust
raised by the haying
from porch and car and garden
chair. We are shorn
and purified, as if tonsured.

The grass resolves to grow again,
receiving the rain to that end,
but my disordered soul thirsts
after something it cannot name.

Mary Kinzie ～

The Bolt

That girl so long ago walked, as they all did, shop girls,
Little cousins, and church friends, to the unflattering
Hack of the hem just where the calf begins to swell,
Felt ruchings of the bodice's stiff panels
Gall the flesh beside the flattening ornate
Armature of underwear (like pads and straps
For livestock, fretted by tooling and bright studs),
So she must yank her knees against
Pounds of rigid drapery in the storm of heat,

Trailing through the pestering, gray heads
Of Queen Anne's lace, wind ravelling
Her hair and sweeping through prolific
Jagged-bladed grass—a wind that pressed down
There like God with both His hands, mashing the air,
Darkening the hole where the dry mouth of the wood
Yawned to drink the stumbling travelers already touched
By the heavy sacs of rain that broke and ran
In gouts down saturated pleats of serge . . .

Here that girl ran last, so long ago, to be run through
By one long lightning thread that entered, through
A slender purple bruise, the creamy skin of her temple.

The instant that it happened, nobody remembered
How she looked or spoke, so quickly had she blended
With this evocation of her having been.

This was the past: a stroke of imagery stare-
Frozen, finished in suspension.

Beautiful Days

Blossoms lift the branches
So the birds move.

The first leaves shine.

These are nice days, shipshape and fair.
Birds over all
Are moving.

But then I think, they
Are happy and gay,

They do not know
What life does.

Carolyn Kizer ～

Twelve O'Clock

At seventeen, I've come to read a poem
At Princeton. Now my young hosts inquire
If I would like to meet Professor Einstein.
But I'm too conscious I have nothing to say
To interest him, the genius fled from Germany just in time.
"Just tell me where I can look at him," I reply.

Mother had scientific training. I did not;
She loved that line of Meredith's about
The army of unalterable law.

God was made manifest to her in what she saw
As the supreme order of the skies.
We lay in the meadow side by side, long summer nights

As she named the stars with awe.
But I saw nothing that was rank on rank,
Heard nothing of the music of the spheres,
But in the bliss of meadow silences
Lying on insects we had mashed without intent,
Found overhead a beautiful and terrifying mess,

Especially in August, when the meteors whizzed and zoomed,
Echoed, in little, by the fireflies in the grass.
Although, small hypocrite, I was seeming to assent,
I was dead certain that uncertainty
Governed the universe, and everything else,
Including Mother's temperament.

A few years earlier, when I was four,
Mother and Father hushed before the Atwater-Kent
As a small voice making ugly noises through the static
Spoke from the grille, church-window-shaped, to them:
"Listen, darling, and remember always;
It's Doctor Einstein broadcasting from Switzerland."

I said, "So what?" This was repeated as a witticism
By my doting parents. I was dumb and mortified.
So when I'm asked if I would like to speak to Einstein
I say I only want to look at him.
"Each day in the library, right at twelve,
Einstein comes out for lunch." So I am posted.

At the precise stroke of noon the sun sends one clear ray
Into the center aisle: He just appears,
Baggy-kneed, sockless, slippered, with
The famous raveling grey sweater,
Clutching a jumble of papers in one hand
And in the other his brown sack of sandwiches.

The ray haloes his head! Blake's vision of God,
Unmuscular, serene, except for the electric hair.
In that flicker of a second our smiles meet:

Vast genius and vast ignorance conjoined;
He fixed, I fluid, in a complicit yet
Impersonal interest. He dematerialized and I left, content.

It was December sixth, exactly when,
Just hours before the Japanese attack
The Office of Scientific R & D
Began "its hugely expanded program of research
Into nuclear weaponry"—racing the Germans who, they feared,
Were far ahead. In fact, they weren't.

Next night, the coach to school; the train, *Express,*
Instead pulls into every hamlet: grim young men
Swarm the platforms, going to enlist.
I see their faces in the sallow light
As the train jolts, then starts up again,
Reaching Penn Station hours after midnight.

At dinner in New York in '44, I hear the name
Of Heisenberg: Someone remarked, "I wonder where he is,
The most dangerous man alive. I hope we get to him in time."
Heisenberg. I kept the name. Were the Germans, still,
Or the Russians, yet, a threat? Uncertainty. . . .
But I felt a thrill of apprehension: Genius struck again.

It is the stroke of twelve—and I suppose
The ray that haloes Einstein haloes me:
White-blonde hair to my waist, almost six feet tall,
In my best and only suit. Why cavil?—I am beautiful!
We smile—but it has taken all these years to realize
That when I looked at Einstein he saw me.

At last that May when Germany collapsed
The British kidnapped Heisenberg from France
Where he and colleagues sat in a special transit camp
Named "Dustbin," to save them from a threat they never knew:
A mad American general thought to solve
The post-war nuclear problem by having them all shot.

Some boys in pristine uniforms crowd the car
(West Pointers fleeing from a weekend dance?),
Youth's ambiguities resolved in a single action.

I still see their faces in the yellow light
As the train jolts, then starts up again,
So many destined never to be men.

In Cambridge the Germans visited old friends
Kept apart by war: Austrians, English, Danes,
"In a happy reunion at Farm Hall."
But then the giant first struck—in the still
Center of chaos, noise unimaginable, we thought we heard
The awful cry of God.

Hiroshima. Heisenberg at first refused
To believe it, till the evening news confirmed
That their work had led to Hiroshima's 100,000 dead.
"Worst hit of us all," said Heisenberg, "was Otto Hahn,"
Who discovered uranium fusion. "Hahn withdrew to his room,
And we feared that he might do himself some harm."

It is exactly noon, and Doctor Einstein
Is an ancient drawing of the sun.
Simple as a saint emerging from his cell
Dazed by his own light. I think of Giotto, Chaucer,
All good and moral medieval men
In—yet removed from—their historic time.

The week before we heard of Heisenberg
My parents and I are chatting on the train
From Washington. A grey-haired handsome man
Listens with open interest, then inquires
If he might join us. We were such a fascinating family!
"Oh yes," we chorus, "sit with us!"

Penn Station near at hand, we asked his name.
E. O. Lawrence, he replied, and produced his card.
I'd never heard of him, but on an impulse asked,
"What is all this about harnessing
Of the sun's rays? Should we be frightened?"
He smiled. "My dear, there's nothing in it."

So reassured, we said goodbyes,
And spoke of him in coming years, that lovely man.
Of course we found out who he was and what he did,

At least as much as we could comprehend.
Now I am living in the Berkeley hills,
In walking distance of the Lawrence Lab.

Here where Doctor Lawrence built the cyclotron,
It's noon: the anniversary of Hiroshima:
Everywhere, all over Japan
And Germany, people are lighting candles.
It's dark in Germany and Japan, on different days,
But here in Berkeley it is twelve o'clock.

Reunion

For more than thirty years we hadn't met.
I remembered the bright query of your face,
That single-minded look, intense and stern,
Yet most important—how could I forget?—
Was what you taught me inadvertently
(tutored by books and parents, even more
By my own awe at what was yet to learn):
The finest intellect can be a bore.

At this, perhaps our final interview,
Still luminous with your passion to instruct,
You speak to that recalcitrant pupil who
Inhaled the chalk-dust of your rhetoric.
I nod, I sip my wine, I praise your view,
Grateful, my dear, that I escaped from you.

Fearful Women

Arms and the girl I sing—O rare
arms that are braceleted and white and bare

arms that were lovely Helen's, in whose name
Greek slaughtered Trojan. Helen was to blame.

Scape-nanny call her; wars for turf
and profit don't sound glamorous enough.

Mythologize your women! None escape.
Europe was named from an act of bestial rape:

Eponymous girl on bull-back, he intent
on scattering sperm across a continent.

Old Zeus refused to take the rap.
It's not his name in big print on the map.

But let's go back to the beginning
when sinners didn't know that they were sinning.

He, one rib short: she lived to rue it
when Adam said to God, "She made me do it."

Eve learned that learning was a dangerous thing
for her: no end of trouble it would bring.

An educated woman is a danger.
Lock up your mate! Keep a submissive stranger

like Darby's Joan, content with church and Kinder,
not like that sainted Joan, burnt to a cinder.

Whether we wield a sceptre or a mop
It's clear you fear that we may get on top.

And if we do—I say it without animus—
It's not from you we learned to be magnanimous.

Ingathering

The poets are going home now,
After the years of exile,
After the northern climates
Where they worked, lectured, remembered,

Where they shivered at night
In an indifferent world.
Where God was the god of business,
And men would violate the poets' moon,
And even the heavens become zones of war.

The poets are going home
To the blood-haunted villages,
To the crumbling walls, still pocked
With a spray of bullets;
To the ravine, marked with a new cross,
Where their brother died.
No one knows the precise spot where they shot him,
But there is a place now to gather, to lay wreaths.
The poets will bring flowers.

The poets are coming home
To the cafés, to the life of the streets at twilight,
To slip among the crowds and greet their friends;
These young poets, old now, limping, who lean on a cane:
Or the arm of a grandchild, peer with opaque eyes
At the frightening city, the steel and concrete towers
Sprung up in their absence.
Yet from open doorways comes the odor of grapes
Fermented, of fish, of oil, of pimiento . . .

The poets have come home
To the melodious language
That settles in their heads like moths alighting,
This language for which they starved
In a world of gutterals,
Crude monosyllables barked by strangers.
Now their own language enfolds them
With its warm vocables.
The poets are home.

Yes, they have come back
To look up at the yellow moon,
Cousin of that cold orb that only reflected
Their isolation.
They have returned to the olives, the light,
The sage-scented meadows,

The white-washed steps, the tubs of geraniums,
The sere plains, the riverbanks spread with laundry,
The poppies, the vineyards, the bones of mountains.

Yes, poets, welcome home
To your small country
Riven by its little war
(as the world measures these events),
A country that remembers heroes and tears;
Where, in your absence, souls kept themselves alive
By whispering your words.
Now you smile at everything, even the priests, the militia,
The patient earth that is waiting to receive you.

Election Day, 1984

Did you ever see someone cold-cock a blind nun?
Well, I did. Two helpful idiots
Steered her across the tarmac to her plane
And led her smack into the wing.
She deplaned with two black eyes & a crooked wimple,
Bruised proof that the distinction is not simple
Between ineptitude and evil.
Today, with the President's red button playing
Such a prominent role,
Though I can't vote for it, I wonder
If evil could be safer, on the whole.

Maxine Kumin ～

Early Thoughts of Winter

It's sweaty work, the getting ready part.
This winter's cordwood split and stacked

seen endwise is as gratifying
as the Pyramids in a steel engraving
each stone etched with equal emphasis.

Spraddle-legged in the humbling steam
of the manure pile I stand shoveling
pickup loads to tuck the garden in
dreaming beyond backache and tedium
of February with each dip, lift and fling

remembering Heidegger, his broad-jawed noun
Geworfenheit, for the castaway's condition
the shipwrecked seeker after news across
the water, the burrower, gleaner I need to be.

I summon up my winter Crusoe-self
the she-who-enters-her-own-stubbornness
who, chilled to rising in the predawn pitch
to stoke the stoves, will overhear the tick
and thrust of seeds inside the sleet's sad tune

and with the wild turkeys, the bachelor moose
the endearing cluster of juncos braving
the barn floor, comrade castaways
demand from February good news
across the water.

Almost Spring, Driving Home, Reciting Hopkins

"A devout but highly imaginative Jesuit,"
Untermeyer says in my yellowed
college omnibus of modern poets,
perhaps intending an oxymoron, but is it?
Shook foil, sharp rivers start to flow.
Landscape plotted and pieced, gray-blue, snow-pocked
begins to show its margins. Speeding back
down the interstate into my own hills
I see them *fickle, freckled,* mounded fully
and softened by millennia into pillows.

The priest's sprung metronome tick-tocks,
repeating how old winter is. It asks
each mile, snow fog battening the valleys,
what is all this juice and all this joy?

October, Yellowstone Park

How happy the animals seem just now,
all reading the sweetgrass text, heads down
in the great yellow-green sea of the high plains—
antelope, bison, the bull elk and his cows

moving commingled in little clumps, the bull
elk bugling from time to time his rusty screech
but not yet in rut, the females not yet in heat,
peacefully inattentive—the late fall

asters still blooming, the glacial creeks running clear.
What awaits them this winter—which calves will starve
to death or driven by hunger stray from the park
to be shot on the cattle range—they are unaware.

It is said that dumb beasts cannot anticipate
though for terror of fire or wolves some deep
historical memory clangs out of sleep
pricking them to take flight. As flight pricked the poet

dead seventeen years today, who for seventeen
years before that was a better sister
than any I, who had none, could have conjured.
Dead by her own hand, who so doggedly whined

at Daddy Death's elbow that the old Squatter
at last relented and took her in. Of sane mind
and body aged but whole I stand by the sign
that says we are halfway between the equator

and the North Pole. Sad but celebratory
I stand in full sun on the 45th parallel

bemused by what's to come, by what befell,
by how our friendship flared into history.

Fair warning, Annie, there will be no more
elegies, no more direct-address songs
conferring the tang of loss, its bitter flavor
as palpable as alum on the tongue.

Climbing up switchbacks all this afternoon,
sending loose shale clattering below,
grimly, gradually ascending to a view
of snowcaps and geysers, the balloon

of Old Faithful spewing, I hear your voice
beside me (you, who hated so to sweat!)
cheerfully cursing at eight thousand feet
the killers of the dream, the small-time advice-

laden editors and hangers-on. I've come
this whole hard way alone to an upthrust slate
above a brace of eagles launched in flight
only to teeter, my equilibrium

undone by memory. I want to fling
your cigarette- and whiskey-hoarse chuckle
that hangs on inside me down the back wall
over Biscuit Basin. I want the painting

below to take me in. My world that threatened
to stop the day you stopped, faltered
and then resumed, unutterably altered.
Where wildfires crisped its hide and blackened

whole vistas, new life inched in. My map
blooms with low growth, sturdier than before.
Thus I abstain. I will not sing, except
of the elk and his harem who lie down in grandeur

on the church lawn at Mammoth Hot Springs,
his hat rack wreathed in mist. This year's offspring
graze in the town's backyards, to the dismay
of tenants who burst out to broom them away.

May the car doors of tourists slam, may cameras go wild
staying the scene, may the occasional
antelope slip into the herd, shy as a child.
May people be ravished by this processional.

May reverence for what lopes off to the hills
at dusk be imprinted on their brain pans
forever, as on mine. As you are, Anne.
All of you hammered golden against the anvil.

Credo

I believe in magic. I believe in the rights
of animals to leap out of our skins
as recorded in the Kiowa legend:
Directly there was a bear where the boy had been

as I believe in the resurrected wake-robin,
first wet knob of trillium to knock
in April at the underside of earth's door
in central New Hampshire where bears are

though still denned up at that early greening.
I believe in living on grateful terms
with the earth, with the black crumbles
of ancient manure that sift through my fingers

when I topdress the garden for winter. I believe
in the wet strings of earthworms aroused out of season
and in the bear, asleep now in the rock cave
where my outermost pasture abuts the forest.

I cede him a swale of chokecherries in August.
I give the sow and her cub as much yardage
as they desire when our paths intersect
as does my horse shifting under me

respectful but not cowed by our encounter.
I believe in the gift of the horse, which is magic,

their deep fear-snorts in play when the wind comes up,
the ballet of nip and jostle, plunge and crow hop.

I trust them to run from me, necks arched in a full
swan's S, tails cocked up over their backs
like plumes on a Cavalier's hat. I trust them
to gallop back, skid to a stop, their nostrils

level with my mouth, asking for my human breath
that they may test its intent, taste the smell of it.
I believe in myself as their sanctuary
and the earth with its summer plumes of carrots,

its clamber of peas, beans, masses of tendrils
as mine. I believe in the acrobatics of boy
into bear, the grace of animals
in my keeping, the thrust to go on.

Ann Lauterbach ∽

Meanwhile the Turtle

for Gloria Jacobs

(Not even the lame grass can answer this *what is this*
Thread of body, injunction to seem,
The ricochet robot blurting its mind
In these aftermaths & retreats, as if singing.
Say you heard it all before in the crisp dawn.
Say you were held delighted in duration:
The giddy kingfisher's clack and surround
Above water while the mower rackets air.
Shorn, divested, complicit asunder or sender
Forthwith enjambed in the yellow sound of yellow.
Maybe someone else was talking in the next room.
Maybe the big man lay with a spoon in his mouth
Lest he swallow his tongue, or was coiled

Sleeping in the stairwell while someone's mother wept.
We had nameless signs we could read.
Nobody told me to confess.
There was an old fear, hearing the planes,
Believing our anthem's threat: the noise is real.
Anyone can see there are gaps in the leaves.
Anyone can tell the sky is in disrepair.
But also an accumulation, being wounded
Similarly with just the wind to embrace
In the pallid sky's stormy indoctrination.
Not just any shard underfoot, but a long nail
Up through the heel, a child's wrist broken) is lost.

Werner Herzog 68 / Iowa City 88

Then this light flipped in the rowboats
Then this anchor lifted from petulant water
Like a stem. Neither chimes nor chills nor vanes,
Wheels wheeling, deadpan, the young man
Had taken his crew so far to this island,
This wind, to find them and, eventually,
To take us there.
               It was a small city
It was
     the light released, skyward, not
Natural and I wondered how many of them
Were dead having gone from the frame.
                    It was
Like a wedding of strangers previously arranged,
The bride in her gown of fetid rosebuds
Forgetting her lines, smiling
Despite the feet in the wall,
Despite the illusion.
          It was
Another film in the small city where a man
Saw the most beautiful woman ever
In the ugliest hat.
          It was a hen trapped in sand.
It was, finally, a young boy not knowing what to say

Now that he was able to say it, a young girl
Singing, twisting up her skirt, her mouth dark.
It was a war nobody had ever heard of, a child
Touching the sleeve of a stranger.

How Things Bear Their Telling

for Joe Brainard

They settle out from their curfew
A splash of redemption, a ploy

Steeped in earliness
Listening is scenic

Uplifted ruffled boughs
Anchor the pond

To be near, tame and graphic
Small derivations drawn mutely forward

Footsteps on the pier
Quickly dry

His white cuffs open
His collar open

To fuse, conclude, adhere
To dangle and arrange

Along the road, a garden is waiting
Along the road, a house will be built

The painter's huge back—
The volume's tent

A celebration among strangers
A bride's opaque face

Where she travels she is
Harpoon in the back of a whale

    *   *   *

Tinctures, sets, rips—
Leaping as conquest, as plot

A mower and an old man's booming voice
A chronology is mislaid

What is palpable is shunted—
The distance between landings

Deep in the foreground like a caress—
The breath draws in

There are these rims
These goggles clouded and abrupt

A narrative resembles a lost ornament
The dying resemble the living closely

Is someone really sawing the night?
Any choice is exclusive

Saying and crickets abide—
They forgot to put up signs

Both dice and sky are loaded—
The night is like Chicago

Seeing through to thought
A nude and voracious stranger

If you are stung, try cool air—
The sun is not a light bulb

    *   *   *

Not so much spinning as raking
Not so much burning as fleeing toward

Days the size of postcards
Voyages along steps

Immediacy precludes reversal—
Jumping, he contained her pleasure

To touch, to refrain from touching
Nearness is its own, inexhaustible law

A temporal clerestory evades the threshold
No smears, no red ink

Stairs, halls, doors—
An incitement to hurt, to be inconclusive.

Dorianne Laux ～

This Close

In the room where we lie, light
stains the drawn shades yellow.
We sweat and pull at each other, climb
with our fingers the slippery ladders of rib.
Wherever our bodies touch, the flesh
comes alive. Heat and need, like invisible
animals, gnaw at my breasts, the soft
insides of your thighs. What I want
I simply reach out and take, no delicacy now,
the dark human bread I eat handful
by greedy handful. Eyes, fingers, mouths,
sweet leeches of desire. Crazy woman,
her brain full of bees, see how her palms curl
into fists and beat the pillow senseless.
And when my body finally gives in to it
then pulls itself away, salt-laced
and arched with its final ache, I am

so grateful I would give you anything, anything.
If I loved you, being this close would kill me.

What I Wouldn't Do

The only job I didn't like, quit
after the first shift, was selling
subscriptions to *TV Guide* over the phone.
Before that it was fast food, all
the onion rings I could eat, handing
sacks of deep fried burritos through
the sliding window, the hungry hands
grabbing back. And at the laundromat,
plucking bright coins from a palm
or pressing them into one, kids
screaming from the bathroom and twenty
dryers on high. Cleaning houses was fine,
polishing the knick-knacks of the rich.
I liked holding the hand-blown glass bell
from Czechoslovakia up to the light,
the jewelled clapper swinging lazily
from side to side, its foreign,
A-minor ping. I drifted, an itinerant,
from job to job, the sanatorium
where I pureed peas and carrots
and stringy beets, scooped them,
like pudding, onto flesh-colored
plastic plates, or the gas station
where I dipped the ten-foot measuring stick
into the hole in the blacktop,
pulled it up hand over hand
into the twilight, dripping
its liquid gold, pink-tinged.
I liked the donut shop best, 3 AM,
alone in the kitchen, surrounded
by sugar and squat mounds of dough,
the flashing neon sign strung from wire
behind the window, gilding my white uniform

yellow, then blue, then drop-dead red.
It wasn't that I hated calling them, hour
after hour, stuck in a booth with a list
of strangers' names, dialing their numbers
with the eraser end of a pencil and them
saying hello. It was that moment
of expectation, before I answered back,
the sound of their held breath,
their disappointment when they realized
I wasn't who they thought I was,
the familiar voice, or the voice they loved
and had been waiting all day to hear.

Homecoming

At the high school football game, the boys
stroke their new muscles, the girls sweeten their lips
with gloss that smells of bubblegum, candy cane,
or cinnamon. In pleated cheerleader skirts
they walk home with each other, practicing yells,
their long bare legs forming in the dark.
Under the arched field lights a girl
in a velvet prom dress stands near the chainlink,
a cone of roses held between her breasts.
Her lanky father, in a corduroy suit, leans
against the fence. While they talk, she slips a foot
in and out of a new white pump, fingers the weave
of her French braid, the glittering earrings.
They could be a couple on their first date, she,
a little shy, he, trying to impress her
with his casual stance. This is the moment
when she learns what she will love: a warm night,
the feel of nylon between her thighs, the fine hairs
on her arms lifting when a breeze
sifts in through the bleachers, cars
igniting their engines, a man bending over her,
smelling the flowers pressed against her neck.

The Thief

What is it when your man sits on the floor
In sweatpants, his latest project
set out in front of him like a small world, maps
and photographs, diagrams and plans, everything
he hopes to build, invent or create,
and you believe in him as you always have,
even after the failures, even more now
as you set your coffee down
and move toward him, to where he sits
oblivious of you, concentrating
in a square of sun—
you step over the rulers and blue graph-paper
to squat behind him, and he barely notices,
though you're still in your robe
which falls open a little as you reach
around his chest, feel for the pink
wheel of each nipple, the slow beat
of his heart, your ear pressed to his back
to listen—and you are torn,
not wanting to interrupt his work
but unable to keep your fingers
from dipping into the ditch of his pants,
torn again with tenderness
for the way his flesh grows unwillingly
toward your curved palm, toward the light,
as if you had planted it, this sweet root,
your mouth already an echo of its shape—
you slip your tongue into his ear
and he hears you, calling him away
from his work, the angled lines of his thoughts,
into the shapeless place you are bound
to take him, over bridges of bone, beyond
borders of skin, climbing over him
into the world of the body, its labyrinth
of ladders and stairs—and you love him
like the first time you loved him,
with equal measures of expectancy
and fear and awe, taking him with you
into the soft geometry of flesh, the earth

before its sidewalks and cities,
its glistening spires,
stealing him back from the world he loves
into this other world he cannot build without you.

Cleopatra Mathis ～

Blues: Late August

Bluefish boil the water silver; they tangle in the chase
and the frantic smelt run headlong onto the sand,
caught by the blinding mirror, the water's

skimming sheet. And in the tide's remove, the knife-like
bodies hardly struggle, laid out in one long row
like silverware by a child's hand. All the bathers

scramble out of the sea, fearful of the indiscriminate
bluefish jaws, and around our heads, the gulls
flail about, sharp-eyed and diving, a frenzy

guarding the feast. All along, the ocean
turns its back to the spectacle, locked
in its usual resolve, but I can't move

for love of the world, its terror and sufficiency.

The Angels

They bring in the knife, they show you
his sleeping body and the spot to strike.
They are quick as shadows crossing,
a knot of confusion. Then one of them
moves apart, separate from their dark impulse,

and claims your hand. She creates
another step, another purpose,
though for now she makes your tears
fall with frustration. She will not let you
do what your body wants; your teen-age body,
made purely of anger, wants to forget
the spirit, the flicker of self
that whispers through you at odd moments.
You do not yet know the art
of seeing and waiting, the way
to make change possible. And what is she
but the secret that bears your life forward.
Charitable toward this mess you live in,
she turns you away, and in that instant
you hear the night birds, the small clamor of their appeal
more lovely because they remain unseen.
A universe of wings is somehow at your window,
claiming a world you have never known
could be righteous. When the moment passes,
your hand, having lost its will,
moves away from his chest, and the chaos
takes over, those truculent voices
of fear. Years will pass before you can live
with their noise, before their presence
grows quiet, and you find her again, the one
who, without reason, made herself your mother,
and you listen.

from *Lessons*

12. Given What Manages

This is for the daughter,
heiress to a fortune in grief, a paradise
and so the loss of one. They made her
heroine of the hurricane: no flattery
to share the female name.
This time she'll get credit,

discovering the eclipse and comet; the romance
hurled to earth, the morning
white in her face, too many kisses
or not enough. By thirty she can't believe
the ugly business of winter: leaf by leaf,
the trees give up everything
to survive. In her own house
crows feet and the widening
network of veins. And this hunger she's got—
an eye for food, the endless
fat or thin, shrink and scold.
Regret for the baby she turned from,
guilt for the one in her lap, how she takes in
the pure air of that little breath.
Destined to be of two minds
she's the heartchip and the nag,
keeper of the sponge,
the bedtime and the bed.
Instead of love, she learns mercy
requires knowledge. She buys herself
a net and a killing jar, and goes out
into the remarkable summer field
(the baby is napping, the ring's on the sink).
Before the summons of that bright yell
she went to the woods, walking to see
the fox and deer. And to repeat the infinite
names from all the books, the regeneration
of wild. Once on her mountain, she discovered
the burrow of the last great rattler, the last poison
that high up in the East.
Fierce for him, she scattered
leaves and brush against the spot,
and hearing human noise, ran
deeper into the trees. As if she were a deer—
then like the deer she could do nothing for,
stumbled finally back to the road.
All through late winter's grip
she walked to find the herds
whose hunger would have forced them
to the bad bark and pencil-thick stems
that rip like cloth the lining of the stomach;
forced them to the crushed and mangled

winter bushes, where to suffer that gnawing
they all lie down.

                    Now squinting in the noon buzz
she gathers the easy weeds, some to admire,
some to eat, rubbing off the dirt with spit.
Uncovered in the glare, the clumsy insects
scatter and fall. And what is it inside her
still holds and releases?
She writes in her book: "Given what manages
to survive on this earth, who are we
to think we could know trauma or triumph,"
and sits until sweat
trails down her neck, between her breasts.
She uses the net to jar what's common,
the horsefly and bee. After supper she'll draw
with clarity and precision.
She'll draw them as they have not been.

Gail Mazur ～

The Acorn

On the way home from school, a child is struck
on the head by a falling acorn. She looks down
at her brown shoes, refusing to give the squirrel—
who must have waited for her, aimed at her—
satisfaction. *You've got to show them you don't care*
her mother taught her. Does this mean
the squirrel knows she's Jewish? She always
dawdles so the other girls who have friends
to walk home with won't bully or taunt her
the way the Leblanc boys did yesterday,
in front of Corpus Christi—
pulling her hair, kicking her, calling her
"kike" and "Christ killer," while Father John

strolled up and down the sidewalk
that glittered with flecks of mica, reading.
Or the way Anna and Mary, the twins, held her down
in the cloakroom to make her show them her tail,
only letting go when the art teacher saw them.
Some days, she wants to be Catholic and make
confessions. Some of the secrets she keeps
from her mother. Why hurt her and what could she do?
Don't be fooled by girls pretending they like you,
the world is full of those rotten bitches—
The acorn.

After the Storm, August

What can I learn from the hummingbird,
a big thing like me? I hardly have time
to study its flash, its momentous
iridescence, before it disappears
into the mimosa, sated with nectar.
I admire the way the greenery trembles.
I remember reading that this bird is
never sated—its whole miniature
life an exercise in digestion. What
excuse does it need to be this useless,
what's to learn from this inscrutable engine?
Why does something in me fly out
to the feathery tree, whirring
so hungrily toward translucence?

Keep Going

It's not only the accumulation of small slights:
your name misspelled on last evening's program;

the party uptown after the ceremonies and readings—
an editor praising C's poems as if you weren't

standing there beside him, craving appreciation
(or you *were* there, dimming, eclipsed);

then D—your loyal old friend, you'd thought—
leaving without goodbye for a midnight dinner,

clearly, you could see, forgetting you'd flown
down together, shared a Yellow Cab

from the Marine Air Terminal, checked in
to your separate funky rooms at the Gramercy;

petty distresses, trivia you're shamed to be
wounded by, the comedy of literary manners—

How to reconcile these insignificant cuts
with the weight—a boulder, really—pressing

on you as you drive (your brain still crackles
normally, well-organized signals steering

the right foot that accelerates or lifts without
thought, from the pedal), Sunday afternoon

on the Mid-Cape Highway to Provincetown:
no, the small slights aren't what's made you,

you feel, overwhelmed, despairing. There's
E's illness, her doctor calling frantically

last week, the latest test results so desperate
that specialist feared her patient was *dead*;

L's depression, months of lassitude, the trap
of his life sprung with no loophole of escape;

an "official" letter your mother just showed you,
her abandoned cottage condemned, a building

inspector demanding she take action. "Take action":
last year, when you'd nailed plywood to her windows,

hauled away the few good sticks of furniture—
even then, the neglected walls were black, mildewed,

the green daybed rich with mold, a hornet's nest
inside the door, the door lock jimmied, broken,

glistering poison ivy crawling across the floor . . .
It's *action* she can't take, and your inaction,

watching her tough little body falter
and fail—the largeness of spirit, sacrificial

generosity you hoped for in yourself,
ceded—or unborn; and K, sweet

unathletic K, examining a box turtle
in your yard two days ago, K jaunty

in his faded red baseball cap, then—that night—
tossed in the air by a drunken car,

his face in the morgue, you're told,
unmarred, only *surprised* by the quick

skull-shattering moment of his death.
And now, you hardly notice your brain

(which you picture as hardening, sclerotic),
your brain shifting signals, so the car slows

until a passing driver yells a high-speed curse
that someone else might take as challenging,

even menacing. *Take action:* you accelerate,
again, keep going until the Sahara of dunes

on one side, the brilliant icy bay on the other,
say you're nearly here, whatever's pressing on you,

whatever rides with you, might shrink
in the scouring briny air. And like the survivor

on Everest, the photographer, oxygen deprived,
beyond cold, who stared at his team-mate's body

"in perplexity," the exposed outstretched hand,
the familiar shoulder and chest, thinking,

without affect, not curiosity or grief,
How could this have happened to Rob?

his own body not having "room for emotion"
as he waited for assistance, a guide to help him

off the mountain to safety, to *life*,
his camera storing the neutral, fatal images—

like that, you can turn off the road, and pull in.

Then

We weren't waiting for anything to happen.
We lived by a lake, no tides to nag us,
no relentless conventions of flow

and ebb. No frantic hermit crabs
dragging sideways in their stolen shells,
nor the drained tidal pools they fled—

Only the soft green surround of pine
and beech, the mackerel clouds, the meek
canoes. We felt enclosed. Safe.

The future looked fictional then,
though I never doubted a lucky life
could break, that rapture and grief

could be handed to me in one hard package,
delivered, and left, however I labored,
whether I rested, or ranted and zigzagged

from morning to evening. I worked
with my back to our life. Moonflowers
bloomed in the nightyard: white,

dazzling, sufficient to the night.

Heather McHugh ～

Past All Understanding

The langouste's long feelers may be the result of a single gush of thought.
EZRA POUND

For it is the opinion of choice virtuosi that the brain is only a crowd of little animals,
but with teeth and claws extremely sharp . . .
JONATHAN SWIFT

A woman there was balancing her baby
back-to-back. They held each other's hands,
did tilts and bends and teeter-totters on
each other's inclinations, making
casual covalency into
a human idiogram,
spontaneous Pilobolus—
a spectacle at which
the estimable Kooch
(half Border and half Lab)

began to bark. He wouldn't stop. The child slid off
the woman's back—now they were two again (and so
he quieted a bit). But they were two who
scowled and stared (now it was I who grew
disquieted). You looked,
I started to explain, like one

big oddity to him. (They weren't appeased.) He barks at
crippled people too. (Now they were horrified.) Meanwhile a wind

rose at the kiosk, stapled with yard jobs, sub-clubs, bands somebody named
for animals. The whole park fluttered up and flailed, and Kooch, unquench-
   able,
perceived the higher truth. The upshot: such a bout of barking
as to make the bicyclists bypassing (bent beneath their packs),
an assortment of teaching assistants (harried, earnest, hardly earning)—
and even the white-haired full professorships
all come to a halt, in the wake
of the wave of their tracks.

What brouhahas! What flaps!
To Kooch's mind, if you
could call it that,
the worst was
yet to come—

for looming overhead, a host of red and yellow kites appeared
intent on swooping even to the cowlicks of the humans—Were
these people blind?—that woman in pink, that man in blue, who
paused there in his purview, stupidly, to shake their heads? He thinks

we're in danger, I tried again
to reason with my fellow-man. But now the dog

was past all understanding; he was uncontainable. He burst
into a pure fur paroxysm, blaming the sky for all that we
were worth: he held his ground with four feet braced

against the overturning earth . . .

Sizing

Where's my hairbrush? Where's the belt?
I want my switch. I need that cane. Just let me get
my hands upon that licking-stick, and then

we'll take the starch right out of you.
Your hide is fixing for a tanning. Just you wait.
What hit you you won't know. The future cannot help

but cut you down to size. Its feeling for you,
more and more apparently parental,
cannot help but grow.

Three To's and an Oi

Cassandra's kind
of crying was

otototoi . . . They translate it
o woe is me, but really it's

less graspable than that—it isn't Greek for
nothing, all that stuttering in tones . . . When things get bad,

we baby-talk. In throes of terror in the night,
when dreads cannot be turned aside

by presences with promises, or dronings of a long
erroneous lullaby, or shorter story lines—

of which the lines themselves
have given rise to fear—we wake up

in Cassandra's kind
of quandary. There's been

some terrible mistake.
We're all about to die.

    *

Each whiplash of a girl, each eddy of a boy
comes reeling back from too much sheer

towardness—clarity from cataract—only to be
drawn in, again:

into tomorrow by today,
into the tune by the gondolier,

into the two by two who turn
the bow toward torrents of *veyz mir*.

Etymological Dirge

'Twas grace that taught my heart to fear.

Calm comes from burning.
Tall comes from fast.
Comely doesn't come from come.
Person comes from mask.

The kin of charity is whore,
the root of charity is dear.
Incentive has its source in song
and winning in the sufferer.

Afford yourself what you can carry out.
A coward and a coda share a word.
We get our ugliness from fear.
We get our danger from the lord.

Ghazal of the Better-Unbegun

A book is a suicide postponed.
CIORAN

Too volatile, am I? too voluble? too much a word-person?
I blame the soup: I'm a primordially
stirred person.

Two pronouns and a vehicle was Icarus with wings.
The apparatus of his selves made an absurd person.

The sound I make is sympathy's: sad dogs are tied afar.
But howling I become an ever more un-
heard person.

I need a hundred more of you to make a likelihood.
The mirror's not convincing—that at-best in-
ferred person.

As time's revealing gets revolting, I start looking out.
Look in and what you see is one unholy
blurred person.

McHugh, you'll be the death of me—each self and second studied!
Addressing you like this, I'm halfway to the
third person.

Lynne McMahon ～

Not Falling

The tree was shaken from the inside
out—the party greenly winding the interior stair—
    then abruptly stilled, as if
drunkenness, resting there, summoned
    the suddenly weighted doubt

    that cypress could support such heavy birds
as these, parting the needles with their tangled hair,
    angels one thrust beyond
their mortal bearings, sixty feet above the dirt.
    Fucking-A, they called down

    to the ones below, and the cypress top
bent to brush a snow of moonlight on their
    upturned faces.
Is it God that keeps his lunatics safe? Or merely wine
    branching through the body's tree

to make of it a natural rhyme
so that five moonlit heads, clustered like
    improbable fruit, could keep,
at least this time, their precious juice and postpone
    an offering to that final truth.

Peace Studies

Though he looks almost exactly the way
we thought he would, slightly grubby serape,
huaraches, the beard of a desert cenobite,
the voice of the guest speaker tonight
is surprisingly brisk and business-like,
few inflections, no gestures, not the least hint
of a power salute—a kind of revised prophet,
like Buddha in a suit, meant
to keep us on our spiritual toes.
Even the group of boys in back, taking
the class for an easy A, who, when called upon,
say the world is pretty much okay and besides,
they don't plan to live in Guatemala
or L.A. in any case—
even they have stopped unspiralling the wire
from their notebook page and fashioning tattoos.
The whole auditorium, in fact, is beginning
to look confused. Surely, at some point in his speech,
he'll begin the castigation? Our apathy, our anemic
good intentions, our greed? If not consumption,
exploitation, collaboration, at least
landfill, river dumping, Lotto . . .
Haven't we failed to vote, purchased plastic,
ignored the petition?
Are we familiar with the term "society"?
But he hasn't yet looked up from his notes
on the nature of prosperity.
He can't, surely, be celebrating our good fortune?
Is this what he's come to after years of rage?
Central heating, he's saying now.
The bowl of milk put down for the cat.

Blankets on our children's beds. Books.
The dogwood and redbud in the Missouri spring.
Spring itself. Winter. Summer. Fall.
Is he trying to break our hearts?
Has he no heart at all?

All quail to the wallowing,

Hopkins wrote, punning bird and verb,
mud and clumsy baseness, and his favorite
entirety "all," near-rhyme with "ah" and
that *ah* his abruptly intaken breath, that awe,
whose *bright wings, my dear, touched*
in your bower of bone, are you! led me
from poem to poem: *ah, there was a heart right . . .*
this air I gather and release . . . the heir
to his own selfbent so bound . . . Ah, well where!
to his final troubling pun, *ah, let life*
wind off . . .
Was there ever a man so tormented, my Victorian
professor asked, twinning *ah* with the frequent *alas,*
ever so circumscribed by the fact of the body?
Hopkins was circumcised six days
after his ordination. Is that something
we need to know? he asked the class.
Or his record-book of sins?
Is the anguish and determined praise
apparent enough in the poems, do we need
the speculation about masturbation
as well? Or his love for Digby Dolben?

(But I would not give up the name. Digby Dolben!
Nor the angelic portrait. Nor Henry James's distinctly
Jamesian assessment of him as someone so attracted
to ritual he was in danger of being thought
"merely imitational, cheaply 'romantic' "—one wonders
what he would have made of Hopkins.)
All quail to the wallowing, indeed,
the mudhole of posterity and its fashionable

interpretations. The professor last week
was in despair over the latest
de-canonizing: a feminist critique reading
"The Wreck of the Deutschland" as gang-rape
and voyeurism, the tall nun as either
1.) erect phallus violating the sky, or, 2.) all women
(that all again) raped by Christianity
while the men on the shore watch
and the poet records.
The male gaze which silences and drowns.
Ah, as the heart grows older
It will come to such sights colder . . .
The poems remain
whether wallowed in or skimmed or sunk
in the dearest freshness deep down things.
I think I may cut back my critical forays
for a while. Let go of the new talk.
Was there ever a man so intoxicated by fields,
so worddrunk and dazzled?
He fathers forth whose beauty is past change:
            Praise him.

Sandra McPherson ～

Outsider: Minnie Evans

Now, because of you, symmetry and asymmetry interest me *equally*.
Paints tinting the cisterns in which they mix
slosh and overflow, but you tend the garden gate.
You are so celestially symmetrical that if
you have a sun rising from the sea on the left
in your picture, you'll put the echo of a sun
rising out of the same ocean on the right, an island for their hub.

You draw portraits of spirits, mount them
on suit-box board and carry the crowd as a deck.

Those little wraith faces in leaves and fruit, cherrylike.
Or heads in urns, one face channeling fire into the mind above.

You were a domestic servant when you made these.
"Draw or die," said a dream.

A symmetrical thing measures itself
according to itself. Shoulders make a vase.
Wings have their own faces. Life-forms
share surfaces and rally into medallions.
Because of the admonition—
which didn't say, "Draw and live."

> *25 Jan 92: I've been in depression for days but felt a sudden rush of change—
> like the push of caffeine—upward—and the whoosh is associated with the
> draft of fire up one woman's head through her hair to the neck of the
> woman's face above—pentecostal chimney! The flame my cremation creates!
> The wings lifting me, the urn by its handles soaring. I am the head of the
> flame. I am handing it up, up, the expression of each wing, the stomping
> and clapping, the women in tongues, the women holding the women falling
> backward and upward, glossy glassy glossolalia, their eyes up where the
> flame goes, the hats dropping to the floor, decorating the hearth on which
> we dance. Handles have to be wings—to lift their burden on their own—
> handles have to be wings.*

And the path out of the vision
is asymmetry.

There it goes, all by itself,
daring its route away.

And out there facing the single fire,
the single sun,
is the one person
who is but one.

Bedrooms

Who are you, coming without flash and standing high
on a chair in the doorway?
    —And who are *you,* living in this room
these twenty years,
testy and messy,
pitching bibelots
more from weariness than from anger—
but casting things aside for
charity, too?
Flannel shadows, caning, a clear
old mirror whose "flaws"
avert the eye
around to the present
shiftiness of surviving—
I see them where you live, do you?

Once I saw a horse
rearing so as to fit
in a tall glass cabinet
in a small bedroom south
of Aliceville, Alabama—
Gladys Hudson's ceramic palomino
among salvaged,
crocheted, framed
fandangles, shaken rugs,
hand-twisted chintz
chrysanthemums.
A horse. And I have
no picture . . .

In a book, in the dark, at the thinking end of one bedframe,
this passage, memorized:
A loon swims
leisurely in the heart of the stream—
seeming to certify
the solitude of the place.
Who is that flat person
slow-kicking with the loon
to rest—

while the green reserve of the unforgotten
is thicker and stiffer
than pages of memoir, more rigorous
than any camera wall?
Is it something to share,
the dream one hopes
will be so comfortingly spectacular?

The light a photograph pinpoints
is for diary writing,
drawer handles, hide-soled slippers,
a single pair.
It says, *I can't*
go on being where you are.
But look close
at the dark
in this actual square
of your life.
I give you back your dream room.
You hallucinate beyond me here.

Genius of Fog at Ecola Creek Mouth

The horse meadow quarters roots as large
as if they'd cantered from the stable.
They lie in salt rush and spiky large-headed sedge.
They recline in bird's-foot trefoil
the horses crop. Loggers' drift-stumps,
they rave at the root end,
but on their misery-whipped plane
light springwood bands, dark summerwood rings,
weathered and fuzzed. Up to the woods of small alders,
they gallop in heavy recumbencies.
One swirling wooden mane holds a crow.

When fog in the spirit of blue harbor seal skin
suffuses this pasture, the great roots can't be told
from beings that change places;
and, superimposed, true horses, in fact, drift

from back in the nebula
to the immediate drizzly foreground,
with the dark burgeoning aspect of old growth logs
tumbled into seeds for birds.
The landscape is felted, hushed, as the line
of horses moves, sinew and tracheid, out to sea.

Crouched on the uprush edge, focusing low to the sand
and tracking coppery, tinny mica tracings—
jet, pewter, bronze, as if tannin gilded a fish-scale
or an oak leaf fell across a vein of pyrite—
I can only see up to the herd's approaching, jaunty knees.
Their burl-brown, spherule, liquid eyes
have not seen me. They are quieted by fog,
their riders as lofty as little trees.
When I evade, spring up like beach wood
twisted by a wave, I am not surprised
they go straight through my station
on the lacy swash.

Such dense luminosity—I inch back
to the inland of grayed black-blooded
Himalayan berries, silvered rummy pink spirea.
But fog makes it all one field of direction,
our bearings and our contours corresponding,
vaporous human torsos, humid pasterns,
fogged-in cannons and fetlocks, misty lungs,
and true fog-mind neither blurred nor mumbled,
amnesic nor censorious. Its genius is to be unafraid
so near breakers you cannot hear,
that do not roar in a climate so huge, diffuse,
and tender.

Jane Miller ~

Giants

Someone's old parents in the desert on folding chairs,
one cradling his face, the other absorbed,

a Jew with blue eyes and a Jew with brown,
and inside, behind a huge plateglass window,

a modern dining area, black and white high-tech kitchen, swivel stools,
a lot of counter space,

and their daughter basting a turkey with orange sauce.
The father has only this morning

confessed his wife's secret—something he never tells her he knows,
though he assumes she knows

her father—who would be near 100 now—never died
when she was two, but abandoned his daughters and wife

and gave Florence and Rachel—lifted from the Bible—the gift
of the public trial of early sorrow,

which each wore far from her nature like a boxed jewel
that escapes down the throat and illumines the heart,

as the throbbing of the cosmos is lit
by what preceded it.

The man in the chair, whose leg won't work when he gets up,
has accepted his wife's anger as depression

and forgiven her, turning down the light
like an orchard lamp, low and steady, for fifty years.

I know them, I have bothered to inhabit every maneuver
until they shrivel and I am sky that darkens over

them—those creatures in the yard, fallen
like lizards into a pool

without water, gesticulating and blinking, wiry, slow,
whom I let slowly go

into a house, settle in front of the console and press the remote
to each memory station—pause, hold, mute, flash.

Sonnet Against Nuclear Weapons

The human sigh commuted to life imprisonment—
it's a sparrow in the hazels and pines.

A log, and so on and so forth,
anti-pastoral and realistic.

There was a dinner, you can see for yourself,
clean napkins, it might have been far worse,

entering a lit room undressed;
an unlit room, dressed.

It isn't anything you want to think about.
And went pale.

With a stranger for the first time in her life.
With a stranger for the first time in the afterlife.

The light in the room on both of them.
I'm writing on the back of a child's drawing,

a snake. Slightly protruding belly, creamy,
round breasts. Sometimes when I think of her

she remembers. Seven eyes of God
play the tape forward a little, stop it, replay it.

The phone's ringing in someone else's place.
—I'll get it.

When she thinks of moving tonight,
the seven eyes of god in the hazels and pines

enter an unlit room, a little
pale on the back of a child's drawing,

slightly protruding belly, and realistic.
It might have been far.

She remembers a human sigh against
the suppression of rights. A snake.

Foundered Star

Little fevered island, blued to closing,
boatmen, tidemen, shademen, men of color
and of peace;

women of the cabbage, women of the carrot-house,
women of the swim;
children squealing and picnicking, doe-eyed
and able-bodied, children of clashing cymbals and chalky
dreams, of milk-lips, of bugs under glass;

come now to the tips of the roofs, come now to the lake
lip, to the entryway of tunnels, to the counting-house;

air the eiderdown, steam the rooms of lovers, break
the fistfights from their arguments, marry the maid—

live a little in the afternoon, asking,
                    —now what do I do?

because this is the way we are alive, though we force ourselves out
of a certain nostalgia, where we first made love
the condition of our lives—
                    a dark room there, but only because
the shades were drawn, it was really midday!, and our clothes stuck

to our bodies like hairy beasts!—we watched the light change
in our eyes, as we dug deeper, pulling out embers—

remember? But the word itself is no longer magical,
the word no longer a living thing . . . a weakness in one of two breakers.

Yet there remains an image, when you water the sun and moon, mouths
coupling and uncoupling, kissing along the ridge the poet
invented, coincident, temporal, carnal, all
so that others might be entertained, changed a nick or two
like a diamond. Who can say whether better or worse, but this much
I can say, I who am always writing
                              to you, my earthship, my
next life—
though no one is now
listening or talking (it's all the same)
though no one is now
laboring or sleeping (it's forbidden)
no one yet exploded, the globe forgives
the night sky gone yellow, the morning sea gone white
and all for a little greed, a little light on the wall,

a view of the other side—oar dipped in ink!—
where we shall never again believe things
about ourselves that aren't true.

Susan Mitchell ～

The Grove At Nemi

Then and *after* were no use to me, nor the desire to make permanent
the impermanent.
The significance everything takes on after rain
was no use to me. I'd come back and it
was not there, not the least shining.
Sometimes there came

one with whom talking went on: *How does foam?*
How does play of light? I would watch the lips
plumping up, the mouth
flapping
its wings, eddying the syllables.
It was like looking down
from a great height.
When below clouded, there was under
with its violaceous twilights, there was down
with its thunders and echoes. On one of my walks
there was a bridge. Was it
ambition I lacked? In its raiments
of cobalt and brown, the river
was naked.
Most sublime achievements, I began.
Bedizenments, I said. *Investiture.*
Toward evening, birdcalls
became stranger, wilder.
What does strange? What does wild? Beyond
the lumber camp, a sound
of flowing,
exultant, indefatigable.
Was it sublimity
I craved? Massive trees were piled up, some
stripped of their bark, and the roots
of a tree dangled
from a machine. In the sky, creamy
utterances. Foamings.
Toward evening, a hugeness.
Some of it moving toward me,
but most of it retreating. Into itself.
Into greennesses untitled.
The flowing splintering, breaking
open, strewing itself.
The surface of the flowing, uneven, bumpy.
In places, the vastness
blurring, opaquing the vacillations, the quandaries
where it hesitated over leaves, over
branches bent into the asides, the digressions.
Toward evening—*What does evening?*
What does open?
What does does?

Golden Bough: The Feather Palm

as if as if as if a hiss a swish of
fake of fraud fraudulent
among the genuine
but why green should be genuine and this other
this bleached this platinum this gold
oh, I can be plain I can be
plain green in the slippery sunlight the oily—
like an extra limb like a fetish
attached to the tree *Cocos plumosa,* the feather
palm, queen of queens, like a fetish
a golden dildo the la-di-la
flies and wasps and bees smear their
mouths and eyes with spangled with vulgar
with not at all good taste like those beaded
curtains hung up as room dividers:
from a distance peroxide and honey, up loud
a xanthous a luteolous a gilded auric
screech, who said the past
was chaste was not this cheap
aroma that whooshes from the flowers
bunched in fascicles, each
petaled gold rolled in bundles
but already starting to
brown at the bend and flank
where the hum the drone the whir:
what smell
holds them there sucking by mouth
fastening and lapping
bits of gold bits of garish
as if the branch
like a breast flowing its slow gaudy flow
and all the bees with their laughing gear
pushed out ready to diddle
the dingle-dangle the ding-dong the dingus,
and wouldn't I
for days on end like the flies
mucked with gold guzzling
fumbling the golden lather the plush
swaying back and forth, to
be lifted like an aroma

Thylias Moss ∿

Last Chance for the Tarzan Holler

1. The season that precedes Dali's *Autumn Cannibalism*

This day, like all days
is a day of reckoning.

Gretel has felt electricity before
while rebaking walls and repairing
the licorice roof, scraping mold

off the stale door
of the loaf in which she rooms
since inheriting the bread house

from the one who died there; her
assistance with the suicide assists
her cruelty. Humperdinck's
Rubylips, witch, bitch ≈ Gretel, baker, widower-maker

G is the mature audience
for the scene of the crime
of comfort in this warm chair

warm as a living thing.
Ruby warming herself
in the stove.

The end.
Aw; tell me more, Mommie,
dearest Medea.

2. Unity, Inc.

This time perhaps the current will follow the blue path
          of veins in arms cuffed in leather. Loop-the-loop, the
Rotor, amusement park centrifugal thrill, Blue Streak, once

a monster coaster. Wet and Wild's giant water slide, big
splash of grief into Dali's *Premonition of Civil War,*
accurate although war can not be suave, gracious, or able
to partake of Susan Smith's southern hospitality, Civil(ity).

Anguish has no edge: entrails, body parts, Ruby's ashes,
bones that remain rounded for everlasting womanhood,
bombs for which bare-breasted women modeled; anguish
is a *soft construction with boiled beans,* soft as kindness, soft
boys: Michael and Alex, strapped in safety seats like the one
in my car, a Century 2000 on which is written:
for the safety and comfort of Ansted Moss.
Every morning he recites this scripture
as we drive past a transformer, farms, the Huron River.

One of Susan's soft-lipped boys plunged
at the age I was for my first baptism, naked
under the white robe and not aware
of how much of my wet self
the preacher's hand covered. He was holy
and I was becoming that way. Last chance
for the Tarzan holler. Those boys too

are believers. Everyone believes something.
Susan Smith will get better, believe it or not.
Premonition of amnesia. She's not alone,

practitioners of Munchausen's syndrome by proxy
feed off sympathy for the sometimes fatal, dreamed up
pathologies of their children; does turned vixen maintained
by salt licks through winter until it is the season to hunt
them down like dogs with dogs, like dogs eating dogs
until they're all gone in a premonition of peace; no
more best friends, nepotism, parricide. She's

not alone. Accompanies those heading
for abortion clinics. These

madnesses, these choices, a little off
the top versus complete make-over, back
to the drawing board of unlimited ideas
where Medea, Gretel are born. It is that easy.

I see everyone at the market, everyone at
the clinic. And they see me. It is
that necessary. Breathe
a little easier for ten minutes

then the Mazda sinks.

—Cells, those drawings torn
out of animated existence are cels; how
I hate homonymity, as if I am singularly composed
of wicked artistry.

3.   Knock, knock.
    Who's there?
    Marrow.
    Whose marrow?

Zaynah is a girl whose match of bone marrow
may depend on boys dead in the water.

Her father loves her without this maudlin push
but after the press conference many others love her too,
including, he hopes, he pleads, the woman who adopted
Zaynah's first cousins when for their safety and comfort
they were removed from risk, maternal as that risk was;
they may be the bearers of the soft, fatty, vascular interior
of bones, collaborators in a life-blood postulated.

Gretel's wicked matriarchy.

    Knock, knock.
    Come in, says the oven.
    But you don't even know who's there!
    Doesn't matter.
    Ah, a paragon of equal opportunity.

In that other house of bread where deacons serve it
all cut up, there is after the light one
a heavy supper of beans, squash, and pork chops.

The cooks sit hot in folding chairs by doors
and windows propped open with hymnals, and suck

a sweet intensity
from well-blackened bones of swine.

There is nothing between life and death, solid
and liquid forms of equivalent sacredness. Between
us, grudges.

Just like *that!*
you're in John D. Long Lake
that does not know a day in which light
does not skim it like a wing,

especially on the October day that a car,
though a chariot is preferred, released two boys,
spirit willing, from their bodies so they could

sink into homecoming, alive
in comfortable seats
that can withstand collisions at 50 mph
if fastened properly—as they were. Susan's

marrow is eligible; Zaynah's life
could depend on the charity of the one
whose marrow is innocent, who did not put
her hands on her own marrow, did
not masturbate, was molested
although, knock, knock, these days
who wasn't?

Susan, I don't mean to be cruel
but   as you know   it is inevitable. She

once took the boys on a picnic near water
cool and effervescing with motherhood
that blew bubbles that emerged
from Michael's right ear when she whispered
in his left, a rummage

of secret disappointments in school, so much
to remember, fix; life imprisoned in ego. Susan
likes Mr. Quixotic, *psst, pass it on—does not—does too*

and wants the time of day from shrugging shoulders,
silhouette

like iron monument in the park. They date
in her dreams and she's the Florence Nightingale
of Hadleyville and Roanoke that someone—Michael
(her son or the angel?)—said she couldn't be, kissing
away hurt until her lips rot

with duty and her ankles swell into cast iron casts,
weighing her down with identity—who did she marry?
Why isn't the love of her new life here under
bandages that she, the Arachne of Hadleyville and Roanoke,
wrapped into parcel, care package saved
for all the rainy days it takes to make a lake?

She kept her eyes on the loophole
in her wedding ring, so where's her Houdini?

Talcum and corn starch fill the air
as Gretel flails trying to escape a bathtub
turned to pudding, trying to escape

the revenge of marrow.

Lisel Mueller ~

Losing My Sight

I never knew that by August
the birds are practically silent,
only a twitter here and there.
Now I notice. Last spring
their noisiness taught me the difference
between screamers and whistlers and cooers
and O, the coloraturas.
I have already mastered

the subtlest pitches in our cat's
elegant Chinese. As the river
turns muddier before my eyes,
its sighs and little smacks
grow louder. Like a spy,
I pick up things indiscriminately:
the long approach of a truck,
car doors slammed in the dark,
the night life of animals—shrieks and hisses,
sex and plunder in the garage.
Tonight the crickets spread static
across the air, a continuous rope
of sound extended to me,
the perfect listener.

Statues

1989

In Prague, or perhaps Budapest,
the heroes have fallen off their horses.
Here lies a general's profile
and here a helmet, there
a ferrous glove still holding the reins.
The horses, so long inert
under the heavy bodies,
are not used to wind and sun,
nor to the tenderness of their flanks
now that the boots are gone,
and their eyes, so long overcast
by bronze or stone, are slow
to take in the gray city,
the heavyset houses. Gradually
they start to move, surprised
by their new lightness. There's a scent
of rain in the air, and something clicks
inside their heads; it has to do
with green, with pasture. They step down

from their pedestals, unsteady as foals
beginning to walk. No one pays attention
to riderless horses walking
through city streets; these are
supernatural times. Near the edge of town,
where the sky expands, they trust themselves
to break into a run
and then drop out of sight
behind a bank of willows
whose streamers promise water.

The Late-Born Daughters

The late-born daughters of famous fathers,
who never knew their fathers
except to sit on their laps
when they visited once or twice,
go up to the attic to read
the brilliant and cruel letters
their mothers kept until they died.

The younger daughters of famous fathers,
born of the late, last marriages,
who watched their mothers grow tongue-tied
when they spoke about their fathers,
go to the library archives,
sign in, sign out, for permission
to search for their missing fathers.

The soft-spoken daughters of famous fathers,
who long since changed their names
and do not answer their phones,
collect the lives of their fathers,
their dead, difficult fathers,
in stories told by neighbors and lovers
and servants and hangers-on.

The aging, late-born, younger daughters
spend the best years of their lives

with their haunted, shipwrecked fathers.
They iron their fathers' shirts,
they cradle their heads in their laps,
they keep their desperate secrets,
they sit up all night with their fathers.

Happy and Unhappy Families I

If all happy families are alike,
then so are the unhappy families,
whose lives we celebrate
because they are motion and heat,
because they are what we think of as *life*.
Someone is lying and someone else
is being lied to. Someone is beaten
and someone else is doing the beating.
Someone is praying, or weeps
because she does not know how to pray.
Someone drinks all night;
someone cowers in corners;
someone threatens and someone pleads.
Bitter words at the table,
bitter sobs in the bedroom;
reprisal breathed on the bathroom mirror.
The house crackles with secrets;
everyone draws up a plan of escape.
Somebody shatters without a sound.
Sometimes one of them leaves the house
on a stretcher, in terrible silence.
How much energy suffering takes!
It is like a fire that burns and burns
but cannot burn down to extinction.
Unhappy families are never idle;
they are where the action is,
unlike the others, the happy ones,
who never raise their voices
and spit no blood, who do nothing
to deserve their happiness.

Happy and Unhappy Families II

According to the director
even Electra was once a child
in a happy family. Hard to imagine
Agamemnon's daughters
batting balloons across the lawn,
while Orestes shouts
joyfully from his rocking horse
and the soon-to-be-murdered parents
smile fondly over their summer drinks.

Only in the catastrophe,
the inescapable horror show,
do they exist for us,
while close to home, in the latest
double murder and suicide,
horror fails the imagination.
Nothing, a blank, We remember
the good times, study the family pictures.
The little girl had a birthday
last week. They had balloons.
They played jump rope in the yard.
The mother always looked pretty.
He was always polite.

In the play, we know what must happen
long before it happens,
and we call it tragedy.
Here at home, this winter,
we have no name for it.

Animals Are Entering Our Lives

"I will take care of you," the girl said to her brother, who had been turned into a deer.
She put her golden garter around his neck and made him a bed of leaves and moss.
FROM AN OLD TALE

Enchanted is what they were
in the old stories, or if not that,
they were guides and rescuers of the lost,
the lonely, needy young men and women
in the forest we call the world.
That was back in a time
when we all had a common language.

Then something happened. Then the earth
became a place to trample and plunder.
Betrayed, they fled to the tallest trees,
the deepest burrows. The common language
became extinct. All we heard from them
were shrieks and growls and wails and whistles,
nothing we could understand.

Now they are coming back to us,
the latest homeless, driven by hunger.
I read that in the parks of Hong Kong
the squatter monkeys have learned to open
soft drink bottles and pop-top cans.
One monkey climbed an apartment building
and entered a third-floor bedroom.
He hovered over the baby's crib
like a curious older brother.
Here in Illinois
the gulls swarm over the parking lots
miles from the inland sea,
and the Canada geese grow fat
on greasy leftover lunches
in the fastidious, landscaped ponds
of suburban corporations.
Their seasonal clocks have stopped.
They summer, they winter. Rarer now
is the long, black elegant V

in the emptying sky. It still touches us,
though we do not remember why.

But it's the silent deer who come
and eat each night from our garden,
as if they had been invited.
They pick the tomatoes and tender beans,
the succulent day-lily blossoms
and dewy geranium heads.
When you labored all spring,
planting our food and flowers,
you did not expect to feed
an advancing population
of the displaced. They come,
like refugees everywhere,
defying guns and fences
and risking death on the road
to reach us, their dispossessors,
who have become their last chance.
Shall we accept them again?
Shall we fit them with precious collars?
They scatter their tracks around the house,
closer and closer to the door,
like stray dogs circling their chosen home.

Laura Mullen ～

House

Where it should have been there were only memories.
They liked it anyhow and lived there. For them
The moment it fell down was the moment it lifted up:
Livable-in at last.
A pantry full of regrets; a garden
Planned out in the shape of a plan, lush
With *what-might-have-been* and *O-if-only*;
A folly where . . . on fine afternoons . . .

And the parties they threw there then, or rather,
Imagined themselves throwing, who had never been
Much for parties, but "Better late than . . ."—and the rest
Of the phrase lost in laughter. Love bloomed
In the nonexistent parlor: the piano
That never was was closed, suddenly,
By the woman who looked at her hands so as not to see
The face of the young man who knelt at her side,
Enrapt. Impossible ever to know
If it was the sunlight which had faded those curtains
So slowly that no one had seen, or whether
They had been wrong about the color from the start.

For the Reader (Blank Book)

The man in the white room next door wrote this, I think: wrote this thinking
I wanted to read it. Our identical rooms pressed up against each other like
the pages of a shut book. One of those blank books so popular a while ago
and still, The Nothing Book. *Put your thoughts here.* And whether they were
laid to rest or came to life hardly mattered, all a part of the cure. The one
dream he'll write in his, over and over, is of waking early or being woken
early by the wife he doesn't have when the light is strange. Something he
thought he killed, she calls to him, is moving awkwardly across the lawn to
the edge of the lawn: the blood an oily smear of almost black against all that
crisp, evenly clipped blue-green. He lingers morbidly over description, oh
yes, in what he likes to call my dream. At the edge of the lawn: woods or
water; some kind of menacing refuge, something he'll never feel safe from.
Dragging its limbs, the thing, mindless determination, making its slow way
back in. Left here to get well some time ago, we are jolted back into all the
attendant symptoms by the rare visits of those who left us, who come back
to check in, *Can we stop paying now?* "For the settlers the wilderness seemed
desolate and evil, something it was necessary to both cultivate and tame." *If
you won't play the piano for me*, the guy in the movie we gather to watch in
the rec room yells, suddenly, *you won't ever play it for anyone again*, and the
cripple's cane comes smashing, on both fingers and keys, down. Ka-*boom*.
We twine hands in the dark and promise to show each other everything,
later. We promise we're going to say, this time, only what we meant. What

an awful noise, the wife he swears he doesn't have sighs, again, but louder. What's *she* trying to recover from? "We would not have survived without the help of our mortal enemies." I dream I'm a pilgrim. I dream I'm knocking on the door just to the right of mine, which might in fact be mine, like the one to the right of that, they are all so remarkably the same, very late or very early, in one of the long white nights or mornings. *Is it over?* Her voice caught deep in his throat, the woman in his dreams says It isn't dead yet darling, you didn't kill it, you only maimed it darling, see, it's still moving. How long is it going to haunt him, I wonder, looking down from above at the plot of cleared land, what little we'd been able to make sense of.

Self-Portrait as Somebody Else

Did it better: pathetic in bathtub, post-
Water. Naked victim of what? In the late
20th century style: hurt-dirty, rage-
Soaked. Language running out, time itself
Just the remembered echo of a choking
Noise from the hole past history's hair-nested
Grate hard water's turned white. Hard luck.
Written out in layers, like music, the dead
Residue—*ash* gray at the reach, or *smoke*—
Begins where it ends: under the over-
Flow vent's chrome cover, the name
Brand of the fixtures apparently forever
Stamped into my distorted, weeping, slightly
Rust-rotten features. And I might be the Nazi
Industrialist's bride, or daughter; bleached
Whale in an equally creamy container, or an-
Other by-product of this over-produced self-
Portraiture, leaving a little something sticky
And stuck here even now (date expired),
Like a long-gone breath still ghosting a mirror,
Unable to come any cleaner, or closer. Seen
Under the scribbled list of greenish figures
Must totals on the tear-stained plastic curtain
Of this theater, I'm the remainder—a bit

Player; a black box cracked among fractions
Of landing gear, scattered; a mess of master-
Pieces in the *oeuvre* of over; fetal in the after-
Math of the orders ("Happily"), feigning death
In the ditch of my life ("ever after")—until flesh
Scorched by cold takes me out of the picture,
Fear the already damp cloth in whose folds
Fading day sulks, guilt the expensive soap.

After I Was Dead

I had time to think about things,
Time for regrets, like.
The glowing vessel of frozen booze
Lists: *Way a minit: wanna . . . 'scuss shumsing!*
Memory overflowing its salt-rimmed dike?
But your version only, "the" truth . . . —

Sliced. Time folds in on itself: bed to couch.
The sheets (to the wind) come clean:
I gave the keys back.
Comes (in hot water) the stain of love, out.
Comes nobody back from the said, *I mean . . . ,*
To say what lies still under all that black

(Ashes cling): nobody, that is, you'd trust.
I sifted myself, things over between us.

Carol Muske ~

Like This

Morituri te salutamus.
LOS ANGELES TIMES, 1927

Maybe it's not the city you thought
it was. Maybe its flaws, like cracks
in freeway pylons, got bigger, caught
your eye, like swastikas on concrete stacks.

Maybe lately the dull astrologies of End,
Millenium-edge rant about world death
make sense. Look. Messages the dead send
take time to arrive. When the parched breath

of the Owens River Valley guttered out,
real voices bled through the black & white.
The newspaper ad cried, *We who are about
to die salute you.* Unarmed, uncontrite.

Gladiators: a band of farmers, entrenched.
And how many on the Empire's side recognized
the bitter history of that bow? Greed drenches
itself in a single element, unsurprised.

Like strippers, spotlit. Tits and asses
flash red-gold, while jets shriek above.
Rim-shot. History, like a shadow, passes
over a city impervious as a bouncer's shove

to dreams. Images tell you what's imaginable.
Here comes another ton. We bathe in
what's re-routed from the source: a fable
of endless water in a dipper made of tin.

The future's in fact a few images refusing to fit
anywhere. For some: heads on pikes, sky-fires.

For others: a kid's painting of a green horse, its
bridle fallen behind. This city never seems to tire

of stupid prophecy, yet seeks no past, ways
Time talks to itself, salutes us as it dies.
We were taught to think: *like that, like this.* Days
of nights, not seeing the simile's power. It tries

to link the unlike and the like, I said aloud
to my special students, so-called troubled youth
who'd packed guns & gang caps. On campus, proud
to scare the shit out of everybody. The truth

is, they wrote *offkey*, like weird singing. So
it was quiet as one of them read his analogy:
The bullet-holes over my door, his voice low,
look like a peacock tail, a peacock fan. He

who'd never seen a shuddering strut of quills,
hadn't seen desire in that many eyes, said *I
don't think like anybody.* And why? He kills,
he's a kid. But look, he sees what we die

from not seeing—how different beauty opens
its different eyes. The expanse unfolds,
many-eyed, iridescent, it holds. Unbroken,
salutes you. The fiery gaze turns gold.

Miracles

for Charles Simic

Think about it:
            The siren finds its migraine, the fix its junkie,
the bomb flowers up under the foot of the Goodwill Ambassador
                        as he turns the ignition key . . .

Miracles, nothing but miracles!
                         I heard the faith healer
complain about his arthritis to his wife, a dwarf, stone deaf.

        Hallejuah! The one person on earth to whom he could
convey his great pain can't hear him. Neither can he, who
lays hands on the afflicted, rolling back his eyes,
                              lengthen her bones one notch.

Stasis and apocalypse, stasis and apocalypse. The stopped wind
and the wind of destruction together deface the spotlit virgin
            and the Good Humor Man shooting up at her feet.

What more can we ask of the miraculous?
When the Holy Ghost appears to a bulldog
(himself a lifelong skeptic), the house catches fire—
the bulldog barks but cannot rouse his master, facedown
                                        on the couch.

O the night is so bright, so filled with possibility!
The hammer finds the thumb, the gas leak the flame—
the long-winded poet, hunched over the podium,
                        struck by a falling EXIT sign

is proof, I tell you! Miracles—
                    nothing but miracles.

At the School for the Gifted

Yes, I wanted them to levitate.
Unfortunately, I hadn't a leg to stand on.
Cut-out camels plodded across the blackboard's high
sill. Yet the desert below refused to unfurl its
mica wings. When I asked them to try to remember,
to release a soap bubble from their marvelous arsenal

of wands, they resisted. They lined up, suspicious
in individual spotlights. The fountain inside

the scissored palm could only rise so high,
maybe just a trumpeted C. Which is high, but
not like those huge blue dreams that used to float by,
shot from cloud atomizers, the original public breeze

on its back in the grass. Let's try to guess who
or what is being borne up by this caravan of thin-
skinned humps, a-bulge, inoculated? I tell you
every one has a rider, a crop. It's been done
this way for some time. If we pause here by the pillars
of sand, up to our poet-knees in anarchy, won't each

gulp of hoarded water from the toppled monument be
sweeter passed hand to hand in the sun-colored dipper?
Up to our thighs in it now, and spared what drills itself into the rock daily, so it can claim to know zero
after zero, and make that nothing into a sound like
silent bells, split parched hooves, plodding.

Blue Rose

Blossoming white in the rose garden,
Plucked at dusk by my daughter's hand:
Colorless rose, it's fate you resemble.

When the young sorceress leans
Over the glass bowl where you float,
Staining the surface with her shadow,

Three dye-drops from a kitchen vial:
She believes she re-invents you.
Here is the passion of the alchemist,

All matter burns before her in that
Pale reconstructive fire. See how she
Clutches the vial to her new breasts?

She desires a sky-colored rose. I
Hear you gasp, drawing the tincture
Up through your veins till each petal

Is blue-tinged, bruised as an eyelid.
Legends warned of your poison blood,
The thorn-prick, deep amniotic sleep.

In this version, harm spirals dark
Up the stem, exacting perfection. *White
Blossoms.* What is this life, corrected

To a dreamed-of shade? Like you,
She is innocent. She floats there,
My vial emptied, running in her veins.

Marilyn Nelson ∽

How I Discovered Poetry

It was like soul-kissing, the way the words
filled my mouth as Mrs. Purdy read from her desk.
All the other kids zoned an hour ahead to 3:15,
but Mrs. Purdy and I wandered lonely as clouds borne
by a breeze off Mount Parnassus. She must have seen
the darkest eyes in the room brim: The next day
she gave me a poem she'd chosen especially for me
to read to the all except for me white class.
She smiled when she told me to read it, smiled harder,
said oh yes I could. She smiled harder and harder
until I stood and opened my mouth to banjo playing
darkies, pickaninnies, disses and dats. When I finished
my classmates stared at the floor. We walked silent
to the buses, awed by the power of words.

Juneteenth

With her shiny black-patent sandals
and her Japanese parasol,
and wearing a brand-new Juneteenth dress,
Johnnie's a living doll.

Juneteenth: when the Negro telegraph
reached the last sad slave . . .

It's Boley's second Easter;
the whole town a picnic.
Children run from one church booth
to the next, buying sandwiches,
sweet-potato pie, peach cobbler
with warm, sweaty pennies.

The flame of celebration
ripples like glad news
from one mouth to the next.

These people slipped away
in the middle of the night;
arrived in Boley with nothing
but the rags on their backs.
These carpenters, contractors, cobblers.
These bankers and telephone operators.
These teachers, preachers, and clerks.
These merchants and restauranteurs.
These peanut-growing farmers,
these wives halting the advance of cotton
with flowers in front of their homes.

Johnnie's father tugs one of her plaits,
head-shaking over politics
with the newspaper editor,
who lost his other ear
getting away from a lynch mob.

Chosen

Diverne wanted to die, that August night
his face hung over hers, a sweating moon.
She wished so hard, she killed part of her heart.

If she had died, her one begotten son,
her life's one light, would never have been born.
Pomp Atwood might have been another man:

born with a single race, another name.
Diverne might not have known the starburst joy
her son would give her. And the man who came

out of a twelve-room house and ran to her
close shack across three yards that night, to leap
onto her cornshuck pallet. Pomp was their

share of the future. And it wasn't rape.
In spite of her raw terror. And his whip.

The Sacrament of Poverty

for Judy Maines-La Marre

All the children on this ward are dying of AIDS.
The sister opens the door to two hundred and ten
quiet cribs lined in such tight ranks
you can barely squeeze between. This is not
an unpaid advertisement: You left your family,
the local value of your surname, your wind-tight house,
electricity, the safe water we turn on and drink,
and went for two weeks to Haiti,
to hold out your arms from a rocking-chair.
One by one babies were handed to you,
their skin smooth as black milk.
Gradually they remembered touch,
met your gaze, surrendered smiles.

One tottered through three wards to find you again;
he stood beside your chair, his cheek pressed to your arm.
All you can do, you said later, *is hold them
and love them. And let them go.*

And now this grief, Judy.
Each day another square to ex through.
You said you were helpless, dumb,
humbled by their pure poverty.
I never even started
your wedding poem.

Lovesong

after Rilke

How shall I hold my spirit, that it not
touch yours? How shall I send it soaring past
your height into the patient waiting, there
above you? Oh, if only I could shut
it up, leave it to gather velvet dust
someplace where it would echo you no more.
But, like two strings vibrating as the bow
ripples them with a long, caressing stroke,
we tremble, drawn together by one joy.
What instrument is this? Whose fingers make
a chord beyond our capacity for awe?
How sweet, how: *Ah!*

Alice Notley ～

A Baby Is Born Out of a White Owl's Forehead—1972

At this time there are few
poems about pregnancy and childbirth

do I find this curious
I want to shriek at
any identity
this culture gives me claw it to
pieces; has nothing to
do with me or
my baby and never will,
has never perceived a
human being.
My baby is quiet and wise, but I'm
a trade name and I'm
chaos
rainwater on a piano—I'm so
scared then but now of then I'd say
I want to make your tunes go away
to have a child is more casual
than, you might say, and more serious than
the definition
for who, frankly, was ever born
or gave birth?

After the usual pain and the well-meaning,
mostly but not all,
intervention of others and others' words and meanings
I find him. Lying next to me yes and being
nursed by me.
I serve him why not he isn't wrong.

I'm infused with a noxious dispirit
as the world makes me be a woman
everything has gone wrong in some sense by now.

———————

Of two poems one sentimental and one not
I choose both
of his birth and my painful unbirth I choose both.
The woman in the photo has a haircut from Vidal Sassoon
wears a black silky synthetic top and probably a long skirt
the baby on her lap in sleepers and
a blue and white Peruvian cap.
They look abstracted in the same way.
He is the baby unchaotic

he is born and I am undone—feel as if I will
never be, was never born.

Two years later I obliterate myself again
having another child
not to be a form of woman
but in allegiance to the process I
can't quite see.
I have begun to be.

I sit with my sons in a barely cared-for apartment
inside from Chicago in the TV's ambience (black and
white, like the snow) purple crocuses there
Ted's becoming sick with a lasting illness
though we are calm while money doesn't press us
a moment of happiness, these bodies are clear
all four finally clear and
still clear

but first, for two years, there's no me here.

1—Towards a Definition

Grief isn't empty it's black and material I've seen it
It's a force, independent, and eats you while you're sleeping
The spring after Ted died I once saw it in pieces
in the air of the apartment tatters
whirled around me like burnt paper

I know I didn't make it what made it
Could hardly stand up some days that year because of it
No luxuriance in this process no dolorous
sea of grief it's a battle
Pieces of myself are hacked away my adulthood is
art a lost story

What's left of me really is a young girl
and to accept her after such war, after the tears of
myself as a general have hardened into semiprecious

ivory or coral, is sad and
defeating no victory
Oh yes this is who I always am
beginning child literal I
I'm myself so, knowing a new thing, that
the universe is ruled by love and countervalent sorrow
Grief's not a social invention
Grief is visible, substantial, I've literally seen it

Mysteries of Small Houses

Poverty much maligned but beautiful
has resulted in smaller houses replete with mysteries
How can something so finite
so petite and shallow have
the infinite center I sense there? There

in the alley house for example
I enter it again, utterly still in the morning and with
shadows around its door mouth and throughout
frontroom bedroom diningroom kitchen room of washtubs and
porch made my room, all
small, small and worn linoleum blue pattern pink
flowers, but now it's all shadows
'cause inside its center I'm, or is it we're
It's I'm that I won't ever know
completely unless I do when I die
                              How
                               do
we manage to base ourselves on dark ignorance so
house of pressed-down pushed-in
origin, is such poverty; or
apartments where people die, again the strange dense
center of the four tiny rooms on St. Mark's Place may be that
Ted died there and so left a mystery vortex inside that fragile
apartment on stilts—Doug, do you think so?
                                    you
lived there. The apartment where we are now isn't
so poor, though it's small

The house must be small and fragile
My grandparents' house too had four small rooms
and no bath or shower and whenever you sat on the
toilet a mynah bird across the lot cried out
Their house had a darkness where they slept
I know I'm not talking about poverty exactly but not
having, why have it's such
an illusion, and the body-self such a shadowy fragile house—

Go in and find that room that secret
is it under it   or inside, it's inside a shadow
if I could just slip into it—and if I do I'm still whole but
mum in old Needles
the motel's too big the churches are too and the mute
low-lying schools
there's the desert beyond them that I try to keep housed from
no thin flesh there no coursing fluid no thought

Naomi Shihab Nye ∽

Steps

A man letters the sign for his grocery in Arabic and English.
Paint dries more quickly in English.
The thick swoops and curls of Arabic letters stay moist
and glistening till tomorrow when the children show up
jingling their dimes.

They have learned the currency of the new world,
carrying wishes for gum and candies shaped like fish.
They float through the streets, diving deep to the bottom,
nosing rich layers of crusted shell.

One of these children will tell a story that keeps her people
alive. We don't know yet which one she is.
Girl in the red sweater dangling a book bag,

sister with eyes pinned to the barrel of pumpkin seeds.
They are lettering the sidewalk with their steps.

They are separate and together and a little bit late.
Carrying a creased note, "Don't forget."
Who wrote it? They've already forgotten.
A purple fish sticks to the back of the throat.
Their long laughs are boats they will ride and ride,
making the shadows that cross each other's smiles.

Across the Bay

If we throw our eyes way out to sea
they thank us. All those corners
we've made them sit down in lately,
those objects with dust along
their seams.

Out here eyes find the edge
that isn't one.
Gray water, streak of pink,
little tap of sun,
and that storm off to the right
that seems to like us now.

How far can the wind carry
whatever lets go? Light
shining from dead stars
cradles our sleep. Secret light
no one reads by—
who owns that beam?
Who follows it far enough?

The month our son turned five
we drove between cotton fields
down to the bay. Thick layers
of cloud pouring into one another
as tractors furrowed the earth,

streams of gulls dipping down
behind. We talked about
the worms in their beaks.
How each thing on earth
searches out what it needs,
if it's lucky. And always
another question—*what if?*
what if?

Some day you'll go so far away
I'll die for missing you,
like millions of mothers
before me—how many friends
I suddenly have! Across the bay
a ship will be passing, tiny dot
between two ports meaning nothing
to me, carrying cargo useless to my life,
but I'll place my eyes on it
as if it held me up. Or you rode
that boat.

Vocabulary of Dearness

How a single word
may shimmer and rise
off the page, a wafer of
syllabic light, bulb
of glowing meaning,
whatever the word,
try "tempestuous" or "suffer,"
any word you have held
or traded so it lives a new life
the size of two worlds.
Say you carried it
up a hill and it helped you
move. Without this
the days would be thin sticks

thrown down in a clutter of leaves,
and where is the rake?

I Still Have Everything You Gave Me

It is dusty on the edges.

Slightly rotten.

I guard it without thinking.

Focus on it once a year
when I shake it out in the wind.

I do not ache.

I would not trade.

Fuel

Even at this late date, sometimes I have to look up
the word "receive." I received his deep
and interested gaze.

A bean plant flourishes under the rain of sweet words.
Tell what you think—I'm listening.

The story ruffled its twenty leaves.

*

Once my teacher set me on a high stool
for laughing. She thought the eyes
of my classmates would whittle me to size.
But they said otherwise.

We'd laugh too if we knew how.

I pinned my gaze out the window
on a ripe line of sky.

That's where I was going.

Sharon Olds ~

First

He stood in the sulphur baths, his calves
against the stone rim of the pool
where his half-full glass of scotch stood, his
shins wavering in the water, his torso
looming over me, huge, in the night,
a grown-up man's body, softer and
warmer with the clothes off—I was a sophomore
at college, in the baths with a naked man,
a writer, married, a father, widowed,
remarried, separated, unreadable, and when I
said No, I was sorry, I couldn't,
he had invented this, rising and dripping
in the heavy sodium water, giving me
his body to suck. I had not heard
of this, I was moved by his innocence and daring,
I went to him like a baby who's been crying
for hours for milk. He stood and moaned
and rocked his knees, I felt I knew
what his body wanted me to do, like rubbing
my mother's back, receiving directions
from her want into the nerves of my hands.
In the smell of the trees of seaweed rooted in
ocean trenches just offshore,
and the mineral liquid from inside the mountain,
I gave over to flesh like church music
until he drew out and held himself and

something flew past me like a fresh ghost.
We sank into the water, and lay there, napes
on the rim. *I've never done that before,*
I said. His eyes not visible
to me, his voice muffled, he said, *You've been*
sucking cock since you were fourteen,
and fell asleep. I stayed beside him
so he wouldn't go under, he snored like my father, I
tried not to think about what he had said,
but then I saw, in it, the unmeant
gift—that I was good at this
raw mystery I liked. I sat
and rocked, by myself, in the fog, in the smell
of kelp, the night steam like animals' breath,
there where the harsh granite and quartz dropped down
into and under the start of the western sea.

Her First Week

She was so small, that sometimes I would walk into
her room and scan the crib a half-second
to find her, face-down in a corner, limp
as something gently flung down, or fallen
from some sky an inch above the mattress. I would
tuck her arm along her side
and slowly turn her over. She would tumble
over part by part, like a load
of damp laundry, in the dryer, I'd slip
a hand in, under her neck,
slide the other under her back,
and evenly lift her up. Her little bottom
sat in my palm, her chest contained
the puckered, moire sacs, and her neck—
I was afraid of her neck, once I almost
thought I heard it quietly snap,
I looked at her and she swiveled her slate
eyes and looked at me. It was in
my care, the creature of her spine, like the first
chordate, as if the history

of the vertebrate had been placed in my hands.
Every time I checked, she was still
with us—someday, there would be a human
race. I could not see it in her eyes,
but when I fed her, gathered her
like a loose bouquet to my side and offered
the breast, greyish-white, and struck with
miniscule scars like creeks in sunlight, I
felt she was serious, I believed she was willing to stay.

Lifelong

When I think of your tail-bone, the tart sweetness
of its skin, and, in the bone, the marrow,
the packed, quartz crystals of Northern
rock, glimmering, after the glacier,
I think of how we travel, easily,
into each other, it is where we go
at night. There is ocean, sky, granite,
there is your father, dead, curled on his side,
mouth open, lips cracked,
and my father, his jaw at the same grim
angle of a salt-cod, and their seed
is there, too. I do not know
where the mothers are, maybe the mothers
are elsewhere, and I can be the only
woman for a while, and love the entire
human in one man. Smooth and planished
under the stars, your tailbone at night almost
phosphors—I touch it as we dive, through a dark
like a cold and unlighted Atlantic, bands
of seed rich as krill in the water,
down to the floor of our life together, and the
door that opens in that floor, and stands open, and we dive.

The Promise

With the second drink, at the restaurant,
holding hands on the bare table,
we are at it again, renewing our promise
to kill each other. You are drinking gin,
night-blue juniper berry
dissolving in your body, I am drinking Fumé,
chewing its fragrant dirt and smoke, we are
taking on earth, we are part soil already,
and wherever we are, we are also in our
bed, fitted, naked, closely
along each other, half passed out,
after love, drifting back
and forth across the border of consciousness,
our bodies buoyant, clasped. Your hand
tightens on the table. You're a little afraid
I'll chicken out. What you do not want
is to lie in a hospital bed for a year
after a stroke, without being able
to think or die, you do not want
to be tied to a chair like your prim grandmother,
cursing. The room is dim around us,
ivory globes, pink curtains
bound at the waist—and outside,
a weightless, luminous, lifted-up
summer twilight. I tell you you do not
know me if you think I will not
kill you. Think how we have floated together
eye to eye, nipple to nipple,
sex to sex, the halves of a creature
drifting up to the lip of matter
and over it—you know me from the bright, blood-
flecked delivery room, if a lion
had you in its jaws I would attack it, if the ropes
binding your soul are your own wrists, I will cut them.

Jacqueline Osherow ～

Phantom Haiku/Silent Film

*Friends part
forever—wild geese
lost in cloud*
BASHŌ

I don't write haiku. I'm no good at silence,
Which may be why I crave those movies so much,
Though someone told me it's the silver nitrate,
The way it so luxuriates in light
That anything relinquished to its lunar reach
Becomes a kind of parable of incandescence.
Take a scene in a nightclub in war-torn France:
The smoke, the silverware, the sequined dress,
The bubbles orbiting a long-stemmed glass—

Who would interrupt them with a voice?
And then there's what happens to a face.
I wonder if I could get some silver nitrate
To take what I have to say and give it back
With a little of that luminescent silence. . . .
Not that I'd show a close-up of my face
Or anything that might be used as evidence;
There's not a single thing I wouldn't leave out.
But in silent movies when the screen goes black

It still feels as if there's something there.
Maybe it's the pervading threat of fire.
That's why they don't use silver nitrate anymore,
It's so flammable—that, and the cost of silver—
But in this case, I'd want it to explode.
In fact, clumsy as it is, it's my metaphor.
I admire Bashō, but I just can't buy
That bit about the wild geese and the cloud.
Unless he meant to float the possibility

That, after a season or two, the geese return.
It might even be implicit in the Japanese,

Which names a graceful but predictable species
Famous for going back to the same location.
You get to invent a poem in translation;
Only what isn't said is accurate.
For my haiku about friends that part,
I'd need the Japanese for *silver nitrate*,
A catchall character for *luminous* and *burn*.

Ghazal: Comet

Amidst our troubles, a sudden blessing:
Look up. There's a comet in the evening sky.

An omen for a pharaoh, caught retracing
Its half-forgotten summit in the evening sky;

Two burning tails—one gas, one ice—arousing
Ancient tumult in the evening sky;

Debris of a lost planet decomposing,
Gypsy diplomat in the evening sky;

Debut of life on earth, its ice dispersing
Facts too intimate for the evening sky. . . .

Traces of comet in us. This burning, this freezing?
Let's just blame it on the evening sky,

The music of the spheres in us, rehearsing
Across the gamut of the evening sky.

But—see?—the comet's already devising
A shortcut past the limit in the evening sky,

And when it comes again, we won't be witnessing.
Who will even claim it in the evening sky?

What's left of us may well be improvising
Our own last-minute plummet in the evening sky.

Villanelle from a Sentence in a Poet's Brief Biography

In '42 he *was conscripted to work on trains.*
An odd thing to mention in a poet's biography.
In '42? In Czechoslovakia? Trains?

I'm trying to figure out what this entry means,
If he sees himself as victimized or guilty.
In '42 he was conscripted to work on trains.

When Dutch workers wouldn't work *their* trains,
They found out that *work makes you free.*
In '42, in Czechoslovakia, trains

Weren't that busy. They didn't start the deportations
In earnest until 1943.
In '42 he was conscripted to work on trains.

But the next line says *after the war,* which means
That he was still at it in '43,
'44, '45. . . . In Czechoslovakia, trains

(What did he do? Run switches? Check the lines?)
Were as instrumental, let's face it, as Zyklon B.
In '42 he was conscripted to work on trains.
In '42. In Czechoslovakia. Trains.

Alicia Suskin Ostriker ～

The Studio (Homage to Alice Neel)

An oily rag at her feet in the warehouse of scents
Releases essence of pine. A steampipe knocks.
A radio urges the purchase of Philip Morris Cigarettes,
Ford motor cars, Saks quality slipcovers.

Welcome to America, Grand Central Station,
Crossroads of a nation. There is no heaven and no hell,

You got to understand, this existence is it,
I blame nobody, I just paint, paint is thicker than water,
Blood, or dollars. My friends and neighbors are made
Of paint, would you believe it, paintslabs and brushstrokes
Right down to the kishkes, as my grandfather would say.
Like bandaged Andy, not smart enough to duck.

Palette knife jabs, carnation, ocher, viridian.
Look at them. And look at me, I'm like Rembrandt,
Poor, omnivorous, and made of pity. Made of love.
Like José on the couch with nostrils like Dante's inferno.
The thing about life in the bughouse, says Alice Neel,
Is it's better than killing yourself. And you get some rest.

Insane asylum, bughouse, madhouse, loony bin,
Snake pit, it's like the Eskimo words for snow.
I never appreciated the nuances though.
After a while the life is only boring.
The food condenses to pudding.
The beds were cold oatmeal in the first place.

The unconscious cruelties of the staff cease to amuse you.
And when you find yourself secretly peeking
Through the window bars at menstrual red sunsets,
You decide you cannot tolerate the other loonies another day.
So you behave sanely and leave. Bye-bye!
And you're back in the basement studio.

The Boys, the Broom Handle, the Retarded Girl

Who was asking for it—
Everyone can see
Even today in the formal courtroom,
Beneath the coarse flag draped
Across the wall like something on a stage,
Which reminds her of the agony of school

But also of a dress they let her wear
To a parade one time,
Anyone can tell
She's asking, she's pleading
For it, as we all
Plead—
Chews on a wisp of hair,
Holds down the knee
That tries to creep under her chin,
Picks at a flake of skin, anxious
And eager to please this scowling man
And the rest of them, if she only can—
Replies *I cared for them, they were my friends*

It is she of whom these boys
Said, afterward, *Wow, what a sicko,*
It is she of whom they boasted
As we all boast

Now and again, because we need,
Don't we, to feel
Worthwhile—
As without thinking we might touch for luck
That flag they've hung there, though we'd all avoid
Touching the girl.

from *The Mastectomy Poems*

The Bridge

You never think it will happen to you,
What happens every day to other women.
Then as you sit paging a magazine,
Its beauties lying idly in your lap,
Waiting to be routinely waved goodbye
Until next year, the mammogram technician
Says *Sorry, we need to do this again,*

And you have already become a statistic,
Citizen of a country where the air,
Water, your estrogen, have just saluted
Their target cells, planted their Judas kiss
Inside the Jerusalem of the breast.
Here on the film what looks like specks of dust
Is calcium deposits.
Go put your clothes on in a shabby booth
Whose curtain reaches halfway to the floor.
Try saying *fear*. Now feel
Your tongue as it cleaves to the roof of your mouth.

Technicalities over, medical articles read,
Decisions made, the Buick's wheels
Nose across Jersey toward the hospital
As if on monorail. Elizabeth
Exhales her poisons, Newark Airport spreads
Her wings—the planes take off over the marsh—
A husband's hand plays with a ring.

Some snowflakes whip across the lanes of cars
Slowed for the tollbooth, and two smoky gulls
Veer by the steel parabolas.
Given a choice of tunnel or bridge
Into Manhattan, the granite crust
On its black platter of rivers, we prefer
Elevation to depth, vista to crawling.

Wintering

i had expected more than this.
i had not expected to be
an ordinary woman.
    LUCILLE CLIFTON

It snows and stops, now it is January.
The houseplants need feeding,
The guests have gone. Today I'm half a boy,
Flat as something innocent, a clean
Plate, just needing a story.
A woman should be able to say

I've become an Amazon,
Warrior woman minus a breast,
The better to shoot arrow
After fierce arrow,
Or else *I am that dancing Shiva*
Carved in the living rock at Elephanta,
One-breasted male deity, but I don't feel
Holy enough or mythic enough.
Taking courage, I told a man *I've resolved*
To be as sexy with one breast
As other people are with two
And he looked away.

Spare me your pity,
Your terror, your condolence.
I'm not your wasting heroine,
Your dying swan. Friend, tragedy
Is a sort of surrender.
Tell me again I'm a model
Of toughness. I eat that up.
I grade papers, I listen to wind,
My husband helps me come, it thaws
A week before semester starts.

Now Schubert plays, and the tenor wheels
Through Heine's lieder. A fifteen-year survivor
Phones: *You know what? You're the same person*
After a mastectomy as before. An idea
That had never occurred to me.
You have a job you like? You have poems to write?
Your marriage is okay? It will stay that way.
The wrinkles are worse. I hate looking in the mirror.
But a missing breast, well, you get used to it.

Healing

Brilliant—
A day that is less than zero
Icicles fat as legs of deer
Hang in a row from the porch roof
A hand without a mitten

Grabs and breaks one off—
A brandished javelin
Made of sheer
Stolen light
To which the palm sticks
As the shock of cold
Instantly shoots through the arm
To the heart—
I need a language like that,
A recognizable enemy, a clarity—
I do my exercises faithfully,
My other arm lifts,
I apply vitamin E
White udder cream
To the howl
I make vow after vow.

Millennial Polka

Using words this way,
Like chopped crockery—
What is it?

A release? An evacuation? Stop
Making sense,
The musicians say.

Express your anger like a swan.

A prayer, at this late date,
God, a little punch
Through your membrane?

We're only peasants here,
Kyrie eleison, we're jumping
About in the full barns

Among the blood berries.

Linda Pastan ∼

An Early Afterlife

". . . a wise man in time of peace, shall
make the necessary preparations for war."
HORACE

Why don't we say goodbye right now
in the fallacy of perfect health
before whatever is going to happen
happens. We could perfect our parting,
like those characters in *On the Beach*
who said farewell in the shadow
of the bomb as we sat watching,
young and holding hands at the movies.
We could use the loving words
we otherwise might not have time to say.
We could hold each other for hours
in a quintessential dress rehearsal.

Then we would just continue
for however many years were left.
The ragged things that are coming next—
arteries closing like rivers silting over,
or rampant cells stampeding us to the exit—
would be like postscripts to our lives
and wouldn't matter. And we would bask
in an early afterlife of ordinary days,
impervious to the inclement weather
already in our long-range forecast.
Nothing could touch us. We'd never
have to say goodbye again.

Agoraphobia

"Yesterday the bird of night did sit,
Even at noon-day, upon the marketplace,
Hooting and shrieking."
WILLIAM SHAKESPEARE

1.

Imagine waking
to a scene of snow so new
not even memories
of other snow
can mar its silken
surface. What other innocence
is quite like this,
and who can blame me
for refusing
to violate such whiteness
with the booted cruelty
of tracks?

2.

Though I cannot leave this house,
I have memorized the view
from every window—
23 framed landscapes, containing
each nuance of weather and light.
And I know the measure
of every room, not as a prisoner
pacing a cell
but as the embryo knows
the walls of the womb, free
to swim as its body tells it, to nudge
the softly fleshed walls,
dreading only the moment
of contraction when it will be forced
into the gaudy world.

3.

Sometimes I travel as far
as the last stone
of the path, but

every step,
as in the children's story,
pricks that tender place
on the bottom of the foot,
and like an ebbing tide with all
the obsession of the moon behind it,
I am dragged back.

    4.

I have noticed in windy fall
how leaves are torn from the trees,
each leaf waving goodbye to the oak
or the poplar that housed it;
how the moon, pinned
to the very center of the window,
is like a moth wanting only to break in.
What I mean is this house
follows all the laws of lintel and ridgepole,
obeys the commandments of broom
and of needle, custom and grace.
It is not fear that holds me here but passion
and the uncrossable moat of moonlight
outside the bolted doors.

Self-Portrait

after Adam Zagajewski

I am child to no one, mother to a few,
wife for the long haul.
On fall days I am happy
with my dying brethren, the leaves,
but in spring my head aches
from the flowery scents.
My husband fills a room with Mozart
which I turn off, embracing
the silence as if it were an empty page
waiting for me alone to fill it.
He digs in the black earth

with his bare hands. I scrub it
from the creases of his skin, longing
for the kind of perfection
that happens in books.
My house is my only heaven.
A red dog sleeps at my feet, dreaming
of the manic wings of flushed birds.
As the road shortens ahead of me
I look over my shoulder
to where it curves back
to childhood, its white line
bisecting the real and the imagined
the way the ridgepole of the spine
divides the two parts of the body, leaving
the soft belly in the center
vulnerable to anything.
As for my country, it blunders along
as well intentioned as Eve choosing
cider and windfalls, oblivious
to the famine soon to come.
I stir pots, bury my face in books, or hold
a telephone to my ear as if its cord
were the umbilicus of the world
whose voices still whisper to me
even after they have left
their bodies.

Molly Peacock ～

Why I Am Not a Buddhist

I love desire, the state of want and thought
of how to get; building a kingdom in a soul
requires desire. I love the things I've sought—
you in your beltless bathrobe, tongues of cash that loll
from my billfold—and love what I want: clothes,
houses, redemption. Can a new mauve suit

equal God? Oh no, desire is ranked. To lose
a loved pen is not like losing faith. Acute
desire for nut gateau is driven out by death,
but the cake on its plate has meaning,
even when love is endangered and nothing matters.
For my mother, health; for my sister, bereft,
wholeness. But why is desire suffering?
Because want leaves a world in tatters?
How else but in tatters should a world be?
A columned porch set high above a lake.
Here, take my money. A loved face in agony,
the spirit gone. Here, use my rags of love.

The Purr

As you stand still in the hall thinking what
to do next and I approach you from behind,
I think behind must be best: your naked
rump scalloped beneath the plumb

line of your spine's furred tree. But
as I catch the concentration in the kind
angling of your head toward the cats and tread
catlike myself behind you, your scrotum

hung like an oriole's nest, I cut
beneath your outstretched arm and find
I'm hungry for your face instead,
hungry for my future. The mysterious thrum

that science can't yet explain awakes a hum
in me, the sound something numb come alive makes.

The Fare

Bury me in my pink pantsuit, you said—and I did.
But I'd never dressed you before! I saw the glint

of gold in your jewelry drawer and popped
the earrings in a plastic bag along with pearls,
a pink-and-gold pin, and your perfume. ("What's this?"
the mortician said . . . "Oh well, we'll spray some on.")
Now your words from the coffin: *Take my earrings off!*
I've had them on all day, for God's sake!"
You've had them on five days. The lid's closed,
and the sharp stab of a femininity
you couldn't stand for more than two hours in life
is eternal—you'll never relax. I'm 400 miles away.
Should I call up the funeral home and have them removed?
You're not buried yet—stored till the ground thaws—
where, I didn't ask. Probably the mortician's garage.
I should have buried you in slippers and a bathrobe.
Instead, I gave them your shoes. Oh, please
do it for me. I can't stand the thought of you
pained by vanity forever. Reach your cold hand
up to your ear and pull and hear the click
of the clasp hinge unclasping, then reach
across your face and get the other one
and—this effort could take you days, I know,
since you're dead. Let it be your last effort:
to change my mistake and be dead in comfort.
Lower your hands in their places
on your low mound of stomach and rest, rest,
you can let go. They'll fall
to the bottom of the casket like tokens,
return fare fallen to the pit
of a coat's satin pocket.

Matins

Rain hisses off the bus and car and taxi tires,
hosing the almost gardened streets; blackened lanes
of traffic seem planned as garden paths;
buildings wired like cemented topiaries
lean into their baths, and it's spring,
we're alive, the city a human-made Eden,
so gray, not green, though there in the fruit stands

jonquils and hyacinths bow in tin buckets and
figures in slickers duck out to shop, a wet parade
of flower heads conveyed along below.
It occurs to me to pray.
In a little seizure, a prayer shudders up,
its spasm quick as a camera's shutter:
Glad you exist to rise up, window.

Lucia Perillo ~

For Edward Hopper, from the Floor

What I like about the women in Hopper's paintings
is their being given postures anyone could hold—no need
to lie on your side propped up on an elbow,
rotating your head until its gaze is directed
backward athwart your shoulder, a pose
figuring so prominently in the book of nudes
you might be tempted to try it, as I was, on the floor.
And hear a muffled unknuckling, as though the twenty-dollar bills
you've been giving the chiropractor to wad in your spine
have all come unchinked as from old cabin boards,
only it's you there issuing the noise the wind makes
groaning through. The chiropractor: call him Dr. Bruce
to distinguish him from his brothers Drs. Bob and Bill—
at lunch they all go out running together
like a pack of raindrops falling from one cloud.
And just to see them makes my bones ache, the way seeing
the old women who scrubbed tile floors in Mexican hotels
pinged the rubber band stretched in the balsa wood of my chest
because I knew should I get down beside them
within a half-hour my knees would be locked
underrib in perpetuity, like the Land O' Lakes maiden's.

But Hopper will let you just sit there, slumped
in that very unergonomic chair, sobering in light
from a not-too-difficult sun, and you don't have

to be slender. And you don't have to pretend
that the collie dog standing chest-deep in the grass
doesn't secretly irritate you with her virtues.
And Dr. Bruce will not crawl into that space
between the hotel dresser and the narrow hotel bed
to demonstrate stomach crunches or those doggie exercises
supposed to pop your sacral vertebrae back in place.
Or Dr. Bob, Dr. Bill—but for the color of their nylon shoes
they are interchangeable, the way Hopper's women
all share the body of his wife, Jo, whom he drew
often with a crumbly rust-colored crayon
called sanguine, I've learned: after the French for blood.

Lament in Good Weather

So would this be how I'd remember my hands
(given the future's collapsing trellis):
pulling a weed (of all possible gestures),
trespassing the shade between toppled stalks?
A whole afternoon I spent chopping them back, no fruit
but a glut of yellow buds, the crop choked
this year by its own abundance, the cages
overrun. And me not fond of tomatoes, really,
something about how when you cut to their hearts
what you find is only a wetness and seeds,
wetness and seeds, wetness and seeds.
Still, my hands came gloved with their odor
into this room, where for days I've searched
but found no words to fit.
Bitter musky acrid stale—the scent
of hands once buried past the wrist in vines.

For I Have Taught the Japanese

whilst sitting with my fanny on the desk,
which is not done in their country

someone who knew later said.
And hectored them in words they did not understand,
though I spoke loudly and clipped each one off
like Don Quixote pruning dead blossoms from a rosebush.

And now that they have long since traveled back
into the pebble gardens of their lives, I wonder
if they remember any more of me than the pretzel shapes
my lips squirmed through, the ones that betrayed
my disapproving their enthusiasm for the mall
where they bought accessories silk-screened with obscure

American cartoon characters like Ziggy—& see
how I raise him now against them like a studded club?
For didn't I envy their aptitude at old, masonic arts
like ballroom dance and bowling, my own wild gutter balls
bounding them to the brink of a genuine sadness
they also fastened to my spinsterhood: "No, really,"

I had to tell them, "it's okay." I was such
an idiot I even tried to apologize more than once
for Nagasaki, their reply held back until one night
when they made floating lamps from paper bags and candles.
And watching the orange smudges ride into the deep
blue-black of the lake, at last I understood

that I understood not one thing about grace, whose anatomy
is mostly silent. Toward the end of the term
they took a class picture then would not show me it
for weeks, so I imagined an open button or a scrap
of lettuce blackening my teeth. But I turned out
I thought normal among them, camouflaged in my blue dress,

and have never learned what about me made them
hang their heads over their desks, the hair
falling down over each face like a puppet-show curtain
shut across the moon, until someone reclaimed the photo
as if taking something sharp back from a child
and elocuted very crisply: There now, Lucia-san, you see.

Marie Ponsot ~

"I've Been Around: It Gets Me Nowhere"

"Cuncta fui; conducit nihil."
V. AURELIUS

I am the woman always too young to be
holding the diamond the baby exulting.

I am the worker afraid of the rules & the boss; my
salary heats the house where I feed many children.

I am packing my bags for coming & going
& going much further than ever before.

> Though elsewhere gets me nowhere
> place is not a problem.
> Feet keep me going,
> the impressive exporters
> of what place is about. Maps—
> gold on parchment or printed
> Mobil travel ads—lay it all out.

> But over every place, time goes
> remote, a cloud-cover question.
> You, in love with your castle, your jet,
> your well-invested dollars
> and I with my moving
> dictionaries & binoculars
> are both almost out of it,
> too far gone to find a bin
> with stores of more time in.
> A decade, a week, a second, then
> time shrugs and shudders out of touch
> into a perfect fit,
> and that's it.

I am the dog I let out in the morning
wagging & panting at the open door.

I am the foresworn child in the swing
arching & pumping, practicing, "More, more!"

I'm the crossword puzzle time & place
bound at the end by their loose embrace.

One Is One

Heart, you bully, you punk, I'm wrecked, I'm shocked
stiff. You? you still try to rule the world—though
I've got you: identified, starving, locked
in a cage you will not leave alive, no
matter how you hate it, pound its walls,
& thrill its corridors with messages.

Brute. Spy. I trusted you. Now you reel & brawl
in your cell but I'm deaf to your rages,
your greed to go solo, your eloquent
threats of worse things you (knowing me) could do.
You scare me, bragging you're a double agent

since jailers are prisoners' prisoners too.
Think! Reform! Make us one. Join the rest of us,
and joy may come, and make its test of us.

The Story After the Story

In bubbles to the elbow, on my knees,
I am washing children. You are laughing,
pleased to observe me at my mysteries.

Antoine & Will giggle as I sluice their backs.
My knees soaked by local tidal splashes
creak as I stand and towel two relaxed

bed-ready boys. I crib them, warm in their
soft shirts, & sit to eat a bruised sweet apple
as I nurse Chris and float on mild air

a story for everyone; Monique & Denis
settle on child-chairs; we are a tangle,
bitch and pups, in the oldest comity.

You like that less, leave us for the kitchen
to finish the fruit and cheese. The ample
story falls short on me. My mind itches.

Sighing & smiling Antoine drops to sleep.
Will lies awake, only his eyes active.
Monique trusts the story somehow to keep

mapping new ways home through more & more world.
Chris drowses. Will's eyelids lift up, lapse back.
Denis' fists lie in his lap, loosely curled.

I am willing them one by one to sleep.
The story wanders in its adjectives.
Chris' mouth clamps down, lets go, breathes deep.

Humming & murmuring I bed them all.
Monique tells a soft story, managing
me into mind with her as she too falls.

I rise in joy, ready, the child-work done.
I find you have gone out. A radical
of loss cancels what we might have become.

"Trois Petits Tours et Puis..."

She gives him paper and a fine-nibbed pen;
he discovers the world and makes a map.
She gives him boots and a Havaheart trap,
Peterson guides, tent, backpack, fish-hooks, then
rehearses the uses of the North Star.

He leaves a trail of breadcrumbs down the road.
He mails back snapshots of himself & his load
borne almost a mile till he thumbed a car
& hitched to where he spread his picnic out.
His assets (food & use of gear) he lends
to the driver. He learns he likes to play fair.
That all this must please her he does not doubt.

His map omits her. His snapshots go to friends.
A fresh music fills her house, a fresh air.

Winter

I don't know what to say to you, neighbor,
as you shovel snow from your part of our street
neat in your Greek black. I've waited for
chance to find words; now, by chance, we meet.

We took our boys to the same kindergarten,
thirteen years ago when our husbands went.
Both boys hated school, dropped out feral, dropped in
to separate troubles. You shift snow fast, back bent,
but your boy killed himself, six days dead.

My boy washed your wall when the police were done.
He says, "We weren't friends?" and shakes his head,
"I told him it was great he had that gun,"
and shakes. I shake, close to you, close to you.
You have a path to clear, and so you do.

Minnie Bruce Pratt ~

Shades*

*"We were landed up a river a good way from the sea . . . where we saw few or none of
our native Africans . . . I had no person to speak to that I could understand. . . . I was
very much affrighted at some things I saw, and the more so as I had seen a black
woman slave . . . cruelly loaded with various kinds of iron machines; she had one
particularly on her head, which locked her mouth so fast that she could scarcely speak;
and could not eat nor drink."*
OLAUDAH EQUIANO

Even before the flat yellow sail of the sun
passed beyond the horizon, Beatrice had stopped
looking. Fog had whited out details,
blurred the landscape, an overexposed photograph.

For that day she had seen enough. She had seen too much.
In the morning she'd worked in a room where arched light fell
unhindered on broken plaster. She'd stood at the blackboard
cuffed by what she was supposed to teach.

She had not drawn the blinds while they had talked
of the Middle Passage: the Yoruba, the Fulani, the Ibo,
the Bambara caught by men as white as ghosts
who shipped some on deck and most in the hold,

who decided which would have sunlight and which the dark
where children drowned in their own excrement, where
men and women remembered another kind of night
spent on their knees beside their mothers' graves,

the air thick with cries and the spirits of those
who had gone before, as wine glittered on the ground
to reconcile living and dead under the moon.
A thousand miles out they were led in coffles to the deck.

There some refused enslavement of their night and day.
They fled into the sea, dived into depths where light
came from no one direction but was present everywhere,
where blackness was refracted into countless shades.

Home for the evening, Beatrice wished to see no more.
She tried to walk out into an uncomplicated dark, down
to the deserted farmhouse to pick the last of the zinnias.
In the garden, pale blooms floated, like specks of foam.

Her hands had to grasp in the shadows for other flowers.
She thought she held burnt orange, red and fuchsia
set on tough green stems. She stood until
she began to see, plain as in the hour after dawn,

the petals, the color of each flower in the night.

*Some of the details in this poem are drawn from a narrative written by Olaudah Equiano (1745–1797), who was born into the Ibo people in what is now modern Nigeria. He was kidnapped and sold into slavery when he was eleven years old. He survived the Middle Passage, the journey of abducted Africans in slavers' ships across the Atlantic to the Americas. From the mid 1400s to the mid 1800s the international slave trade claimed the lives of untold millions of African peoples. Equiano, also known as Gustavus Vassa, was the first native African and former slave to write the story of his life without a white ghostwriter or editor. See *The Interesting Narrative and Other Writings*, (ed. Vincent Carretta (1789; rpt. New York: Penguin, 1995); the epigraph is from pp. 62–63.

The White Star

Inside the White Star it was warm, tumbled clothes
and humming revolution of unsteady washer-dryers.
It was a whirligig blur of red black blue yellow
that Beatrice watched like a TV, next to her lover.

Last night she'd looked into lighted windows
bitterly, as if she'd been evicted, things thrown
out on the sidewalk, cracked lamp, books sprawled
by the mattress, sheaves of paper spilled, all
looking small and naked, exposed, like her once
in a bad dream of childhood.

            Not yet, except
they'd been kicking some people out on her street,
not her, not yet, not for skin or rent money,
but always perhaps if she forgot to draw her curtains
when she kissed the woman who was not her sister,
when they slowdanced in the kitchen before supper.

Not yet, but already to her. The children taken,
no place of hers, lit or dark, fit for home.

Not yet here to her, but already to a white woman
on the block, standing out by her clothes piled out
to draggle-tail in the dirt, in the getting-dark time,
clouds neon pink, birds going to roost so fast
they leave only a single wingbeat in the air overhead.

Already to a brown woman under a mound of blankets
piled by the corner, her head emerging at footsteps,
cautious, fearful, wrinkled turtle neck.
                                          Already
to the sallow woman on a laundry bench, wine skin
hot as a blanket, asleep in the clean drunk room.

Tonight in the White Star muzak was playing old
brittle raindrops. Beatrice leaned sideways against
her lover, smelling her hair and the clean clothes.
Next bench, a man muttered stones, a woman stared away.

        The padlocked doors, people bending in the rain
        to salvage one obscure object, people shouting
        to no one: *We live here. You can't throw us out.*

    She closed her eyes and wished they could dance
    in this lit public place. Mouth against the other's ear,
    she began to hum: *Go in and out the window, go in
    and out.* How the glass would crack under a desperate fist.
    Go in and out the window as we have done before—

Eating Clay

Face damp on a lover's thigh and scratchy
pubic hair, she sighs in the wet dirt smell,
steam rising from hot ground and underbrush,
the hollow place, bottom of the hill, where
cars stopped for it seemed no reason, until
one day she saw a young thin woman digging up
the yellow-brown clay, crumbly as cornmeal
put in a paper sack. She'd never tried the dirt
but thought the woman had a power she did not,
tasting that mysterious meal late at night.

Now Beatrice envied no other's power, licking
acrid delicate salt from her lips. Not anymore,
as she lay back pliant in another's steady hand,
thou-art-the-potter-I-am-the-clay. Surrender.
Oh yes, the way she'd never done in church.

> Closest then she'd ever come was in the shed
> cool as a scooped-out cave, beside a dirt road
> miles from nowhere, in a world that went on with
> no help from her, even Ed could not do a thing
> when the wild turkey hen and her chicks crossed by
> but wish for his gun. The world went on around.
> Breathe, rot, eat and be eaten, regardless.

> In the shed, grey rows of pots dripped wet, just born,
> some small as a hand, some thick through the body.
> When the potter let her kick the board, the wheel spun
> heavy as a car on muddy ground, the squat clay lump
> sliding in her hand. The slightest touch changed
> everything. Thumb, hooked as if to peel an orange
> at the navel, suddenly would plumb the earth's core.
> Her fingers laid mountains low into glistening bowls.

Soon they'd breakfast off plates lifted whole from that place.
She'd set the table with a thump, ready for the morning news,
the next story about women like her, the same question,
What made you the way you are?

She'd say straightfaced it was
the dirt she ate.

And in the coming night she'd shiver.
In the candle's flame the blue eye of a waiting kiln. Touch
scorches her breasts, her belly fattened with desire. The other
woman, panting, digs between her legs. Candle shadows
eat the wall, nether light swallows up the fire.

Sweat glazes her pale skin, done, undone by one touch
and terror, never knowing whether what will come will be
surrender, the tongue's flame in the furnace of the mouth.

Claudia Rankine ～

Testimonial

*

As if I craved error, as if love were ahistorical,
I came to live in a country not at first my own
and here came to love a man not stopped by reticence.

And because it seemed right
love of this man would look like freedom,

the lone expanse of his back
would be found land, I turned,

as a brown field turns, suddenly grown green,
for this was the marriage waited for: the man
desiring as I, movement toward mindful and yet.

It was June, brilliant. The sun higher than God.

*

In this bed, a man on his back, his eyes graying blue,
It is hurricane season. Sparrows flying in, out the wind.
His lips receiving. He is a shore. The Atlantic rushing.
Clouds opening in the late June storm. This,
as before, in the embrace that takes all my heart.
Imagine his unshaven face, his untrimmed nails, as all

the hurt this world could give.

*

Gnaw. Zigzag. The end of the alphabet buckling floors.
How to come up?

The blue-crown motmot cannot negotiate narrow branches,
but then her wings give way, betray struggle,

intention broken off in puffy cumulus.
I wished him inside again.

Touched him. Feathery
was the refusal,

drawing together what thirsts. His whole self holding me in,
we slept on the edge of overrunning

———————————————————

with parakeets nesting
in porch lights and dying hibiscus covering the ground.

(a dry season choked in dust, etched cracks in dirt roads,
children down from the hills in the sweat of night

to steal water.

                        Plastic containers in those hands,
over the gate to my house. I lie here, my head
on the prime minister's belly, listening: urgency
swallowed by worried stillness

enveloped again by movement, before, finally,
the outside tap turns tentatively on—

*

Lower the lids and the mind swims out into
what is not madness, and still the body

feels small

against such flooding hurled through the dull and certain dawn.

You, you are defeat composed.

The atmosphere crippled brings you to your knees. You are
again where we find ourselves   dragged.
Your hand, that vagary in shadow.
So soon you were distanced from error. Nakedness
boiled down to gray days: hair in the drain, dead skin
dunning shower water. The morning cannot

be picked through, not be sorted out. Clearly, you know,
so say, This earth untouched is ruptured enough to grieve.

Hilda Raz ～

Before John and Maria's Wedding

In front of the throb
space opens in the skull,
space where the garden reassembles
without shrubs, golden yews flanking the gate,
pseudo angels, the light at four sword-like . . .

Instead, reassembling behind gauze,
the thin time between now, over coffee, safe in company,
and flight—the airport, bus, and the blessing,
the exchange of rings, the lock sprung on the apartment

next door, your assault on the common wall
to make an extension, a tent, a shelter, a bond.

You, older son, will be married in the sight
of the company, blessed, and the common veil
of light will drape us all—great composer
and his wife, Elliott and Helen Carter, the assemblage
of blood—both sides—and the ancestors dead
on one side at the hands of the other, fled
from the scene—my mother who wouldn't leave
the car, not for anything, so her foot
wouldn't touch soil your new wife springs from.

Time, thin fabric, the scrim Yawah plays behind,
bless our children, two at the front
of this fleshly company, the other holding my hand.

The flesh will have to do now, this marriage
a healing you make for us, yourselves
who were never broken. Let our blessings
be sufficient here, the garden you move through
together, covered now by time and light.

Volunteers

Out the window, a kid-robin on a branch
shows me her size, the same as mama's
but fuzzy, an outline and then,
turning, her all over splotches.

At the back of the yard, a blighted pine
shows a beige fringe in the emerald sumac,
they're big feeders, you've got to tend them
so everything else stays healthy.
That pine's dying from something. A storm?

On the radio, a story about customers
come to the clinic for mary jane,
$40 a dozen for marijuana cookies

or $80 an oz. for the best stuff
and the police won't close it down
because they'd have to cart us off
in ambulances!—a snort of laughter—
this one with lesions on his arms,
thin, and open sores and bruises.
Poor guy buys cookies as an appetite
stimulator. What would become of him?
What will become of me?

Dark letters, welcome! What a deal!
I'm gonna grab a cup of joe, java, and a cookie
before the gas guys come to cart off the old grill
we cooked hamburgs—upstate NY talk—
and hotdogs on. Flaky rusted now.
Here I am, happy and healthy, tip tapping along
one minute at the time. Eating.

Even though I don't believe this mess is worth saving,
writing is like digging in clay the sumac plays out of,
black letters, the sound of Mom's voice, the crisp edge
of Papa's celluloid dresser set: buttonhook, shoehorn,
brush, mirror, comb, and what's that odd receptacle with the hole
for hair combings? To make jewelry? Papa bald as an egg.

He holds me, listening to the radio
night after every night, each night a story.
I wouldn't lie down without a headphone later
after surgery, a novel or poems for the heart.
Mama, read to me. Papa, I'm fuzzy, read me a story. Like that.
Or on paper. Like this. Tip. Tap.

Fast Car On Nebraska I-80: Visiting Teacher

Early sun on fields.
A pheasant flushes and skims
the north ditch on air.
Students, I say out loud, rehearsing

in the car, *this morning*
our subject is nouns,
how to pin them down.
Gold is the color of freedom,
I say, *the fields Mennonites farm*
to yield more than an acre can.

Later, the most compelling noun
is *car,* fast skimming away from a class
I've asked to describe death
in terms of silk tatters, the smoking gun, for example,
of a brother shooting over his sister's head.

The girl in the front row
who daubed her eyelids purple
wrote about *the-one-who-is-gone,*
meaning her sister. And wrote
about *the-one-who-did-it,*
meaning her brother who shot the gun,
whom she ought to hate—and doesn't.

She doesn't. She misses the black hair
of his head, his brown eyes, her sister's
pale skin, now gone *dead-white.*
I don't make her read out loud.

First things they said, this is a Mennonite community
and a boy killed his sister here two weeks ago.
But they forgot to mention the family, other kids in school.

Early Monday, driving through wet air at seven
I'd noticed the horizon did a good job
on my heavy mind: what had seemed a knot
so snarled I couldn't get a nail in
began to unwind as I watched through the windscreen.

Here, the town is groomed, each stubble lawn smooth
in a yellow fallow. The houses are brick.
Each child in grades two through twelve
is spruce and well-dressed. Some seniors
they tell me in class, drive Thunderbirds,
or go visit China in the summer. In the library

I have a glassed-in office usually reserved
for the Monday-Wednesday speech teacher.
I work undisturbed. Nowhere here
is violence I can see, only the peace of community.

Not here, or in the deep ditchen where pheasant harbor,
or the deer. Who couldn't be happy here?

Martha Rhodes ∽

Behind Me

I think he was behind me.
I think he wore a hat.
I think I ran inside a store
and asked if I could wait.

I think I called my husband.
I think he was asleep.
I know he didn't hear the phone
that rang till I gave up.

I think he was behind me.
I think he grabbed my arm.
I know a car door opened next
and then he disappeared.

I think I took a shower.
I think I saw a bruise.
I think my husband was asleep.
I think he wore a hat.

Bare Windows

There weren't any curtains in my parents' house,
not while we lived there. Who's there now,
who drapes the windows on every floor
so no one can look through anymore?

I drive slowly past expecting to see
Father in the hedges creeping underneath,
under my window, pretending to weed.
It's Saturday. I'm sleeping.

Mother wanted curtains but he said No.
He built this house, he did, not her,
and he demanded windows that stay bare.
So wherever I dressed I crept down low.
Even now, away from there.

Inside Father's Pockets

I was sticking my hands into his pockets,
changing jacks for quarters
and spitting one wet marble
into each shirt pocket
so he'd look like a woman.
I was making him nervous.
He sat me on the couch across the room.
I climbed down twice.
When he carried me to bed,
ordering me to sleep, I lifted
for a kiss, my arms
around his neck and pulled him down
and pulled him down. He breathes,
You always want more, don't you?

Don't I.

All the Soups

All the soups I've made in my life—
slow-cooking easy broths, red thick
puréed blends. Churning it all up
alone in my kitchen, tasting,
covering, uncovering, remembering
spat-out carrots pinched between Mother's fingers
and pressed back into my mouth, Mother
wanting to get done with those meals, running
upstairs before Father comes home, Father
grubbing through drawers looking for pints,
both sisters up in the field getting plastered
and laid, me stuck in that chair,
locked behind a metal tray, not knowing
who's slamming the screen door so hard
that waves in my milk cup spill to my lap.
There's always a pot of soup on the stove.
I trace cats and houses on the damp kitchen wall,
waiting for anyone to come home,
waiting for one person
hungry enough to come home.

The Robe

After his shower he reaches for
her robe, not the sexless terry
but the white satin down to the floor.
And she imagines softness and curves on him
as he walks around the kitchen,
drinks his coffee, bends to pet the cat,
reaches for more sugar, bends again,
wiping what he's spilled from her foot.

How will she love him like this, should she
pull him by the sash to bed
or bare his shoulders, oil him first

then slowly rub him dry with her palms?
Where are the breasts and wide hips
she thought she saw? What do they want
each other to want—both of them
standing here shy.

Adrienne Rich ～

Letters to a Young Poet

1
Your photograph won't do you justice
those wetted anthill mounds won't let you focus
that lens on the wetlands

five swans chanting overhead
distract your thirst for closure
and quick escape

2
Let me turn you around in your frozen nightgown and say
one word to you: Ineluctable

—meaning, you won't get quit
of this: the worst of the new news

history running back and forth
panic in the labyrinth

—I will not touch you further:
your choice to freeze or not

to say, you and I are caught in
a laboratory without a science

3
Would it gladden you to think
poetry could purely

take its place beneath lightning sheets
or fogdrip   live its own life

screamed at, howled down
by a torn bowel of dripping names

—composers visit Terezin, film-makers Sarajevo
Cabrini-Green or Edenwald Houses

   ineluctable

if a woman as vivid as any artist
can fling any day herself from the 14th floor

would it relieve you to decide   *Poetry*
doesn't make this happen?

    4

From the edges of your own distraction turn
the cloth-weave up, its undersea-fold venous

with sorrow's wash and suck, pull and release,
      annihilating rush

to and fro, fabric of caves, the onset of your fear
kicking away their lush and slippery flora nurseried
      in liquid glass

trying to stand fast in rootsuck, in distraction,
      trying to wade this
undertow of utter repetition

Look: with all my fear I'm here with you, trying what it
      means, to stand fast; what it means to move

    5

Beneaped. Rowboat, pirogue, caught between the lowest
and highest tides of spring. Beneaped. Befallen,
becalmed, benighted, yes, begotten.
—*Be*—infernal prefix of the actionless
—*Be*—as in Sit, Stand, Lie, Obey.

The dog's awful desire that takes his brain
and lays it at the boot-heel.

You can be like this forever—*Be*
as without movement.

    6

But this is how
I come, anyway, pushing up from below
my head wrapped in a chequered scarf   a lantern helmet on this
        head
pushing up out of the ore
this sheeted face this lanterned head facing the seep of death
my lips having swum through silt
    clearly pronouncing
Hello and farewell

Who, anyway, wants to know
this pale mouth, this stick
of crimson lipsalve Who my
dragqueen's vocal chords my bitter beat
my overshoulder backglance flung
at the great strophes and antistrophes
my chant my ululation my sacred parings
nails, hair my dysentery my hilarious throat

my penal colony's birdstarved ledge my face downtown
in films by Sappho and Artaud?

Everyone.   For a moment.

    7

It's not the déjà vu that kills
it's the foreseeing
the head that speaks from the crater

I wanted to go somewhere
the brain had not yet gone
I wanted not to be
there so alone.

1997

In Those Years

In those years, people will say, we lost track
of the meaning of *we*, of *you*
we found ourselves
reduced to *I*
and the whole thing became
silly, ironic, terrible:
we were trying to live a personal life
and, yes, that was the only life
we could bear witness to

But the great dark birds of history screamed and plunged
into our personal weather
They were headed somewhere else but their beaks and pinions drove
along the shore, through the rags of fog
where we stood, saying *I*

1991

What Kind of Times Are These

There's a place between two stands of trees where the grass grows
        uphill
and the old revolutionary road breaks off into shadows
near a meeting-house abandoned by the persecuted
who disappeared into those shadows.

I've walked there picking mushrooms at the edge of dread, but
        don't be fooled,
this isn't a Russian poem, this is not somewhere else but here,
our country moving closer to its own truth and dread,
its own ways of making people disappear.

I won't tell you where the place is, the dark mesh of the woods
meeting the unmarked strip of light—

ghost-ridden crossroads, leafmold paradise:
I know already who wants to buy it, sell it, make it disappear.

And I won't tell you where it is, so why do I tell you
anything? Because you still listen, because in times like these
to have you listen at all, it's necessary
to talk about trees.

1991

Mary Ruefle ～

Controlling Factors

You might not think Toulouse-Lautrec and Mother Teresa
have much in common, though if he were a twentieth century
child in Calcutta, living on the street as he did, she might
take him in. And if she were in Paris living the night life
late in the last century, who's to say? She might have
slapped him. But this much we know: *I am a pencil* he cried
one night and she replied to the reporter *I am a pencil
in the hands of God.*

I went to school with a pencil box, long and narrow
with a sliding lid. A little coffin for my friends.
And lucky Nabokov, after a boyhood illness, was given
a pencil five feet high with an eraser tip he could kick
like a ball. Year by year he must have watched himself grow
until at last his head reached the graphite end.
Then the polygonal Faber took control.

The girl grew to be pencil thin. King Kong picked her up.
Her mouth fell open. When you walk into the jungle,
the controlling factors are impossibly high and all things
are impassioned. I can't blame him for what he did. It's
a primal need. Like the screaming girl with scribbling legs

who thinks of her luggage, the carry-on case with her initialed
name. The alligator top pops up: there's a mirror inside.

School of Denial

First sign of fall: yellow chalk
on the green blackboard. Then the leaves.
Finally, the orange ones, warning us
their pornographic state is soon to follow.
The man's hand brings down a beer.
He loves to watch. He's got orange gloves,
a vest and hat to match.
Is it the devil's tail or the cat's eye or the coal's breath
before the ash? The school bus stopping on a leafy street.
The red eyes on the back of its head. The hiss
of the door opening. Things falling from trees
and people loving it. The deer: not his bushwhacking
crown, not his hooves covered with mud,
but the tip of his tail, white
before it flickers out. I don't think anything actually happens
in the film. Some deer die, sure, but in Woodford,
on the opening day of the season, more men get shot in the foot
and we see their bleeding toes.
So there are some funny parts before the end, before
the last shot of the dead doe roped to the hood
and the car going over the Whitestone Bridge in a fog,
the doe's eyes and nose black and glistening. Whatever
happens in the woods is implied and this heightens
the effect of the nose and the eyes darkly glistening
on the Whitestone Bridge in the fog.
But we don't actually know.

Minor Figure

At one point, you have to sift the sand to even glimpse
the eroded smile of God's exhaustion. And He is exhausted.

He's been playing Ozymandias backwards and forwards.
He loves to watch the sand leap up and form a throne. He loves
to watch it fall. He loves the archeologist, unearthing his first
bone. He loves Nebraska, where the wheat plays *boules* with itself,
and the memory of Poulenc's occlot walking in the *bois,* the sky
after sunset strangely blue. A Dutch landscape painted in Italy
is especially exhausting, as is anything intensely observed
in the dark: fungi, wild cabbage, the rotting stumps of birch.
All the immaterial factors: some matches, a bent spoon and
broken button asleep in the ditch. A couple of coins in the drawer
back at the motel. They belong to the archeologist who will never
claim there, who has lost as many pennies as there were concubines
in the Byzantine harem. Should a portion of God's earnest work
be wasted? Colonel Mustard in the conservatory with a candlestick.
He loves all these things equally, with the same amount of
exasperation and regard you might have for a statue, or the desert,
or the moths that sometimes settle in bags of flour, surprising you
when you open the flap and some of the flour appears to escape.
He no longer knows what is divine and what is human, and His
favorite example is how Adam Pynacker, a nobody, just last November
stood in his Andean castle near an open window and watched
a piece of cloud break off and wander into the little room.

Stopwatch

So your daughter had a white dress, and once you saw
a polar bear, yellow against the snow.
I do not think there are any sights in paradise,
except a woman on her hands and knees
washing the road between two cities
who has the impression she is wasting her time
while the earth is doing something differently.
When soap falls from her bucket the moon almost
glows. I believe everything you've ever done encroaches
on your being. Draw a wheat field with a reed pen
in brown ink, and afterwards your hands are straw.
Why were the martyrs eye-bitten, hand-bandaged, boiled alive?
I have sixty seconds to answer that. Let's go back
to the beginning of their lives and do a study

of death in its infancy: a baby in a bowl, bath time,
skin as blushed and firm as perfect fruit.
A painter can't look too closely at his model.
He'll be devoured like the bones of a churchmouse
in the jaws of an owl. When I look up
at the wish-washed sky, the crosshatched breath
of my boomerang comes back: why do we waste our time
while the faucet continually drips, a clock
with as little accuracy as the moon?
The last thing the martyrs saw was an eraser
of sorts, chalk drifting downwards out of felt. Star
pupils! They thought the perfection of a day
required years. In this manner they all passed.

Kay Ryan ～

Why Isn't It All More Marked

Why isn't it all
more marked,
why isn't every wall
graffitied, every park tree
stripped like the
stark limbs
in the house of
the chimpanzees?
Why is there bark
left? Why do people
cling to their
shortening shrifts
like rafts? So
silent.
Not why people *are*;
why not *more* violent?
We must be
so absorbent.
We must be

almost crystals,
almost all some
neutralizing chemical
that really does
clarify and bring peace,
take black sorrow
and make surcease.

The Woman Who Wrote Too Much

I have written
over the doors
of the various
houses and stores
where friends
and supplies were.

Now I can't
locate them anymore
and must shout
general appeals
in the street.

It is a miracle
to me now—
when a piece
of the structure unseals
and there is a dear one,
coming out,
with something
for me to eat.

Surfaces

Surfaces serve
their own purposes,

strive to remain
constant (all lives
want that). There is
a skin, not just on
peaches but on oceans
(note the telltale
slough of foam on beaches).
Sometimes it's loose,
as in the case
of cats: you feel how a
second life slides
under it. Sometimes it
fits. Take glass.
Sometimes it outlasts
its underside. Take reefs.
The private lives of surfaces
are innocent, not devious.
Take the one-dimensional
belief of enamel in itself,
the furious autonomy
of luster (crush a pearl—
it's powder), the whole
curious seamlessness
of how we're each surrounded
and what it doesn't teach.

If She Only Had One Minute

What would she put in it?
She wouldn't *put*
she thinks; she would *take,*
suck it up
like a deep lake—
bloat indiscriminate
on her last instant—
feast on everything she
had released, dismissed, or
pushed away; she would make
room and room as though

her whole life of resistance
had been for this one purpose:
on the last minute of the last day
she would drink and have it; ballooning
like a gravid salmon or the moon.

Elephant Rocks

Here and there,
at the edges and marges,
a bit of an elephant surfaces—
a dome and a dip, a haunch
or an aspect of head—
some worn-away soft and yet
angular hump of the
shambling elephant armature,
up through the earth—a bump
or a knob with the elephant signature.
The ancient, implacable creature
comes ambling back; a bulge
reemerges, that sober, that
giveaway gray. The dirt
rubs away from a treasure
too patient and deep to be lost,
however we've hurt, whatever
we've done to the beasts,
whatever we say.

Mary Jo Salter ～

A Rainbow Over the Seine

Noiseless at first, a spray
of mist in the face, a nose-

gay of moisture never
destined to be a downpour.

Until the sodden cloud
banks suddenly empty
into the Seine with a loud
clap, then a falling ovation

for the undrenchable
sun—which goes on shining
our shoes while they're filling
like open boats and the sails

of our newspaper hats
are flagging, and seeing
that nobody thought to bring
an umbrella, puts

up a rainbow instead.
A rainbow over the Seine,
perfectly wrought as a draw-
bridge dreamed by a child

in crayon, and by the law
of dreams the connection
once made can only be lost;
not being children

we stand above the grate
of the Métro we're not
taking, thunder underfoot, and
soak up what we know:

the triumph of this *arc-
en-ciel*, the dazzle
of this monumental
prism cut by drizzle, is

that it vanishes.

Distance

From up here, the insomniac
river turning in its bed
looks like a line somebody painted
so many years ago it's hard
to believe it was ever liquid; a motorboat
winks in the sun and leaves a wake
that seals itself in an instant, like the crack
in a hardly broken heart.

And the little straight-faced houses
that with dignity bear the twin
burdens of being unique and all alike,
and the leaf-crammed valley like the plate
of days that kept on coming and I ate
though laced with poison: I can look
over them, from this distance, with an ache
instead of a blinding pain.

Sometimes, off my guard, I half-
remember what it was to be
half-mad: whole seasons gone; the fear
a stranger in the street might ask
the time; how feigning normality
became my single, bungled task.
What made me right again? I wouldn't dare
to guess; was I let off

for good behavior? Praise
to whatever grace or power preserves
the living for living . . . Yet I see the square
down there, unmarked, where I would pace
endlessly, and as the river swerves
around it, wonder what portion of
love I'd relinquish to ensure
I'd never again risk drowning.

Absolute September

How hard it is to take September
straight—not as a harbinger
of something harder.

Merely like suds in the air, cool scent
scrubbed clean of meaning—or innocent
of the cold thing coldly meant.

How hard the heart tugs at the end
of summer, and longs to haul it in
when it flies out of hand

at the prompting of the first mild breeze.
It leaves us by degrees
only, but for one who sees

summer as an absolute,
Pure State of Light and Heat, the height
to which one cannot raise a doubt,

as soon as one leaf's off the tree
no day following can fall free
of the drift of melancholy.

Liam

He's down again, aswim in a dream
of milk, and Teresa who is far
too tired to go back to sleep goes back
to the table where she tests the nib
of her pen, like the nipple on a bottle.

Into a bottle of permanent ink
she dips her pen and begins to trace
over her pencil-marks on the face

of the spiral scrapbook the name they chose
for him who has never dreamed of a name.

It's *William*, like his father, but
she has only got as far as *Will*
(the doubled *l* another spiral
to the *Liam* they now call him), which
leaves her still three letters to spell

the man who's curled up in *I am*.
—The stranger in the crib who seems
longer each time they lift him out
and will find that while they named the story
it is his to write.

Leslie Scalapino ～

from *New Time*

there's still on the rim of night (having been in it) which is (in night) there as his horizontal lying rest in snow—breathing in breath 'at' the light day

overwhelming the mark being 'by' his 'action'—there—only. one's—only breathing in breath—not night or day.

past cold, the man kneeling in snow—outside, one—which is horizontal waiting—in 'falling snow' overwhelming the mark, the other being in it—only. as being the only overwhelming of rim.

that he's—'running'—by being forward 'lying' which is waiting (outside): 'by'—on the ground in rim of snow dropping on sky and floor only.

*   *   *

him—having an—action—snowing falling itself as the only overwhelming the rim—flowing on it:

night's dropping—'there:' as itself overrunning horizontal lying resting itself. his (this other person's) overrunning is at rim—only—not 'fighting' as: freezing snowing in it—only.

*   *   *

structure in reverse is the black sky—inside
    defining (as, one)—blue destroying—not—gap—where is fig-
ures—is dawn
    being the reduction of the sky by (one's) structure not seen after merely but in being after only.

*   *   *

interpretative—blue destroying—itself—their—structure in being after only

'it's itself interpreting'—reordering only—as it

*   *   *

the pressure is violent cumulation of series, in earlier youth (*now*, which isn't it)—isn't it, is caused by it (?) (series)

at that present

 rain: falling in sheets at the time. sitting floating (not in it) (fictive there while occurring)

*   *   *

they think (of it, this) knowledge is of one—inner. only. woman carried can see inner. this is some don't hate everyone. this is being. people need the thought of comfort. there's no comfort.
        the physical body has comfort
        sometimes
        (enervated)
        whereas this doesn't

*   *   *

        enervated—extended
        not itself
        the physical body has
            comfort—this is inner

people don't hate everyone is to the physical body's inner

*   *   *

peace has been cumulative there, in the cubicles of light, outside of which is the river through the meadows,

they're clear. (haven't been in war for some time.)

*   *   *

cubicles, of only city, from high up where people live—separated by a river with a vast meadow on either side, people fishing at a far distance on it—unknown how one makes a living or anything, as there are no connections, while there are companies—people 'communicate' only to people

        the physical body
        is only on that
        of cubicles

*   *   *

(the neck cut out—and being the earlier life—is the inner.)
fighting. made up. yet the sole movement is fighting from one throughout. at present.

others, one can't stand the existence—and fight to have existence.

there's no relation, of one to being and the inner—

*   *   *

The movement in the frame (of one's) throughout years, in youth —not imposed, so it's sole—yet accumulation as that even, and so heavily weighed—have no images

mud, the mind in heavy cumulated series—so 'mud' is a relief to have in 'the neck being taken out' to make the earlier start/ 'earlier life', while at *this* time (later)—and to have only the relation to real as only death of one's frame—moves

*   *   *

pressure that's on rim of surface running over it—almost crying —as (at) have no images

the 'mud' as a 'favorable' near clear in the cumulated weight—
that's not in one's frame in movement (that's) in youth, rather than
now, but caused by it or is it—so that its relation to seeing real (death
of frame as law) is clear pressure

clear pressure (only 'having' to—and so without images, though
'mud' as the mind *is* one) as a law

*　　　*　　　*

not (at) one's frame, or at existing, while (though) pressure is in
it, is it (the physical frame)
only

*　　　*　　　*

Grace Schulman ⌒

False Move

Hearing a thud, as though a ball had struck
my window pane, seeing a feathery mass
cling to the spot, I peered outside, fearfully
braced for some creature, writhing or inert.

It was a grackle, changing glass to air.
Dead still, the bird was on his feet. Too dazed
to fear my hand, he tilted a stiff head,
opened a knifelike beak but made no sound,

hunched an iridescent back. He's done for:
that polished purple, ebony and brown
will sink. With glassy eyes, he saw a clearing
larger than his cage of air allowed,

tested its limits, darted as though worlds
could bend. My ground is cumbrous earth that sun

can fire, storms erode. Those silver hills
beyond the hemlocks actually are mountains:

I've scaled their ledges, narrowly escaping
grooves. One step too far, one double image
can kill, I knew, and faltered. Then the bird
lowered his nape, compressed his body, flew.

Crossing the Square

Squinting through eye-slits in our balaclavas,
we lurch across Washington Square Park
hunched against the wind, two hooded figures
caught in the monochrome, carrying sacks

of fruit, as we've done for years. The frosted, starch-
stiff sycamores make a lean Christmas tree
seem to bulk larger, tilted under the Arch,
and still lit in three colors. Once in January,

we found a feather here and stuffed the quill
in twigs to recall that jay. The musical fountain
is here, its water gone, a limestone circle
now. Though rap succeeds the bluegrass strains

we've played in it, new praise evokes old sounds.
White branches mimic visions of past storms;
some say they've heard ghosts moan above this ground,
once a potter's field. No two stones are the same,

of course: the drums, the tawny pears we hold,
are old masks for new things. Still, in a world
where fretted houses with façades are leveled
for condominiums, not much has altered

here. At least it's faithful to imagined
views. And, after all, we know the sycamore

will screen the sky in a receding wind.
Now, trekking home through grit that's mounting higher,

faces upturned to test the whirling snow,
in new masks, we whistle to make breath-clouds form
and disappear, and form again, and O,
my love, there's sun in the crook of your arm.

Notes from Underground: W. H. Auden on the Lexington Avenue IRT

Hunched in a corner seat, I'd watch him pass
riders who gaped at headlines: "300 DEAD,"
and, in their prized indifference to all
others, were unaware he was one who heard
meter in that clamor of wheels on rails.

Some days I took the local because he did:
He sank down into plastic, his bruised sandals
no longer straining with the weight of him;
there, with the frankness of the unacquainted,
I studied his face, a sycamore's bark

with lichen poking out of crevices.
His eyes lifted over my tattered copy
of his *Selected Poems*, then up to where
they drilled new windows in the car and found,
I guessed, tea roses and a healing fountain.

All memories are echoes: some whisper,
others roar, as this does. Dazed by war,
I, who winced at thunder, knew that train
screeched "DISASTER!" How it jolted and veered,
station after station, chanting *Kyrie*

eleison, while metal clanged on metal,
and bulbs went dim. Peering at tracks, I heard,

"Still persuade us to rejoice." I glimpsed
a worn sandal, turned, and then my eyes
met his eyes that rayed my underworld.

Two Trees

For David and Rhonda

Ancient borassus palms, masculine and feminine,
rise on this coast as they soared in Eden,

and yearn to join yet stand, earth, sky between them.
See them now, after the storm—

call it a whirlwind, or someone's cross phrase—
cracked the mangos' trunks, but spared these trees.

Each closes leafy fans above hard wood
that wraps the visionary self inside.

In a Van Eyck painting, man and wife are seen
and see: a convex mirror throws back curtains,

well-wishers, outside the viewer's province;
and, in a Beckett play, a man listens

to himself on a reel-to-reel recorder
speaking of a brighter, but unwanted, summer.

So the self gathers, multiplies, alone.
In this replanted Eden, newly grown

palms breathe free, unbent by other palms,
and bear fruit when they are ready, in their time.

Maureen Seaton ～

Malleus Maleficarum 4

Now you lean across the table, fingers
gold and sticky with apricot preserves,

dishing up the third degree. *At the Witches'
Tower in Hesse, victims were hung*

*fifteen feet above ground in niches, slowly
baked to death over a low fire.* I'm

infected with a nasty tongue, you say,
heresy the devil himself must have loosed,

the nerve to intuit insanity. Wolfenbuttel,
Germany, 1590: *There were so many stakes . . .*

the place resembled a small forest. Como:
one thousand dead. Strasbourg: five thousand.

Nine million women over three hundred years.
What's one more, father? I'll tell you

about magic. It's the slow ticking
of a woman's heels on deserted city streets,

hair haloed in cold lamplight, eyelids
heavy with Chicago river smog. The knife

she carries against her hip is subtle as sin
and nothing bad will happen to her tonight

for she knows how to snap the blade, like this,
and carry you with her into hell.

Tagging

There's something we call a game show with all kinds of dings and glitches
going on in the next room, and outside the Queen of Angels points her
    steeple

at something we call heaven. We say Chicago's more polite than New York.
Driving around, you sometimes find a person who will give you a break.

He or she will signal for you to pull out in front, and if you're from New
    York,
you will wave and wave until he or she is lost in your rear-view mirror. We
    say

we're safer here. Lately I've been reading something called the *new* physics,
the kind where nothing's sure and that's just fine: Dissipative structures,

inconclusive theories, discontinuous motion—one big *huh?* at time and
    space,
one small question leading to others we ask and ask until we're giddy, all
    those

unexpected foldings into a seamless universe. We say brazen electrons
    leaping
into invisible orbits. We say blood invisible as Jesus. I was star dust

when the first atom exploded on Chicago's South Side. Now
our children discover ways to kill each other without metal—they scoot

through detectors like excited shydrogen armed with plastic guns they call
    gats.
They scatter down Clark and land beneath a sheet outside our front doors.

Their wars are small, American. They name themselves *the people* and
    the folks,
tag the land as if there is anything left that's free. Nothing in the universe

exists separately—us, our kids, fear, blood, grief. First,
a man and a woman spin a wheel and then they try to guess a phrase, and if

they're lucky they win a car or money. We call this *The Wheel of Fortune.*
I'm holding my breath as an architect from Los Angeles uncovers a sudden
rush

of vowels. I love the vowel *a*. It's round or flat and beautiful and free.
In New York we say cat, hat, tobacco. In Chicago we say cat, hat, tobacco.

We say we are dissolving into sky, our breath is piquant with rumors,
our whole body frantic for the leap and the sweet light that follows.

Cannibal Women in the Avocado Jungle of Death

They say it's the iron in the blood that resists transformation.

It is also said that no creature can learn that which his heart has no shape
to hold.

When she left him alone he found women who douched,
women with eel-skin legs and simpler schedules,
women obsessed with pumice and Q-Tips.

It is said that she lay in bed three days and two nights while her body slept
off enough pills to kill a horse and he entered her regularly, and on the third
day she awoke to the sound of water breaking and left her bed to begin a
new life.

The best casserole in the world has no avocado. Therefore the following is
    written:

1. Chop some leftover meat.
2. Cook some noodles.
3. Sauté some onion and green pepper.
4. Mix it all together with a can of Campbell's Cream of Something Soup
    and a small amount of horseradish.
Bake at 350° for one hour.
(Do not forget the horseradish or the casserole will be ordinary.)

There were nights of apple pies made with macs from upstate and enough cinnamon to make you cry. Days of attic living on Maple down the street from the folks with the Disney characters on their front lawn and the artificial deer. Near the river where you could see the nuclear power plant and get the willies thinking about it. And Bear Mountain where they went on their first date and she couldn't wait to have sex with a man who made love as if his life depended on pleasing her and it did.

It is written that only a pig can see the wind and that the wind is red.

Cannibal women in the avocado jungle of death step from behind the waterfall and their breasts are enormous. You could hide in those breasts for days, thinking only of guacamole. (Add chopped tomatoes, cloves of garlic crushed beneath a pestle made of stone, juice of a lemon, and you have the kind of guacamole men die for.)

He thought: casseroles, chipped beef, shrimp if you can get it.

She thought: *guacamole*—and disappeared like garlic into avocado, piquant as death, quiet as the whoosh of creation.

The Man Who Killed Himself to Avoid August

That night you looked like a little androgyne in your silk tie
and braids that touched your breasts or biceps depending
on the way the wind blew in Washington Square Park.
I was femmed-out in my new skirt with the built-in wrinkles
and queasy from just missing that glass of Dewars,
remember? *Why'd you want to go and do that for, you crazy?*
This is how crazy we were: I'd almost drowned in an ounce of scotch
and you'd almost slugged me. August: Too hot for some folks.
I had a friend who killed himself to get around it. You'd
been reminiscing about the addicts you were once fond of,
how you lost your virginity on the front seat of a Plymouth
to a disease-free white boy from Brooklyn
where your grandmother kept clean towels and enough change
to get you sober and back to Manhattan.
Behind you were two whispering waitresses,

the type I never trusted with Jersey accents and enough mental slack
to balance out Kerouac, their interest piqued
by the way you leaned over and kissed my hand. Oh,
honey, any clue how long it takes Irish blood to reach fever pitch?
When I was six, I tripped a toddler who looked
just like the Betsy-Wetsies yukking it up near the steam machine.
I was sitting angelically beside our picture window
while Poe chased the milk truck down the road
and my mother brewed coffee for her guests and my foot
shot out. Just like that, the kid down and wailing. That night
the air was a drunk's thick tongue, people circling
slow as sharks on MacDougal. The man who killed himself
sounded like a movie star from Yonkers and played with gender.
He was searching for his Dean Moriarty, he would say,
and once walked due West and slid quietly into the river.
That night the waitresses were cutting up Manhattan
into huge pieces of pie. You could feel the blade,
you could take the air in your hand and squeeze Kahlua
into your iced cappuccino. Subcultures swarmed. Some
blended in like cream, some debated drug cost near the teeter-totter.
We were swimming underwater, slick and seasoned as rats.
We were gaining on the waitresses from Jersey where
the Palisades grew all the way down to the center of the earth.

Rebecca Seiferle ～

Welcome to Ithaca

Since *metaphor* derives from *transferring*
a burden from one to the other, it
was clear, then, from the beginning,
that blood-drenched hall, that it would be easier
to silence pleas for mercy
if heard as the unintelligible
chirping of birds—easier
to string servant girls up like pigeons.
So, Odysseus' heart was a *dog*, its hackles

rising when he saw the women caught up
in the suitors' arms, someone else's pets,
and only in a dream did Penelope weep
for her slaughtered geese, their soft white strewn
round the water trough. When Telemachus strung
a wire between two trees and began hanging
the servant women, one by one, noosing
them in a line, the dying women
were described as thrushes spreading their wings,
doves or larks caught in a spring.
They were killed as a flock of birds, as undeserving
of the death of a single human being.
Though, first, in a colder, waking moment, the undisguised
Odysseus ordered the women to remove the corpses
from the great hall, to stack their lovers
in the yard. One cradling each beloved head,
another clutching at the feet,
the women became mere things—
their flesh a rag for scouring the furniture,
trying to scrub clear the appalling
table. Their last task
before being strangled—to dispose
of the earth itself, the blood-soaked floor
that Telemachus meticulously cut out,
so in the future—that narrow corridor
down which so many would be driven—a visitor
would not know she was invited into
a charnel house.

The Catch

We were looking for a paradise, a place
we could return to again and again,
its waters thick with life,
but four-wheeling into the swamps
of a river's mouth, we were driven away
by the exhausted look of clay banks,
punctured with prop sticks, entangled

with lines, and, lost, veering
among the white joints of pipelines
protruding from the earth.
Finally braking at the edge of a mesa,
burdened with tackle, we scrambled
down an eroding slope and reached
an eddy of a reservoir, its waters,
a thick sulfuric yellow. Two dogs,
baying hell hounds, scoured the other bank,
while we settled onto our haunches and waited,
poised, as if praying, all our energy gathering
at the end of the line. Waited
for a strike, some sign of life,
as the waves slapping against the shore
made our lines go slack, again and again,
until the span of attention went slack in ourselves.
All we caught was a tiny bullhead, the murky gold
of the cove, reeled in, unknowingly,
when my husband retrieved his bait. Having heard
that a fish could absorb a lure into its flesh,
as eventually the knot of stitches
in his own shoulder would supposedly dissolve,
he cut the filament, left that jag of metal
in the back of its throat. Released,
the fish wobbled a moment on the muddy shelf,
then slipped away, its recovery,
as vague, as uncertain as the presence of hope
in those depths where nothing exists but the wound.

Mother Tongue

So here I am again thinking of you—
out in the garden, sweeping up
the pink scentless clusters of the bougainvillea,
torn apart by an unexpected cold spell.
Behind the heavy clay pots of the jades,
their succulent leaves like fat thumbs cocked
at the sun, I find the forgotten
maidenhair fern—what is left of it, shoved

so long ago into the shade to recover—
its stems, wires of shorn hair
bristling out of a black mound
of root and soil. I don't know
if it's alive and dormant, if
it will ever thrive. I could blame
the aridity of this climate, but you know,
even in humid Wisconsin, years ago, I couldn't
revive the two you asked me to keep. "Maidenhair,"
"Venus hair," they call the delicate fronds
like the hair of the goddess rising
out of the damp shadows of a forest,
or the scalloped edges of a mountain stream.
The last time I saw them growing in the wild,
was in Arizona, at Montezuma's Well,
a spring as round as a blue eye, enormous,
sunk into stone, thousands of gallons of water streaming
out of the desert rock, fluid mother
tongue. Only soft-shelled turtles
and a unique species of microscopic life
could inhabit the unusual acidity
of the water, and—where a prehistoric people
had carved a ditch at the base of a cliff, directing
the earth's outpouring toward their small patches
of pumpkins and corn—the maidenhair ferns
luxuriantly, shading the hacked, hewn channels.
I thought of your hair—that striking mane,
and that delicate thatch of a deeper, more intimate, color
like the maidenhair fern, *mons veneris*, softly
swelling above the pubic bone.

Vivian Shipley ∼

At Fifty

Too young for congregating in the praying corner at church,
you don't want to be stuck in Harlan County forever.

Your husband's done in by the mines, the hoot owl shift.
Black lung got so bad he couldn't do anything but hawk
up gunk. There's got to be another better town where you

could rake grease back on the griddle. Frying eggs *looking
at you* or *shipwrecked*, you're tired of getting ragged about
the piddling bit of grits you dish up by rolled cigarettes
attached to a lower lip. Puzzling over the license plates
on out of town cars is about as useful as waiting for your

brother to grow a square tomato that'll fit his sandwich.
Any town has this kind of work to offer, coffee to refill.
Take a boat, take a plane. Go to Italy. It's Genoa if streets
go up and down with houses above and below. Get caught
in the rush of wind between them. You are in Turin

if straight streets never end as you look out over railings
of your balcony where a double row of trees fades away
into white skies. In fields of fog, Milan's houses will turn
their backs. It will always be the same room in every town.
Keep your suitcase unlocked, open for the next trip. If you

put your stuff in dresser drawers, stack it so it's ready
to be packed again. Dust will smart in your eyes, pocket
stuffed with newspapers, want ads. You will always keep
the look of the first-time traveler until you're seated, back
home, ready for the preacher to shout, *Do I hear an Amen?*

The Faithful Daughter Dreams of Spring Break While Installing a Bird Feeder for Her Mother by a Window in the Courtyard of Safe Harbour

No Bharatpur Bird Sanctuary in India, or Pantanal
in Brazil. I'm heading for Papua, New Guinea,
the Tari Valley. No novice, I can reel off 43 species,
20 genera of birds of paradise. Eight were spotted

last year at Ambua Lodge where I will palm time,
not close it into a fist. I'll keep notes in present tense:

true plume birds, flagbirds, riflebirds, perching birds,
birds of paradise ranging in size from thrush to magpie.

The largest and best known is *Paradisaea apoda*
whose cinnamon-yellow head and neck, emerald throat,
reached Europe on Magellan's ships. No such luck
for a gray squirrel in Connecticut eyeing kernels I pour

into three funnels. Like Satan in Milton's *Paradise Lost,*
this squirrel contemplates *His sad exclusion from
the doors of bliss.* Even without wings, his paws
will find a way to sunflower seed. *Just like a man,*

my mother says. Startled as if by a voice I didn't know
was in the room, I'm encouraged, tell her males spread
plumes in courtship, hang upside down on trees to begin
breeding season, sit on twigs as if over a dance floor.

Diphyllodes magnificus spreads a yellow, erectile cape,
two long wires coil from the tail. *Lophorina superba*
raises a black velvet cape all the way over its head.
My mother whispers she never saw my father naked.

No need to tell her males don't participate in nest life.
The faithful daughter, I give my mother what of earth,
of heaven, I can mount on a pole. If not *Paradisaea,*
then feathers of cardinals wrens, robins, pigeons, crows.

A Heart with Little or No Bedrock for Anchor

Hulls jut out of sand, sink, emerge as if from black holes
where I imagine all music, baritone or tenor, ever sung
for each death whirling in notes of an endless memorial.

Outer Banks, North Carolina is at the mercy of tide, wind,
can't keep pocked timbers buried. With no foundation
on which to build new life, ships vanish, people disappear

like Sir Walter Raleigh's colony of one hundred twenty
on Roanoke Island in 1590. Their only words were *CRO*
and *CROATOAN* gouged into a post and live oak.

Mounding seven to twelve feet above sea level, the beach
I walk is hostage to ocean that sucks inlets, then buries
barrier islands which are swallowed only to be spit out.

Rain cycles the Atlantic then evaporates to drop back
as years layering me do that can rise to the surface
in flashes of memory triggered by bourbon, Sinatra,

wood smoke. Repetition, recurrence, reincarnation.
Ribbed remains surface with quirky tides of the Atlantic
or when storms roil the beach like specters disgorged

from shell: Georgia, Henry G. Fay, the Momie T.
Six hundred wrecks tombstone my AAA plan. Markers
are for off-shore sites of an American turkey shoot

Germans held during the first three months of WWII
when Nazi U-boats ravaged all Allied shipping off
the Carolinas. I could scuba the York, Benson, Buarque

downed before the U.S. surfaced Germany's U-85.
Diving into bones of sailors who are flesh to mothers
won't float their graved bodies, only stir sediment

like a mezzo-soprano, inhaling grief and desire, long notes
bosoming like wooden breasts thrusting from the bow
of Blackbeard's ship. Now, he was a man who knew

how to dress for battle; multicolored ribbons wired
to his sable beard, half dozen pistols, a brace of cutlasses
and lighted cannon fuses hung from his hat. No daredevil,

I will wave a Jolly Roger while parading mile long
Jockey's Ridge. Four thousand feet wide, rising
one hundred and ten feet above sea level, gamblers

gathered there every Saturday a century ago to race
wild horses. Stronger than the twelve steps of AA,
I can smell their whiskey. I am afraid of the taste

Carolina tobacco leaves on lips, of pirates, of the quest
for doubloons. I stay ashore, knowing, like love, waves
reaching beyond my calves will catch me in the undertow.

Aleda Shirley ～

Late Night Radio

Some of us are telling secrets
but most of us are just listening to other people
tell theirs. What do I expect

beyond the mild voyeuristic thrill
of hearing about faithless husbands,
various addictions, troubled teenaged children?

Is part of me hoping to hear a voice
I recognize, Steven's from Houston
or Paul's from Pittsburgh, saying

he's never gotten over someone
who is me? I don't think that's it,
though it's another variation on a common fantasy,

the one that has you dying right after
an argument, and making the other person
sorry, real sorry, he'd been so mean.

No, I listen because I have trouble sleeping
and I like secrets, hearing
from strangers the private things

only a close friend would usually say.
Because, between confessions, I hear
what the weather is like in Charlotte

or Fort Wayne, and the talk show host's
always offering up hints on how to meet people,
what clothes to take on a cruise,

the etiquette of sorrow. I listen
because I believe I'll hear,
one of these days, a tip I can use

and that it's snowing in Chicago,
or a voice, disembodied between spikes of static,
talking about someone who is like me, or me.

Long Distance

A man in California says he understands me,
and I don't object. Only the faithful believe
in edges, as if a clear boundary between something

and something else were proof of God. Lately
I've sensed a tidal movement in the past
as it moves into the present and out again,

and in the dead shimmering from death into dreams
and standing like thin silver trees at the foot of the bed.
I take solace in a thing that is absolutely itself

or itself no longer. And what's the difference
between those presences who come in the middle
of the night and the man who asked me to sail

down the waterways that thread the Atlantic coast,
the east side of the country where the sea releases
the sun in the morning? The boat was made of wood:

it shone. Or the woman who could bend and open
light, suspend it in the palm of her hand like water
in the deep bowl of a wineglass. I'm talking

about the night of the night, a length darker
and deeper when night is most itself; even the watchman
in the warehouse dozes for a while then jerks

himself awake at the sound of a car horn,
the sharp edge of a motion sensor in the parking lot.
A clerk at a convenience store makes change,

gives a ten back when she means to give back
a five. In California my friend is awake
and not because it's earlier there. We talked

for hours one night; I described the waterways
as the trees changed from latitude to latitude,
the estuaries and finger lakes,

the birds moving north as we sailed south.
Of course I was talking about something that never
happened, which is a way of saying no all over again.

Are you happy is one of those questions people
ask each other only when they've been apart
a long time. Later, when I looked east, I was looking

for two things, two things at least. One was morning.
I asked him to tell me how to give up.
Tell me how you do it, I said, and then go on.

Betsy Sholl ～

To the Dregs

I saw my own children leaning
against the corner church. In the streetlight

their eyes glittered, hard as the empty
pints and fifths they cast off—my own
smoldering kids lifting a bottle
of gasoline to their lips, flicking the lighter's
elongated flame, so their breath erupts.
Overnight, I was not a woman, not
even human, just two useless eyes.
What could I pour on a flaming child?
What could I do but drop like God's own grief?
Drink this cup, is what he said,
Stop and let it drench you—

Something to Say

Hyped up on caffeine and Thorazine
you tried to explain the jailbreak from Houston,
3 A.M. in my kitchen, pacing, exhaling.
Your favorite aunt, I sat on a backless stool,
wilted and limp, blown away

watching your eyes dart
as you tuned in channels from some snowy
galactic void, playing an on-off switch so fast
in your mind the screen enlarged itself
till the whole world was inside and you
were its hired prophet.

You rode the bus from Houston,
pulling smokes from your blond kinky hair,
radiating unease through the crowd—watch this guy,
don't mess around.

You had gotten incredibly strong—
half workout in a gym on doctor's advice,
half drumbeat of whatever you found to dance
through your veins, *to hide*

you explained, from the grinning baby
you were just then bugging your eyes out for,

when some inner stalactic voice began chanting
stab, stab. I never saw you again.

Cops picked you up in Austin. Stolen car,
sawed-off shotgun, couple of machetes.
Crouched on the floor, eyes darting, ready to
shoot out a squad of translucent nebuloid hit men—

you weren't expecting bluecoats, no that was all wrong.
You blinked, went along without resisting,
strangely relieved by their frisking hands.

For the broken immunities of your mind
they locked you up in a hospital, gave you pills
to make your feet drag, slur your speech.
The doctor is too earnest, you told your mother.

Pissing on couches for revenge
like some lobotomized grandmother, you cried—
Is this any way for the son of Stagmite Avenger?

Nights in the county jail taught you
how to use an overlooked hanger, how to count
between bed checks. Still, it was pure chance
that made the clothes rack strong enough.

"Let God take me now
before something worse does," you wrote
and I think you meant that.

So God give me something to say
stepping into my house near midnight,
feet wet from a slush puddle, and the phone's ringing
which'll be my sister again having to tell me
she can't make the pain go away.

The Past

I love hanging out laundry, bright linens,
billowy tables of air, and how when the pins slip,
wind like a mad lover tumbles a sheet
up gusty ladders, over treetops and roofs.

Birds flitting from branch to branch,
bright leaves, smoke from the neighbor's roof—
everything rises. Why should smoke hesitate
on the chimney's edge? Why should it

stiffen and fear sheet-fall, dog-snap, rag-rot,
the fire roaring below? In the book of Acts
our mother read to us, there's a chapter
where if you circled the words *rise, stand, get up,*

those whisper-thin pages would be full of eyes.
And if those words did what they said, there'd be holes
to see through, like stepping into brightness,
the sidewalk glittering outside of church,

or getting our cards back when Sunday is over,
the game my sisters and I loved to play,
its object to cheat and get caught, accuse
and roar with laughter. I like to think

there are rules in the Bible like that, God
shuffles the deck with great leaping arcs, deals in
the one standing on the edge sucking her lip.
Maybe we get aces slipped off the bottom,

and the game shifts so fast, everything's wild,
loser takes all. What was our mother thinking
when she put away those cards, took our matches
and pennies, called everything she didn't want us to be,

common? In her Bible with its dog-eared pages,
isn't it hustlers and cheats who fall on their knees?
I used to pray for another childhood, and here it is,
my son's, here's the dog I never had, a sweet one,

we name *Stray* for the way she came to us,
loping out of nowhere, worm-ridden, mangy,
tearing sheets off the line, and every time my son
calls her in from the fields, we can almost hear

God calling the used, the thrown out, the scolded,
a child with her head down, hands twisted
around a wad of blue dress, who ought
to just hush now, who ought to be ashamed

for the way she slammed into those wet sheets
with her dirty hands, whooping it up, pretending
they were walls she could pass through—
but that is the past now, now she has to let go.

Maurya Simon ～

All Souls' Day

I ask you, Is your soul still open?
Does the sound of Gabriel's trumpet
Install in you the glory of God?

I am a weak creature: I find fault
With the universe and its creator,
Who—or whatever—that may be—

And there are days when I'm undone
By a nameless grief, by my marrow
Singing only to itself for alms.

And there are weeks when love
Appears to me—in the form of a dog—
And I can no longer bear to call it.

So, I ask you, Where does it dwell,
This thing called soul, this mirage
I feel pricking my nerves with gall,

This clear shadow made manifest only
By doubt and doubt's sister, trouble,
Or by doubt's beleaguered bride, faith?

I have waited, like a saint, alone
On the Bridge to Nowhere, and I swear
To all that is unholy and sacred:

My soul, my perplexed spirit, keeps
Its vigil all night, awaiting a sign,
Like a ship that can never dock.

Coward

If God had a wife, she'd be a doozy,
A siren tart with luscious hips and bee-stung lips,
A master blackmailer, pedophile, Ms. Universal
Misdemeanor whose toxic bones ooze ambrosia—
A mercenary of transubstantiations,
A barefoot confection, Countess Miracula—

If God had an aunt, or a sister, a pal,
Or a grandmother, daughter, or a winsome niece,
She'd bash in the brains of all those men
God favors, then drink their hot blood sweetly
From a glass slipper, before calmly bowing
The cello wedged between her sultry knees—

If God had a girlfriend, a *chua*, a squeeze,
She'd be a monstrously pretty killer,
A slayer of archangels and liars, of mayors
And virgins and libertines—Bam! They're dead!
If God had, if only God had her: his soulmate,
His extension ladder, His only friend.

Doomsday

Slowly, like a hot tear tracing the skin's folds,
God drew His finger along my parted lips,

Then down, down along the round swelling of my chin,
Then slowly He skimmed my curved nape of neck—

Soft as a dove's throat and bare of any scent—
Turning delicately around my wingless collarbones,

His finger pulled its burning torch down to my breast
That pounded so I shook, down to my hardened aureole,

Its tiny halo enflamed, engorged with milk—
Where He hesitated only a millisecond before

Letting His finger meander further down, gravity
Lowering my eyes too, as slowly His fingertip undulated

Along the corrugation of my ribs, and down again,
Grazing now across my taut expanse of belly,

Where He paused momentarily to circle my navel softly
Before His finger moved on further down, down

To my tenderest mouth flushed with blood, blushing with
God's breath upon it, His finger rousing me there,

Stroking my trembling nether lips, rubbing them gently,
First the one, then the other, then the tiny tidal wave

That rose to meet His finger's playful, painful touch—
The aching, rising pitch of flesh turning everything to fire—

And then, all the universe—extinguished:
God took His hand away.

The Search

I'm sick of celestial whodunits, wherein God
multiplies Himself like the eyes of a fly,

and blows another version of redemption
into the golden pores of the sunflower,

and inflates the tulip's mansion with ghosts.
The rubied maple leaves bloody the ground

with tattered clues to the afterlife;
acorns concern themselves, like plump nuns,

with the sacraments of summer that worms
sequester as holy grails. I have lost my way.

I'm weary of the world of deeds and men—
oh world of ten thousand leavings and losses.

The Great Sleuth of meaning divides Himself
too thinly for comfort and dwells alone

in this patchwork universe, surveying our sins
of omission, the falling stars His hot tears,

and love's the only grace binding us
to each other with invisible threads.

Where does my wandering take me, but down
into the deepest pit of bewilderment,

where my own death stares back at me,
unadorned, unforgiven, unknown?

The only mystery that counts is the one
I cannot solve. Such is my burden, my hope.

Cathy Song ~

Journey

My father is looking at the end of his life,
and it looks like the end of the world to him.
There is no one left from his town to say good-bye.
His childhood friends are saying
good-bye to their own lives.
He says he can see it coming,
the long trek into silence,
the idea of himself
seen through a distant lens—
a black figure disappearing into a tunnel of snow.
Wind enters his shoes, his mouth
with the sound of his heart
muffled in ice, buried
beneath the layers of fur
he's traveled with. All the things
he thought he could live without.
A map, a compass, a pocket
watch and a scattering of coins
spray across the snow.
I am lightening my load,
so I will be ready
when the dogs lie down and die.
All day I hear him
making the necessary provisions.
Night whittles a sled of moon.
Shavings of wood
drift to the far
corners of the room.

Leaf

for my sister

It was after we laid the infant
clothes in the rosewood chest,
after you wept at the scent

of your boys' soft
lingering in the flannel folds
where you last received and held them,

that the moon broke its light
on the lawn
and your small daughter tiptoed through

the broken dishes of grief.
Sidestepping hoops of moonlight and milk,

she slipped past porcelain
mingling in the dry wind
of wind chimes, bronze leaves

that kept falling in your sleep.
A restless lullaby,
you tossed in a glass sleep.

December's dry wind
rattling the glass house
made advice difficult,

arriving swift in fruit baskets.
The bronze leaves
kept falling in your sleep,

upsetting plates and cups and knives
in a slow downward upheaval—
the tongue's dull bell,

silent,
unable to finish
its sentence of grief.

Golden

With this kiss,
like the thousand you have lifted
out of my mouth—
Husband of the long haul,
I pull you into my mouth, my body,
the history of its dark breath
coming up in waves
raw like beef shank, globe
of garlic, knotted ginger,
stink of kitchen
sweatshop, sweetshop, and labor,
a labor of love, these acts of devotion.
Witness the beadwork on the embroidered jacket,
the infant's tiny slipper,
the delicate stitchery of the episiotomy.
Knives in the womb,
chop! chop! Soup stock
of aunties, nursemaids, midwives
haggling over a bone a dog
would wag his tail for,
a collar of bone, ripe marrow,
flint of the butcher's block,
piss stream of a river
trickling past watercress bundled in newspaper,
fish heads, black hens, birds of paradise,
the protea opening its furry mouth to the sea.
Words of feathers, petals, words of teeth.
No star-gazing on this voyage,
this body of water,
ocean broth, berthside.
A recovery of memory links
a chain of islands between us,
volcanic ash and debris,

a remedy of sunlight, sea-
water, shell, and salt.
Long ago you pointed out that green
flash on the horizon,
flame of the serpent,
turned it into gold.

Elizabeth Spires ∽

Worldling

In a world of souls, I set out to find them.
They who first must find each other,
be each other's fate.
There, on the open road,
I gazed into each traveler's face.
Is it you? I would ask.
Are you the ones?
No, no, they said, or said nothing at all.

How many cottages did I pass,
each with a mother, a father,
a firstborn, newly swaddled, crying;
or sitting in its little chair,
dipping a fat wooden spoon
into a steaming bowl,
its mother singing it a foolish song,
One, one, a lily's my care . . .

Through seasons I searched,
through years I can't remember,
reading the lichens and stones
as if one were marked
with my name, my face, my form.
By night and day I searched,
never sleeping, not wanting to fail,
not wanting to simply be a *star.*

Finally in a town like any other town,
in a house foursquare and shining,
its door wide open to the moon,
did I find them.

There, at the top of the winding stairs,
asleep in the big bed,
the sheets thrown off, curled
like question marks into each other's arms.

Past memory, I beheld them,
naked, their bodies without flaw.
It is I, I whispered.
I, the nameless one.
And my parents, spent by the dream
of creation, slept on.

The Robed Heart

They come in white livery bringing the sun,
the Robed Heart astride her white mount,
crowds lining the royal road in anticipation.
Ahead, the castle flying the new colors,
a queen's great labors come to an end.
A shout, and the cord is cut,
the crown placed upon my head.

And I am, Mother, I am!

The Rock

For a day and a night
I sat on the rock,
and the sun went down
and the sun came up,

and the tide rushed in
and the tide rushed out,
and I was the center,
the fixed still point.

Behind my back,
row upon row,
the little white houses
were carefully stacked,

one, two, three,
up the hill of stone
that stony forebears
had built the town on.

Did more time pass?
Did a year go by? Two years?
Three? As I held fast
to the rock of my life.

Wind and snow, rain and hail,
the world whirled round me,
whirled my will,
but I was a holdout,

proud by a mile,
who would burn or freeze
before I'd retreat
or drop to my knees.

Before my eyes, the sun
would rise, unblinking eye,
sketching the scene in
with or without me.

Whose will ran the world?
Drew it in its entirety?
But the screaming gulls
wouldn't tell, wouldn't tell.

Finally the cry came,
and the world was words again,

the water, lapping at stones,
cold as a flame is hot.

The cry came. From above
or below? Or was it my own?
Give in, give in, give in.
Give up, give up, give up.

Pamela Stewart ～

August

three resolutions

In the tall orange marigolds, some bees
linger for hours. The big dog sleeps.
Soon this lush, spooky summer will close down.

Looking out on the Connecticut River
with its slow push between tobacco fields,
you feel a wind from recent volcanoes arrive.

It's been telling you all along
what will happen. Within this wind
a helicopter grumbles, the sky gets torn.

Still, a spray of goldfinches gilds the shaken trees.

*

Tonight, despite heat and sweeping rains, nothing
unties the birds from their shadows.

In Holyoke, men and women sit on their cooling steps.
Guns shine in the dark. Upstairs

beside television-noise, one baby's night sweat breaks.
Birds tuck up beneath wet leaves.

In the far-off forest, a vixen stretches awake.

Restless, you step out, touch the mildewed leaves
of phlox. Lavender and pink

their blossoms brighten the evening damp.

*

This night of exceptional falling stars,
the pinched scent of marigolds follows your dog into the house.

Trees lean in, keeping out the world.

If only one tall pine could reach up far enough
to spear a piece of showering light,

then rage might quiet. And

your child, tugging on the black dog's tail
would absorb such brightness you'd lay down your arms

and language, return to her and stay.

What It's For

is different now. The body.
It gets me from desk to store.
It does the work, and when it hurts
the mind goes busy with another list or sings
up memory. (Or perhaps
pain—that otherness, deft
and taut as a parental voice—
ropes back the heartened brain.)
From the body late blood
flows heavy and serious. The solidity
of barn, the dogs, cellar chores
guides me through the hours. But at night
that blood won't lie down beneath the blast

of moonlight on those pulled,
shared sheets of time. It's different now.
Desire's heat flushes the mind. The body
drags toward sleep holding hard
to its small, baffled self. Then,
practicing, lets go.

Martin

It was just this summer I began to forgive. I was six, all cow-
lick, mouth and bones. Those nights he'd slam back home,
his fists would crash like stones so I'd wonder which room my
head was in. All the coffee, stew, and yelling couldn't help.
Our dog, long gone down the cellar stairs, would hide with
me if I made it to that one space we shared behind the boiler.
We'd curl away until Dad went down hard as an ox and the
small house shook toward sleep. When my Mom with her
torn hair wept, and his hands left marks along my shoulders
and jaw, we all kept silent. Those next raw mornings, what
could I do but dream myself a hero? So once I stayed up late
with the star-spangled radio and a pile of comics. The flung
door cracked the wall behind it as he roared and smashed
through the hall, bang-swaying up the stairs past where Mom
had locked herself away. He staggered door to door until I
heard that bottle roll across the spare room's floor. The bed-
springs wailed. When I heard his rasp and snores, I tore off a
handful of pages then snuck close and slipped the matches
from his coat pocket. I crawled into that small darkness beneath the bed, felt the mattress brush against my hair. As
those cartoon faces crumbled, I struck a match and set my
father's bed on fire. The air began to craze, my throat tore
apart. He tossed and snored while my sudden mother rushed
to fix everything before she screamed. I guess I'm sorry, but I
remember how warm the space was beneath that bed, a place
where my whole body fit and felt briefly safe. That night I
began a journey of years away from him. I was six. Look how
long it's taken to see my own face repeat and crumble into the
glass. Just like his. . . .

Against Silence

Alone in the field, I touch
where the panicked colt kicked my leg
and feel, deep within my thigh,
the bruise rising. Soon
it will be a harvest of blood
rimming beneath my skin and I'll say *See?*
It hurts! Right here . . .

*

Decades ago a man in jail, in Watts I think,
needed to show just where the cops
had beat him. How bad it hurt. Locked away
and bruised all over, no one believed him
since he didn't bleed.
What he said was taped and later
a composer looped those words toward a relentless music:
I opened up the bruise
and let the bruise-blood come out
to show them.
                    (and I—so crazy for the man
who played that piece for me one gray
Baltimore afternoon—was married.
I'd lied to be with him.)

*

Once or twice a year something hurts
like that and I hear again *come out   come*
out to show them—words
layering over themselves
until that song takes shape the way a secret
grows. What's changed
since that daft romantic afternoon?

                              Despite
the bright-eyed pumpkins burning, wind-
thrown leaves, or our assaulted language pleading—
we still bruise and flare.

I rub my leg. Words—those words. Or any.
Nothing works until the bruise
opens—

Susan Stewart ～

The Arbor   1937

A thousand bees were tensing
on the blueblack grapes and the daylight

seemed to thicken
with hum and juice and shadow.

> Coming back
> there are two there, and the little
> one can't be more than five,

> does all the talking, while the old woman's
> steadiness is certain.
> The air is still and hot;
> they've taken everything under the leaves.

The leaves ruffled coolly, the tendrils curled
like treble clefs.

> It must have been September,
> the month of her birthday. In later years
> this would seem like another coming
> forward into the world. But it turned then, turned
> in its way from tragedy to cynicism, as if
> somehow the sweetness of the dead became unbearable
> and a kind of hardness would be a stay against
> denial—a steadiness
> that might be its own inheritance, or
> just a distraction from the real—

The cushioned lid was thrown back, open-mouthed
from the basket; the clear drawers gaping

with flosses, spools, and thimbles.
The scissors had been forged

as spread-beaked storks
and were plugged by then

with crabgrass and the knotted ends
of threads.

a theatre of forgotten scenes:
on the boards small dots and crosses
that could be followed, but the point of beginning
is the difficulty.

The naked rag dolls splayed
their muslin limbs, while the newer

rubber girls lay stiffly, their blue eyes
forever snapped open.

Her grandmother had measured
each bust, waist and hips,

a ruff of pins held tightly
in her close-pursed lips.

To explain sewing, and the shell:
the point is the whole struggle
from two to three dimensions, from the mirror to the body

extended, for what is made must move with us—it is
not something entered into, but what is donned or assumed
only after a meticulous labor—
the given, her gift.

At their feet spread all the quarter-moons
of bodices, facings, and skirts—pinked

from the collars and cuffs and hems
of otherwise vanished housedresses.

> A burden, for whose willing is this—
> what compels us to repeat ourselves, and to repeat
> what we never intended?

> That is all she can remember,
> and when she remembers, it is in a certain
> order, but the intention
> *frays*, at an irrecoverable edge . . .

How the old woman rose from the crackling wicker chair
and sat down on the grass with a sudden ripe weight,

her look distracted, given up, as if
another needle had been lost in the dusky shadows.

And how she leaned back all at once
heavily on the lattice, with her eyes closed,

her hands slightly open on her lap
so that the needle did slip, glinting

from her fingers, into the tangle
of grass and threads.

> And then the last thing,
> the part she can't forget—

the downy leaf that fell

from the grasp of the vines, a muted
green leaf exactly

the shape and size of a five-year-old's handprint

> When I look for symmetry, I cannot turn to this world,
> because what is known must be in movement to be true.
> The metaphor is relentless, coming up with an ease

that seeks to deny every aspect of time and care
    ... handprints in plaster, the date scratched
in with a nail, the constant measurement of palm

against palm, finger to finger, an encroachment
    that nevertheless accomplishes
distance. I cannot recall it, but it comes

without effort, the way the foot hits a brake
and the right arm flails out, ready, able
to save what needs saving.

as if her own hand had floated

down so softly
to land on the cheek. And how it stayed there,

unspeakable—its fall and its stopping.
How it stayed there, fast,

as if the wind had ended,
as if the sky had been emptied
of its air and its heavens;

Look to the end and
the start is gone,
to one side
and the other is lost.

how it stayed there
    until at last the parents came back at dusk, found
the two of them there,
    beneath the humming arbor.

What comes back, comes back from another
place, and doesn't save us, but alters
and, even in denying us, can turn us.

I had asked for a third term, and it came
in time, and was time in the garment
of our recognition.

Ruth Stone ～

Hummingbirds

Driving the perfect fuel, its thermonuclear wings,
into the hot layer of the sugar's chromosphere,
hummingbirds in Egypt
might have visited the tombs of the Pharaohs
when they were fresh in their oils and perfumes.
The pyramids fitted,
stone slab against slab,
with little breathers, narrow slits of light,
where a few esters, a sweet resinous wind
might have risen soft as a parachute.
Robbers breached the false doors,
the trick halls often booby traps,
embalming them in the powder of crushed rock.
These, too, they might have visited.
The miniature dagger hangs in the air,
entering the wild furnace of the flower's heart.

Earth Quake

The moon rises as Shizu rises from her couch,
still in the shadow of her husband
who puts her to work early at his vegetable stand.
The mountains take the light.
Her calligraphy, the dark brush stroke
with which she frees herself,
lies in loose sheets on her drawing table.
The tide recedes, the tectonic plates
grind into the flesh of the peninsula.
She is one grain of sand
in the rippling ground swell;
a fan opening and closing.

Up There

Belshazzar saw this blue
as he came into the walled garden,
though outside all was yellow,
sunlight striking the fractals of sand,
the wind striating the sand in riffles.

Land changes slowly, the fathoms
overhead accruing particles,
reflecting blue or less blue.

Vapor, a transient thing; a dervish
seen rising in a whirl of wind,
or brief cloud casting its changing shadow;
though below, the open-mouthed might stand
transfixed by mirage, a visionary oasis.

Nevertheless, this deep upside-down
wash, water color, above planted gardens,
tended pomegranates, rouged soles of the feet
of lovers lounging in an open tent;
the hot blue above; the harem
tethered and restless as camels.

This quick vision between walls, event,
freak ball, shook jar of vapor,
all those whose eyes were not gouged out,
have looked up and seen within the cowl
this tenuous wavelength.

Reading

It is spring when the storks return.
They rise from storied roofs.
In the quick winter afternoon
you lie on your bed

with a library book close to your face,
your body on a single bed,
and the storks rise
with the sound of a lifted sash.
You know without looking
that a servant girl
is leaning out in the soft foreign air.
A slow spiral of smoke
from green firewood
is reflected in her eyes.
She moves down an outside stair
absently driving the poultry.
The storks are standing on the roof.
The girl wraps her hands in her apron.
Small yellow flowers
have clumped among the tussets
of coarse grass.
She listens with her mouth open
to something you cannot hear.
Your body is asleep.
She smiles.
She does not know a cavalry is coming
on a mud rutted road,
and men with minds like ferrets
are stamping their heavy boots
along the pages.

So Be It

Look, this string of words
is coming out of my mouth,
or was. Now it's coming
out of this pen whose ink
came from Chattanooga.
Something tells me
Chattanooga was a chief.
He came out of his mother's
body. He pushed down
the long tube that got

tighter and tighter until
he split it open and stuck
his head out into a cold
hollow. Holding his belly
by a bloody string he
screamed, "I am me."
and became a cursive
mark on a note pad that
was a former tree taken
with other trees in the
midst of life and mutilated
beyond all remembrance
of the struggle from seed
to cambium; the slow
dying roots feeling for some
meaning in the eroded
soil; the stench of decay
sucked into the chitin
of scavengers, becoming
alien to xylem and phloem,
the vast vertical system
of reaching up. For there
is nothing that is nothing,
but always becoming
something; flinging itself;
leaping from level to level.

Stephanie Strickland

from The Red Virgin, *a book-length poem sequence about political activist Simone Weil*

Absent from Dances, 1925

Black, Byzantine eyes
seize us like falcons.
We are defended, a bit,

by the wire-rims;
by lips, unreasonably
full. Awkward hips, long

tent skirts. Stuffing an inkpot
down the pocket
of her beige one—the stains,

huge, black suns
spreading on
the skirtfront, Simone!

at sixteen
you should have been more lady-
like, less mood, less

burning.
At fourteen,
I thought of dying.

My brother, his exceptional
gifts, brought
my own

inferiority
home to me. I did not mind
the lack of visible

successes . . . what did
grieve me . . . being excluded—Truth
reserved for genius.

Fig Tree

One is Genius Itself—the other Beauty,
a neighbor said, pointing
to André,
then Simone, praising
children to their mother.

Simone says, *a beautiful woman*
looking at the mirror may well believe
the image is herself;
an ugly one knows it is not—

She says, she *knows*
it is not, but she shudders, believing
she is the barren, *the parable*
fig tree: naturally
impotent and cursed for her impotence.

Gustave Thibon, How Simone Weil Appeared to Me/2

Her magnificent eyes alone
triumphed in that shipwreck of beauty.

Green immaturity: a terrible self-will at the heart
of the self-stripping; a temptation
to verify all from within.

And the way she mounted guard around her emptiness—

I found her unshakable; I never found her
touchy. Unyielding
green fruit.

A poor judge of people, leveling up.

Invincible reserve.

Gustave Thibon, How Simone Weil Appeared to Me/3

Kisses and embraces disgusted her.
I never saw her cry.
She loved tobacco.
Of all the things belonging

to material life, tobacco
was the only one
she was almost certain
to accept. *This smoke*

has been transformed into pages
covered with writing
in my copybooks, she said.
She was counting out one time

the money she had earned
harvesting grapes. I told her
I had no illusions about
the destination

of this sum, whereupon
she replied with disarming
spontaneity, *But*
I shall certainly also buy a few books.

Gustave Thibon, How Simone Weil Appeared to Me/4

We are *all*
bargaining with heaven—
Simone Weil's whip

calls us back to order.
The only non-heresy is silence.
Silence,

itself, a kind
of treason. She said, *Truth*
is on the side of death,

and it may be so,
but still, it is
too hard for me, that saying.

Gustave Thibon, How Simone Weil Appeared to Me/5

I can still hear Simone's voice in the deserted
streets of Marseilles as she accompanied
me to my hotel in the small hours. She was

commenting on the Gospel. Words issued
from her mouth as a tree yields its fruit.
Her words did not so much translate the truth

as pour it into me, whole and unadulterated.
I felt as if I were being transported
beyond space and time, so that I virtually fed

upon light. The systematic side of her work,
so weak and flat, intelligence in flashes
that can't be strung together. Not pearls.

Intact

Simone, laying her life in Perrin's hands, has yet
escaped him, has refused the conclusion
of their intimate conversation,

but he has her in his head, safe: no one else
can defame, since she never
confided to paper, but only to him

what had been, till then, intact,
inviolable.
And he, from high-mindedness, will keep it.

Beyond the migraine a music, heard
at Solesmes. Pain
is not gone, but the bondage of pain

is gone. *Fear,* she says,
even a passing one,
sways, or tautens, the mind.

Terese Svoboda ～

The Goddess Corn Finds Her Dress in Disarray

with apologies to Herrick

Imagine corn new-discovered, tassels
showing up in fashion, and bucketfuls
of ears gracing fancy dress balls.
Why, to intimate your lover's teeth, all
a-glistening, were like new corn
said much for the seventeenth-century lovelorn.
The goddess on the boxfront
of cornstarch is all that's left of the ancient
American idol
in her accoutrement bridal.

Europeans deny their envy—
let Freud or Lacan explain it. Trotsky
died in corn country but never
rallied to her honor.
'Tis she! 'Tis she! Guns
exploded in unison, Mexican
thugs happy to avenge her lest she be
unreconstructed, the
dialectics of food, like sex
or politics, all interest.

That is, the principal is spent and no
supply exists. To return to the flow
of season whence this aforesaid corn
makes frolic the lark, if you're born
nine months later
perhaps it's allergies that your mother
hid from, naked and quilt-covered,
while in the field for days haze hovered,
storms of propagation
permitting no human reason.

Traditionally fate fills her bucket
and it leaks. Thus: to market, to market,
a pagan harvest of Saffoil
and plastics—what everything boils
down to. Why praise corn,
her seeming assets, when squeezed and shorn,
pregnant women eat and inhale
birth defects, their genes matching the new-failed
kernels zigzagging as crazy
as spray planes over Jersey?

For ashes to ashes, read soap. Last year
she appeared on the Schlitz sign downtown, beer-
cap-crowned, almost Guadalupe
(no tribute to Trotsky)
and entreated civil
disobedience, corn hoarded, the evil
Empire evacuated.
Few did more than honk. She miscalculated,
counting on pure beauty
and our lack of fertility.

Appomattox

That's me, arguing for another effort,
not enough signatures. One of the other me's
insinuates and squanders breath on Thanks. Thanks
for the fight he says with his big Dad body
like the others were boys.

But we are all
boys fascinated with fighting. Uncle! Uncle!
breaks out until we are not arguing,
we are nodding and signing
and the horses, waiting like women
with eyes down,
scrape at the earth underfoot.

Should they shoot the horses too? They want to know.
      Or put dirty holes in the white flag?
            We have to let them cartoon in
        Michaelangelo putting the reach on god
because we can't see the whole picture,
      we don't have the aerials and besides,
they say, Let that be a lesson.

And who are the they but two parents
      silhouetted in the front seat
         by oncoming traffic,
      and on their radio is some tune
sung along by the very back,
         traitors, all shrill brothers?

Epithalamion

Beyond that first domestic kiss
where we're all Odysseus,
the Mediterranean sways enigmatically.
But believe me, the depths scare

all the sailors. It is the cruise
to the vanishing point
where Scylla weds Charybdis
and the gulls cry Divorce!

where the faces you once admired
ghost up, only partly bodiless,
that makes you declare all love art.
Late at night, on deck,

the moon dims all prior scars
to mere regret because
even becalmed, the fish
throwing themselves

into the boat, the compass
too hot to consult, you must find

each other. You don't have
to go back, history's a lesson

no one's required to take over.
So what if the Cyclops rages,
wanting all your attention,
and Calypso's doing an odalisque

on the back deck—it's your ship,
the wind is good, and ardor
is all you need in place of weather,
the stays creaking forever.

Ann Townsend ⌐

Purple Loosestrife

is too good to be true, in all its definitions.
Once beloved, once beautiful: today the wildflower magazines
apologize for including it. It induces wrath
in water-gardeners everywhere. Crews of volunteers
uproot and burn the plants from marshes in Minnesota.

Like the remedies of revisionists, it does the job
too well—like kudzu, or hybrid trout, anything introduced
with good intentions. It wipes out the competition.
Where it grows best it is least desired.
You can't buy it in any nursery.

Doing its enterprising best it seeds itself,
driving out local weedy growth, what fits, what came first.
Best named of all wild things, for those who love the names,
it casts itself into the swamps and will not quit.
Like an imperialist, it has changed the landscape forever.

Rouge

That morning she stood in the kitchen
and considered the chair, its ignoble lines,

its wood of no interest or value, no grain
to coax out with a brush, no grace to enhance

with the tools one uses to strip away old varnish.
So she bought a can of spray paint,

thinking, I'll just cover it up.
She laid newspaper onto the clean linoleum.

She crouched beside the chair and worked
from the legs up. She thought she was a genius—

the paint swirled around the chair and settled
without streaks. Cherry red, barn red,

razzle red. Blood red as the thin spray floated
in the soft air. Only day by day,

as the chair hardened in its new skin,
as she cooked the same indifferent meals,

did she see the wash of color she had cast over the room.
Lit by a deeper light, one grade darker shadow,

the kitchen reddened, as if it had been pollinated
by the most wrathful tropical flower.

It came off on her fingertips, on the sponge
she drew across the counter. And the white stove

held the shadow of the chair across its hinged door
like a photographic negative, or the silhouettes

of the dead on the late night detective movies,
drawn on the floor where they fall.

Outdoor Chums in the Forest

(after Captain Quincy Allen)

a boy's life, circa 1911

The war isn't on yet, though all the toys of battle are ready
in these, the novels of my grandfather's childhood—the Rover Boys
on the Plains, in the Jungle, out West, *lively stories, full of vim
and vigor.* The Deep Sea Series, the Railroad Series, Tom Swift's

thrilling life. The twentieth century opens in a haze of gasoline
and electric energy for Grosset and Dunlap's team of serialists,
their vicarious fast cars, big boats, electric rifles, the wireless and submarine.
Tom longed for a motorcycle and got one unexpectedly.

A question of bravado: will Bluff shoot the mad dog that runs
through the village street? The poor and cowardly
climb trees, and cry out to him in thin voices.
His nerves became like steel and the gun no longer wavered.

He did what a manly boy must, born of invention and optimism,
motherless, sisterless lad, born confident and upright, born
to handle gun, camera, rod and reel, any outdoor adventure,
to feed and defend himself against bear, viper, and quicksand.

The etiquette of the forest—obey the laws of nature, hunt only
in season, kill every vicious thing, pity the poor but keep your distance
—revealed in the author's guarded tone. *Lucky is the boy
who can take a joke, even when he is the victim.* He helps them

swagger in these woods. He lays it out for them, a carefully planned
obstacle course with a landmark catastrophe every twenty pages.
The woods have many lessons, but no beauty. Little men on patrol,
they stay up all night, taking turns, cradling the rifles they love.

They never fall asleep or fail to turn surprise to good advantage.
The language is jocular and inarticulate, the cloudless sky
always right for navigation, and the Negro appears just in time
with the canoes they have ordered from home. The world is getting ready

to explode. The boys of the Midwest are turning the pages, to learn
what they need to know (*Price, 40 cents per volume*), saving their allowance

for the next installment, when the chums go after Big Game,
proving themselves heroes, in the best old sense of the word.

Chase Twichell ～

Tea Mind

Even as a child I could
induce it at will.
I'd go to where the big rocks

stayed cold in the woods all summer,
and tea mind would come to me

like water over stones, pool to pool,
and in that way I taught myself to think.
Green teas are my favorites, especially

the basket-fired Japanese ones
that smell of baled hay.

Thank you, makers of this tea.
Because of you my mind is still tonight,
transparent, a leaf in air.

Now it rides a subtle current.
Now it can finally disappear.

Kerosene

Here comes a new storm, roiling and black.
It's already raining up on Cascade,
where lightning makes the clouds look like

flowers of kerosene, like arson at the end
of the match. Lightning comes straight

from childhood, where the burned-out storms
still glitter weakly, tinsel on the dead trees
in the January streets. Back there a kid is still

learning why her parents need that harsh
backlight to see each other.

Private Airplane

On the grass airfield, a wife
is waiting in her four-wheel drive.
Soon her husband will appear
like a tiny black angel,
and when the winds and commotion

of his landing have come and gone
and I'm alone here again,
I'll carve a little memento of the evening—
a poem. As far back as I can remember,
this is how I've borne my attachment

to the world, trying to understand
what I am, scanning the sky for—what?
A god to tell me
why I'm the airplane,
and not its passenger?

My Taste for Trash

I've got a taste for trashy thrillers,
their psychological sex and violence,
sometimes two in a night.

They're like heavy velvet curtains:
no stray light spoils the darkness,

no sound of the world comes through.
The real is elsewhere.
The real guns, cold to the touch.

The real boys, their eyes opaque,
no longer human.

And when they die,
they turn to stars in the star-clogged night.
This is a tale you could tell

any place on earth, in any century,
and people would already know it.

Horse

I've never seen a soul detached from its gender,
but I'd like to. I'd like to see my own that way,
free of its female tethers. Maybe it would be like
riding a horse. The rider's the human one,
but everyone looks at the horse.

Leslie Ullman ～

Rose Quartz

Flush of fever in spring. The heart's
true color. So much light cresting
makes me write and rewrite
to you as some soft hand in me

reaches out, groping—aargh, why
do I keep all my doors and
windows closed while the desert
fills with the outright perfume of blossoms
I still haven't seen?
The afternoon glazes to caramel
at 80 degrees, and all I want to do
is wander on the mesa, or sit in the blue chair
stroking the cat, or step into the circle
of your arms for a long, slow dance.
Is that why I'm staring into this rocky
pink heart, its hollows and edges softened
by water to resemble the odd froth
that clings to sand, harboring shells of
delicate animals after the tide
has withdrawn? What lies at the heart
of foolishness, the heart offering
itself belly up, or the mind
trying to nudge something
soft, fluid, into even wedges?
The pink of these crystals
is without blemish or darkness,
is simply pink, blooming from stone
broken from deep cave walls.

1945

My parents were married the year
Europe cheered and returned
to the wreckage of her cities.
No hint of me beneath my mother's
flowered silk, the jaunty
shoulders—that dress lived
for tea dancing and long nights
on the town, officers on leave,
the muted brass of big bands
oozing caramel, as the sea
beyond Manhattan soaked up ash
and the rumbling of the last trains.

By the time I was born, Europe
was patched with old brick
and my father's Navy whites
hung in darkness, our nation quiet
at its borders. Every night at six
this family of four sat
down to dinner and smiled
through white teeth like TV people
while the dog who didn't know better
stalked other dogs in neighbors' yards.

By the time I was born
the schmaltzy music had faded away.
Everyone slept eight hours a night.
I came into the world
without a single memory.

Resolve

It's a sudden hue
of feeling. The tint
that softens the edge between
act and dream. Blue as the bay
at noon, the huge
eye through which I swim

once I've stopped looking back.
It's the flow of words after
a moment of doubt—drought
in the throat. It's the slow rain
that fell this morning
on freeways and fields,

not the cold wink of cash, not
the steel or titanium
I thought it was, forged
by a man in goggles wielding fire,
not sword
or bolt out of the blue—

it *is* the blue, the translucent
cup whose accomplice
is gravity. It's the cup's water
born of polar ice and ozone,
the element that washed us
ashore and held us

while our cells felt their
way into marvelous
folds, peninsulas and ridges,
and we stretched,
then opened our eyes, then
tried our legs for the long climb.

Jean Valentine ～

x

I have decorated this banner to honor my brother. Our parents did not
want his name used publicly.
FROM AN UNNAMED CHILD'S BANNER IN THE AIDS MEMORIAL QUILT

The boatpond, broken off, looks back at the sky.
I remember looking at you, X, this way,
taking in your red hair, your eyes' light, and I miss you
so. I know,
you are you, and real, standing there in the doorway,
whether dead or whether living, real.—Then Y
said, "Who will remember me three years after I die?
What is there for my eye
to read then?"
The lamb should not have given
his wool.
He was so small. At the end, X, you were so small.
Playing with a stone
on your bedspread at the edge of the ocean.

The One You Wanted to Be Is the One You Are

She saying, You don't have to do anything,
you don't even have to be, you Only who are,
you nobody from nowhere,
without one sin or one good quality,
without one book, without one word,
without even a comb, you!
The one you wanted to be
is the one you are. Come play . . .

And he saying,
Look at me!
I don't know how . . .

Their breath like a tree's breath. Their silence
like a deer's silence. Tolstoy
wrote about this: all misunderstanding.

The First Station

The first silver work of kindness,
my hand, your hand and your eye, and then the gold play
of watery car lights across the child's white quilt
we slept under and on top of, that February . . .

The rude walnut smell of the hibernation nest.
Sleeping I thought

If there was a hole through you
and a hole through me
they'd take the same
peg or needle
and thread us both
through the first station
and there we'd lean
and listen and listen . . .

The Under Voice

I saw streaming up out of the sidewalk the homeless women and men
the East side of Broadway fruit and flowers and bourbon
the homeless men like dull knives gray-lipped the homeless women
connected to no one streaming no one to no one
more like light than like people, blue neon,
blue the most fugitive of all the colors

Then I looked and saw our bodies
not near but not far out,
lying together, our whiteness

And the under voice said, Stars you are mine,
you have always been mine; I remember the minute on the birth table
when you were born, I riding with my feet up in the wide silver-blue
    stirrups,
I came and came and came, little baby and woman, where were you taking
    me?
Everyone else may leave you, I will never leave you, fugitive.

American River Sky Alcohol Father

What is pornography? What is dream?
American River Sky Alcohol Father,
forty years ago, four lifetimes ago,
brown as bourbon, warm, you said to me,
"Sorry sorry sorry sorry sorry."
Then: "You're killing your mother."
And she: "You're killing your father."
What do men want? What do fathers want?
Why won't they go to the mothers?
(What do the mothers want.)
American River Sky Alcohol Father,
your warm hand. Your glass. Your bedside table gun.
The dock, the water, the fragile, tough beach grass.
Your hand. I wouldn't swim. I wouldn't fly.

Death Asphodel

—I feel like I've buried somebody inside of me
   Parts of her
   I don't remember yet
   Parts of myself I don't remember yet

—Yes you mean
   there is somebody blind and gummy
   lying next to you when you're asleep

—Yes that's it. Goodbye,
   down the elevator,
   something about flowers,
   about giving flowers. Me
   to my daughter?
   My daughter to me?
   My mother to me. Green flowers soon to bloom.

Yield Everything, Force Nothing

Years circling the same circle:
the call to be first,
and the underlying want:

and this morning, look! I've finished now,
with this terrific red thing,
with green and yellow rings on it, and stars.

The contest is over:
I turned away,
and I am beautiful: Job's last daughters,
Cinnamon, Eyeshadow, Dove.

The contest is over:
I let my hands fall,
and here is your garden:
Cinnamon. Eyeshadow. Dove.

Mona Van Duyn ～

One Strategy for Loving the World

To accept this vale
I have had to believe
every death must entail
leaving someone to grieve.

Starved beggar, DeathRow man,
street drunk or O. D.,
beaten child or bought woman,
unclaimed refugee,

though no stone rolls away
let one cross that they bore be:
a life that's now clay
never read its own story.

Deep lies the fossil
manuscript, still unbleached,
of its truest witness,

some loving apostle
whose gospel never reached
the heart's printing press.

Late Flight of The Love God

In one late dart,
exhausted, blind,
he missed a heart
and lit in a mind,

a huge, open shelf
full of rustling things.

He lost himself
among other wings.

When he opened his eyes
his wings had grown
for undreamed-of-skies.
He had never known

so rich a rest,
an aim so blest.

Poets in Late Winter

For Joe Summers and Albert Lebowitz, birdwatchers

I

The poets of Missouri stare at astonishing winter.
On the windshields of their disabled cars they can see
rain, snow, hail, sleet, fog
all at once. Only the river still runs with pity.
The white sandwich they live on is snow between slabs of ice.
For three weeks no one can walk. Perhaps
sold-out salt will float in, they can sit beside
their stricken friend, iced in without guides or maps;
throw enough friction under their skidding souls
to pick up the news thrown on their own front yard
(One man who fell and lay helpless outside his door
clutched his paper and bellowed to wake his lifeguard,
who hunted the house up and down for her husband's voice);
can carry hot food to the trembling next-door widow
(self-immured for ten days from the poisonous glass)
without a steel-point stave to poke down to snow
while wearing golf shoes to crack-step across the lawn;
can send a serious verse to the humorist
who smashed her thirty-year-old hip. For three days
no mailman comes. Never was mail more missed.
Books and small screen pall, poems that hail
Into the cold mind coldly rattle like ping-pong.

In St. Louis seventy mailmen are hurt in falls
the day they try again. It goes on too long.

After two weeks the poets of Missouri hear
that their wintering-over birds are going to die.
For too long the inches of ice on top of snow
on top of ice have kept them from seeds, though they fly,
searching everywhere, through the freezing storms.
Each dried-berry-hung bush is iced off from a bill.
There is no water, each pond and stream stays solid.
Such innocent song to suffer the earth's ill-will!
In city, village, farm, frantic, the poets
set out to save the lovely reds and blues
of cardinal and jay, the cocky mocker,
junco, chickadee, waxwing . . . pulling their golf shoes
on and off all day, they balance warm water
again and again, fill feeders, their mittens smeared
with peanut butter, fat, raisins, breadcrumbs.
From wind and sorrow their face-scarves and eyes are teared.
And the little ones come from the woods, at least some, bedraggled,
too starved and thirsty to scare when food is thrown,
sparrows and starlings too, crows, pigeons, everybody.
Old bird books wake and call out birds unknown.
In his bright beret even the huge red-bellied
woodpecker hunches down to the holes of the feeders.
"If we stick together," he says to the poets of Missouri,
"The earth will re-print for its most devoted readers."

II

The poets of Missouri, in color, are dreaming
a TV drama that troubles their sleep:
when they sailed to these shores of being and seeming
they were met by a giant in exquisite motley
who became their faithful servant. Whatever
they asked he brought or did, though he
was mute except for a high little hum
(as he went about his magical work)
which they took to be happiness. Bang of drum
and now he appears, arms at his side,
dressed like a robot in Reynolds Wrap.
He is looking at them. Used to the big wide
billboards of human grief and desire,

they're unable to understand such a look.
Next a zoom to his heart. If he should aspire
to a heart, they supposed it crisp, firm, green
like Granny apple. But what runny chaos
is this that erupts all over the screen?
Whatever it was is now worn, rancid,
its form weakened by lack of care,
lack of gratitude, praise. Amid
its weary, mushy straining to live
are runnels of need and pain. Their paper
feelings crumple as they cry, "Forgive . . ."
How *could* they have guessed that the generous monster
loved them? The camera shifts and he turns
transparent. Heart fills his throat like fur.
"Our word, our world," they cry, "we've been wrong!"
He tries to hum again, but chokes up
and ends that tiny, unearthly song.

Ellen Bryant Voigt ~

from *Kyrie*

.   .   .   .

All ears, nose, tongue and gut,
dogs know if something's wrong;
chickens don't know a thing, their brains
are little more than optic nerve—
they think it's been a very short day
and settle in the pines, good night,
head under wing, near their cousins
but welded to a lower branch.

Dogs, all kinds of dogs—signals
are their job, they cock their heads,
their backs bristle, even house dogs
wake up and circle the wool rug.

Outside, the vacant yard: then,
within minutes something eats the sun.

. . . .

When does a childhood end? Mothers
sew a piece of money inside a sock,
fathers unfold the map of the world, and boys
go off to war—that's an end, whether
they come back wrapped in the flag or waving it.
Sister and I were what they kissed goodbye,
complicitous in the long dream left behind.
On one page, willful innocence,
                                on the next
an Army Captain writing from the ward
with few details and much regret—a kindness
she wouldn't forgive, and wouldn't be reconciled
to her soldier lost, or me in my luck, or the petals
strewn on the grass, or the boys still on the playground
routing evil with their little sticks.

. . . .

Nothing would do but that he dig her grave,
under the willow oak, on high ground
beside the little graves, and in the rain—
a hard rain, and wind

enough to tear a limb from the limber tree.
His talk was wild, his eyes were polished stone,
all of him bent laboring to breathe—
even iron bends—

his face ash by the time he came inside.
Within the hour the awful cough began,
gurgling between coughs, and the fever spiked,
as his wife's had done.

Before a new day rinsed the windowpane,
he had swooned. Was blue.

. . . .

My brothers had it, my sister, parceled out
among the relatives, I had it exiled

.

in the attic room. Each afternoon
Grandfather came to the top stair, said
"How's my chickadee," and left me sweet
cream still in the crank. I couldn't eat it
but I hugged the sweaty bucket, I put
the chilled metal paddle against my tongue,
I swam in the quarry, into a nest of ropes,
they wrapped my chest, they kissed the soles of my feet
but not with kisses. Another time: a man
stooped in the open door with her packed valise,
my mother smoothing on eight-button gloves,
handing me a tooth, a sprig of rue—

. . . .

O God, Thou hast cast us off, Thou hast scattered us,
    Thou hast been displeased, O turn to us again.
Thou hast made the earth to tremble; Thou hast broken it;
    heal the breaches thereof; for it shaketh.
Thou hast showed Thy people hard things; Thou hast made us
    to drink the wine of astonishment.

Surely He shall deliver us from the snare.
He shall cover us with His feathers, and under His wings,
    We shall not be afraid for the arrow by day
    nor for the pestilence that walketh in darkness.
A thousand shall fall at our side, ten thousand shall fall,
    but it shall not come nigh us, no evil befall us,
Because He hath set His love upon us . . .

                        Here endeth the first lesson.

. . . .

Hogs aren't pretty but they're smart,
and clean as you let them be—in a clean pen,
hogs are cleaner than your average cat:
they use their nose to push their shit aside.
And not lazy; if a hog
acts sick, you know it's sick.

As long as I've known hogs, I've known sick hogs,
especially in the fall, the cold and wet.

Before the weather goes, you slaughter hogs
unless you want to find them on their sides,
rheumy eyes, running snout.

It's simple enough arithmetic,
so don't you think the Kaiser knew?
Get one hog sick, you get them all.

.   .   .   .

All day, one room: me, and the cherubim
with their wet kisses. Without quarantines,
who knew what was happening at home—
was someone put to bed, had someone died?
The paper said how dangerous, they coughed
and snuffed in their double desks, facing me—
they sneezed and spit on books we passed around
and on the boots I tied, retied, barely
out of school myself, Price at the front—
they smeared their lunch, they had no handkerchiefs,
no fresh water to wash my hands—when the youngest
started to cry, flushed and scared,
I just couldn't touch her, I let her cry.
Their teacher, and I let them cry.

.   .   .   .

Maybe the soul *is* breath. The door shut,
the doctor, needed elsewhere, on his rounds,
the bereaved withdrawn, preoccupied with grief,
I pack each orifice with hemp, or gauze,
arrange the limbs, wash the flesh—at least
a last brief human attention,
                                not like
those weeks the train brought in big wicker
baskets we had to empty and return,
bodies often so blue we couldn't tell
who was Colored, who was White, which
holy or civil ground to send them to,
plots laid out by dates instead of names. . . .

Have you ever heard a dead man sigh?
A privilege, that conversation.

Belle Waring ~

Look

Your street at sundown.
Your window, the only one lit up

in all those apartments
stacked silhouette black

against the sky—what a color!
like Sargasso—

loud, like they threw blue dye in it.
Citizen, look up,

the sky god is speaking.
Man, that blue is talking:

You on the old old earth,
listen to me, don't blast yourself.

There: the woman on your balcony.
The woman you let slip—

her forearms on the railing
letting the breeze mess with her sleeves.

Behind her in the room
the books unbend

hover off the shelves
and like a small space station

they wheel like electrons in her skirt—
the books open up to the lines you want

open like air
like water that opens wherever you already are.

Man, look up. Even a small child
has sense enough to drink that blue

whose beauty wounds him so precisely
he knows his life is worth saving.

So Get Over It, Honey

First bout of Shanghai flu, sweat the bed without you
First night walking west over Ellington Bridge
    spy Marilyn's face in the mural over HEIDI'S LIQUOR,
    yearning, so I say *Don't kill yourself* but this is ridiculous
    without you
First conversation with my mother who tells me I'm selfish
    without you
First movie I see, matinee about Monk whose wife and mistress
    looked after him so he could play but still he cracked, he was a
    genius without you
First Dorito binge 'til my lips turn into the slugs I poured salt on
    when I was a kid without you
First talk-the-talk with Dave who says you're a schmuck so I
    should go get laid without you
First drive to Carolina where my cousin Mason's wife takes the babies
    and leaves the state and he crawls into detox—not easy, but simple
    without you
First Christmas I wish I was Buddhist without you
First death, it was Dom, he was 27, lung cancer and that's all I know
    without you
First time I tutor the kids at the shelter and say, *Tell me what you like to do*
    and one says, *Go see Grandma* & the other says, *Stupid! Grandma's dead*
without you
First January thaw, I find a 1943 penny in the alley without you

First period, Oh there is a God without you

Baltazar Beats His Tutor at Scrabble

If Myra counts fifteen cows and Alfredo counts nine,
how many more cows did Myra count?

Baltazar counts on his fingers.
I wish I could stay here 'til morning, he says—cool,

matter-of-fact. Thirteen, sixth grade. All this week
he's been late. Lip swollen and split. *I have nightmares*, he says,

Like falling. Pours out a Scrabble shower of blonde wood chiclets.
Crow black hair, square competent hands. Two grades behind.

Ten points for a Z, Baltazar. I spell PASS.
He spells ZAP on the Triple Word Score, has to multiply by three.

—*You tell your mom you can't sleep?*
—*She lets me lie on the sofa and watch TV.*

I spell ZOUNDS—God's wounds, a Shakespearean oath:
Zounds, I was never so bethumpt with words.

Baltazar doesn't forget where he's from, how beautiful it is
and how fraught. In a flurry of Spanish he spells

MUCHACHO then GRITO then spells I GET UP AT FIVE TO HAUL
    THE WASH
DOWN TO 14TH AND V, HAVE IT HOME FOLDED BEFORE DAD
    WAKES UP

'CAUSE MOM IS ALREADY GONE TO WORK.
I spell DID HE BUST YOUR LIP

The odder the letter, the higher the score.
He spells I WANT TO STAY HERE 'TIL NIGHT PUTS ITS HANDS IN
    THE AIR

Blanks spell what you like—you rub them like luck,
the polished wood suave as a horse's neck.

Blanks goof around—propped in your eye sockets, you squint
like smiling against the sun on the skirts of the mountains,

on your grandmother's face, calm, waking you up.
On the words she would sing, and the music not separate from them.

Rosanna Warren ～

Hagar

And the water was spent in the bottle, and she cast the child under one of the shrubs.
GEN. 21:15

Was it a mountain wavering on the rim
of sky, or only air, shaken like a flame?
Dust stung my nostrils. Lizards fled
over the sharp track where my feet had bled.
My sandal thongs were broken. The water was gone.
I cracked the jar, it cracked like an old bone.
Lord of the desert, did you bless
that birth? Bonded to Abraham, did I guess
his wilderness? He thrust
us out from the squandering of his lust
after I'd framed its future. Hers as well,
griping mistress whose belly would not swell,
witch whose hair I brushed and wound in braids,
whose robe I stitched, whose veil I decked with beads
to snag his pleasure. What was left my own?
Not my bought body, surely. Not my son.
Only that core of shock from which he surged,
the spasm that unbonded me, and purged
me of Master and Mistress and the Lord.
I pressed my knees to the rock, and poured
my body out like sand across the sand.
Not to see him die, I pressed my hand
into my sockets, but his cry broke through
all bone and fiber, shattered the sealed blue
of heaven to wound your vast and hovering ear,

Lord of the desert, Lord who cannot hear
our prayers, but the deathwail of a child
startling from the rootclutch in the wild.
You are the God of stone and stony eyes
and water dripping through stone crevices
to the swollen tongue that cannot taste your name.
Lord of thistle and mica. Here I am.

His Long Home

for RPW, 1905–1989

I

Of Course

From lips notched in the pinebranch bled
no confession, but a clot of resin.
Such currency
in winter. No need to notch

the stream, ice-choked but still
greenly slurring
past boulders and scragwood to some ever-lapsing
period not even January

can grant. If you and I
stand, in silence, to observe
that pregnant snowcloud stalled
on Stratton's frozen stoop

it is in the knowledge
that what courses between us, runs
under the rind of winter
so deep, no blade can coax it.

II

Storm, Summer

At first a numbness
gaining on the surface of the pond,

a twitching in birch and poplar leaves,
tremor in the flat, symmetrical branchtips of balsalm pine.
Then thunder surges, thudding from ridge to ridge,
a seizure of rain
sunders spiderwebs, pummels leafmold,
drowns out the true confessions of the brook.
While we cower on the porch
it passes
like a spasm,
heaves itself into the valley
over the notch.
Sky shimmers in the pond again,
breeze fondles the leaves.
We're still here. Waiting.

III

Your skin

as fragile, pale, and infinitesimally moist
as erasable bond;
your look, a startled bound
of apprehension, subsiding
into its lair.
You coil away from us:
we hunt you down.
Groping, you half-rise:
we escape, leave you there.
What intersections can we appoint
between your knowledge
and ours?

IV

Two days before

you died, we saw your death
funneling in at the eye, your pupil fixed,
tiny, waking neither
to light nor to shade

so that your wisdom drained
inward where only
reverberations of our
voices fathomed.

yet you held us still
kindly, having foreknown
the sere flame tasseling
the roof beam, the palace wall

sinking but invisible
to the chorus; and in the teeth
of our denial
had already greeted

the strange man you alone
saw loitering by the porch,
had wrenched up your
emaciated smile: "Come in! Come in!"

Song

A yellow coverlet
    in the greenwood:
spread the corners wide to the dim, stoop-shouldered pines.
    Let blank sky
    be your canopy.
Fringe the bedspread with the wall of lapsing stones.
    Here faith has cut
    in upright granite
"Meet me in Heaven" at the grave of each child
    lost the same year,
    three, buried here,
a century ago. Roots and mosses hold
    in the same bed
    mother, daughter, dead
together, in one day. "Lord, remember the poor,"
    their crumbling letters pray.
    I turn away.

I shall meet you nowhere, in no transfigured hour.
    On soft, matted soil
    blueberry bushes crawl,
each separate berry a small, hot globe of tinctured sun.
    Crushed on the tongue
    it releases a pang
of flesh. Tender flesh, slipped from its skin,
    preserves its blue heat
    down my throat.

Man, That Is Born of a Woman

It is in slow choking
that leaves flare.
And that single spider strand
flung between shrubs
catches nothing but sun splinters.
Each leaf an hour.
Look, look, the hours
shudder against the regulation blue.
Warm palm on granite:
it's only my own
pulse cantering
as it did against your
cold and stiffening hand.
All around me, life
grips: the oak leaf stem
holds hard the throttling twig,
lichen and moss seize
the Precambrian ledge, wild
grapevines strangle
the beech: my
hand, gripping
this granite glacial
shelf, could clench as surely
an alto-cirrus wisp,
as freely
let it go.

Rachel Wetzsteon ~

Learning from the Movies

In the world of the high jump, if something can go wrong
it will. First he makes it over but brings
the pole with him; next he jumps too early, landing
up to his face, upside down, in dirt; finally
he finds the right pace, looks good, gets ready,
and the pole—standing for friends?—falls down.
So he skips off and tries another sport, just as

the sailor who, finding himself in a hall
of mirrors, having seen his lover's husband
shot down, his false lover downed also, struts out
vowing to forget them both. Where we'd stay
and look for wounds on ourselves or our simulacra,
he smells blood and gets out as fast as he can,
as fast as the woman in the big-shouldered suit

who can laugh at a slap and teach men to whistle
settles into the rhythms of an occupied backwater town,
its bar songs and shoot-outs. Not to give up but
to become a wise fool trying; not to linger in
chambers of vain reflection; never to forget that to sing
"Am I blue?" is to conquer blueness—these things
the seeming goners, towers of raw strength, show us.

Thoughts While Walking

I hate the travel logs that tell you
more about the pain than the place,
yet here I am again, narrating

the same old story to myself
time after time. The papers circling
in an alley, watched by a hunchback,

mimic my plans and their preventer;
when an old man treats the drycleaner
to a lengthy sermon on spotting,

I collect it; bloated clouds spell
messages that people stopped hearing
long ago, and as for the hag

who runs at me, arms open, mouth bleeding?
She's my future, my terrible double.
Always I head out, hot for details,

and always the details start revolving
around brave ingenues who put their
innocent hands in wicked bonfires.

I could never go for ten minutes
without seeing fissures as faces,
and I confess a hopeless weakness

for the types who come back from travels,
gather their fans around and tell them
stories of order or of wonder:

seashores and meadows sometimes get so
muffled and many-voiced that tourists
storm in and do their talking for them—

it's addictive, magical, vital.
But I've observed how, more and more, these
promising outings are becoming

meta-walks and mechanized phrases:
"When I ventured into the outback,
how it blared back echoes of me,

my bright dreams and tragic uniqueness."
Meanwhile forces of good and evil
squirm and flourish under the carpet,

mocking the visionary moment's
sweeping appeal. I'll go on going
out for scenes of horror and pleasure,

but I'll start pursuing clues leading
to the return of that enormous,
fertile ground between shouting and silence.

Surgical Moves

Lights dimmed, the scraper scraped, and I could feel
the change begin; it was the kind of pain
you brace yourself and bear, imagining
all the unfolding options that the cuts
make possible. The red that rolled away
gave rise to thoughts of rolling hills, and so
I told myself, it is a pinch that pays.
Just in the nick of time, I'm hardly doomed
but free to choose my way and free to find
great pleasure in the choosing: jumping off
the table, throwing down the bloody smock
and bolting from the operating room,
I'm the poor fool who stumbles up the aisle
and I'm the sweet face at the other end
who blesses and forgives; I'm in a cloak
behind a pillar, spying on a thief
who answers to my name. Come find me on
the summer lawns, the moonlit winter rinks
and drag me back to where the spongy lumps
coagulate and darken; counsel me
to get down on my knees and look at what
I left behind; implore me to admit
that all the red is realer than the roads
I hastily, unthinkingly pursued;
however many stumps are floating in
the pulp like ghosts of shapes that might have been,
however many stares are telling me to
clean up the mess, it is no mess of mine.

Susan Wheeler ～

He or She That's Got the Limb, That Holds Me Out on It

The girls are drifting in their ponytails
and their pig iron boat. So much for Sunday.
The dodo birds are making a racket
to beat the band. You could have come too.

The girls wave and throw their garters
from their pig iron boat. Why is this charming?
Where they were nailed on their knees
the garters all rip. You were expected.

The youngest sees a Fury in a Sentra
in a cloud. This is her intimation and she balks.
The boat begins rocking from the scourge
of the sunset. The youngest starts the song.

Song for the Spirit of Natalie Going

> qui s'est réfugié
> ton futur   en moi
> STÉPHANE MALLARMÉ, *A TOMB FOR ANATOLE*

Small bundle of bones, small bundle of fingers, of plumpness, of heart,
predicate, prescient, standing and wobbling, lit in the joy,
lachrymose GA, your bundle oh KA, the unfolding begun of the start,
of the toys, of witnessing, silly, the eyes startled and up, re-
enveloped now and fresh with the art, chordate, devoted,
sunk in dreaming of wisps and startled awake—*This is morning.*
This is daddy. This is the number eight—spacey, resplendent,
in seersucker bib, overalled, astonished, in dazzling fix
on the small crawling lights in their spaceship of night and the
plug and the cord and the big one's delight, pausing,

mezzed by mobile HEH HEH and again, stinging the shopkeepers
the monkeyish mouth, *knees, child knees—need to have the child
here—absence—knees fall— and* falling, a dream, a final
singsong UH HAH in the starkest of suns, the heart now a blanket
now a song of your soul—Such a sharp love there is! Such a loud
love there beats! Such a filled hole you leave, in the dusk in the room,
in the wobbling hours of what refuges here, your future in me.

That Been to Me My Lives Light and Saviour

Purse be full again, or else I must die. This is the wish
the trees in hell's seventh circle lacked, bark ripped by monstrous dogs,
bleeding from each wound. We see them languid there,
the lightened purse a demon drug. *Less, less.*

At the canal, the dog loops trees in a figure eight—
a cacophony of insects under sun. A man against a tree nods off.

Let there be no sandwich for the empty purse.
Let there be no raiment for someone scint.
Let blood run out, let the currency remove.
Let that which troubles trouble not.

My father in the driveway. Legs splayed behind him. Pail beside him.
Sorting handfuls of gravel by shade and size. One way to calm
a pecker, compensate for stash. *Dad!* I lied.

The man shifts by the tree and now grace is upon him.
The slant of sun picks up the coins dropped off by travelers and—lo!—
grace enables him to see. The demon dog fresh off an eight barks, too,
standing, struck by the man, by the coins, barks at their glare;
the man reaches in scrim at the glint in the light and thinks *Another
malt.* The flesh is willing, the spirit spent,
                                        the cloud passes over—
grace is not what you think, not the light. Regard the barking
dog now tugging at the dead man's leg becoming bark.

You be my life, you be my heart's guide,
you be the provision providing more,
you be the blood—stanch the sore!—
you be failing

proportion (mete) . . .

Steward of gravel squints up at the girl who is me.
What?, defensively. Out of the east woods, a foaming raccoon spills.
Palmolive executive? Palmolive customer? Palm's stony olives
on the embankment of limestone or soapstone or
shale. Leg of the man clamped in the dog's mouth. Mouth
of the man open and unmoved. Voice of the man:

*Three dolls sat within a wood, and stared, and wet when it rained
into their kewpie mouths. They were mine to remonstrate to the
trees at large, the catalpas and the fir, the sugar maples in the
glade turning gold. To each is given, one doll began, so I had
to turn her off. You see your honor how it was for me—*

Flash of the arrow and the foam falls down. Three balletists
ignoring pliés bound onto the long lawn and its canalward
slope. I am underwater and they haze in the light,

mouthe
but do not sound. In the arrow's blink they start.

Decimal as piercing of the line—
Table as imposition of the grid—
Sum as heuristic apoplex—
Columns in honeysuckle cents—or not.

Just this transpired. Against a tree I swooned and fell, and
water seeped into my shoe, and a dream began to grow in me.
Or despair, and so I chose the dream. And while I slept,
I was being fed, and clothed, addressed—as though awake
with every faculty, and so it went. Then: blaze, blare of sun
after years uncounted, and synesthesia of it and sound,
the junco's chirp and then the jay's torn caw, arc
of trucks on the distant interstate, your *what the fuck*
and then her call. Beside me, pinned to a green leaf,
in plastic and neat hand, a full account. I had indeed still
lived, and been woke for more. So, weeping then, I rose.

Eleanor Wilner ∼

You, Failed Pronoun

Direct address to the swans: you, whose feet
are now unbuttoned from the snow, your wings
spread wide and white, heading out of here,
back to the breeding ponds of spring, away
from freezing lakes whose sudden ice closed in,
when you had thought yourself south enough, and safe;
you had to be cut loose by the Wildlife Service,
and so make your escape, entirely out
of vision's range—gone even your ghosts at Coole.

Once you have flown, the slate is blank,
the great mimetic circle cleared of imagery,
dark as the inside of a camera when the lens
is closed. Now what shall we do for a *you*? Now
that the winged ones are gone, the moon drowned
in the pond, shattered by a tossed stone, the wheel
a drone in the darkened air—to whom should the voice
address itself, and who should the speaker be?
For who, anyway, are we?

Silence. Arrows of asparagus stand fastened
to the ground. Green fence against thought,
image from the armory. Everywhere: thickets,
thorn bush, briar patch, hedge—screen that
dims the light; grids of complex, senseless
green. Dense, ambiguous web. Mind's wallow.
In it, a chartreuse flash, slim bright thread
on a dark ground. Eft. Splash. Gone.

Judgment

When they removed the bandages
from Justice's eyes, she had long since

gone blind. She had been too many days
in the dark, too long alone with
the scale in her numb hands; she could
no longer tell the true from the false.
She had stood so many years in the cold
outside the courts, as the law rushed
past, clinging to the sleeve
of power—until the chill
had turned her veins to marble,
her eyes to opalescent stone.

Yet those who tore the veil away
could swear they were being watched,
and though it must have been a bit of glass
that caught a ray of sun, it was not unlike
a bright, appraising eye. Whatever it was,
they felt caught out, ashamed,
and late at night, at home, they locked
their windows tight and slipped into the room
where the children slept, and looking down
on them—for what they couldn't say—they wept.

Her Body Is Private

                              in spite of all
the sweet inducements to disrobe
in the public eye, to sunbathe
in the hot glow of the spotlight (not be
forgotten for a minute, maybe two);
                        in spite of all
the cash that flows to those
who wear their heart, not on their sleeve
in that old innocence, but on their naked
wrist, or butt, like a tattoo;
                        in spite of all
emoluments, of shrinks who swear
that secrets eat the lining from the guts
and that the more you tell, the less

you burn in hells intestinal;
                              in spite of all
her memory, like her body, is
her own, and serpents guard it
like a tree with treasure in a myth;
if you approach, she'll turn
the blank side of her words, a shield
to the light, to fix your face
in the bright circle
of its mirror. This time Medusa
has the shield, and the last word.

All the Wide Grin of Him

is hovering in the air, there, in the highest
branches, like the fading crescent moon,
tipped in that odd way of what's waning:
a crooked smile, God's grin, the Cheshire
Cat in Wonderland—the smile outlasting
the cat. It fades but refuses to go, hanging
like the pall of ash and smoke over a city
for weeks after the bomb. On a billboard
above Times Square, the man in the Camel ad
has a hole for a mouth, and smoke
puffs out, little o's dissolving like Cheerios
in a bowl of milk.
                    Grennian, Anglo-Saxon
root of grin: to show the teeth, to snarl.
Grendel mutters, turns in his long sleep.
The lake has eaten back the boats, the Lady
has withdrawn her arm—sword and all,
and Arthur, all the wide grin of him,
royal jester at the last, his skull
grinning up from a snarl of weeds,
mirror image of the cat-grin above, drowned
moon, or a trick of reflection: the lake
staring back, wearing tradition's bony grin.

While high in the willows, in a tangle
of branches, the wide smile of the Cheshire
Cat, bright as a Japanese lantern, still swings
in the tree with the wind, and the wind chimes
tinkle their sparkle of tunes, and tomorrow
sleeps like a kitten, curled in time's side,
soft, unsuspecting, milk rimming its grin.

Abstraction

They came that morning, in gowns of pale green and white,
sliding through the slim trees like slants of an unsparing light;

they were noiseless in their coming, and faceless,
except for their eyes, and behind them came a noise,

a clinking, light touch of steel on steel, wind chimes
in the corridors of bone; it followed them, the sound,

as a wake follows a ship, that ruffled disturbance
of what had been even and seamless, a placid

surface, so unperturbed in being what it was.
And when they came, as a wave parts, everything fled

before them, had fled hours, days, before they came,
having sensed their coming from a long way off,

the way snakes know before the seismographs
that the earth will move, and even the mountains

will break, slide in great sheets of mud and rubble,
and swallow the valleys, the inhabited hollows

whose houses were crammed with the unsuspecting,
living like dogs in the dumb incomprehension

of the habitual. The morning was torn where they came,
riven between the slim trees, which were rooted

and could not flee from their own forest nature
like the birds and the insects, the raccoons, opossums,

deer, and the rodents, who had vanished before, leaving
only the stillness behind, and the tension of waiting

which kept even the leaves from stirring, and the wind
held its breath, fearing that the least movement would

shatter the leaves like glass. Every space that once
was the passage for air and light, and the small scurry

of squirrels, became a wound as they entered there,
a legion in the gowns of their office. They were

the priests of postponement, their gifts were subtraction,
pain, and extension of days. They had their rituals,

their instruments, their secret language and passwords;
the forest was not their home, and they had never

heard its secret language, for it always fell silent before
them, and what they came to was only a vacant

room, like the shell of a village that had fled at the news
of an army approaching. And from the edge of the scene,

so composed, and so silent, except for the strange clink
clink of the steel, the trees so straight in their dark lines,

the trunks an abstract study in stripes, rows of harsh light
between them, the figures gliding into the foreground—

from vision's periphery, something begins
to seep, slowly at first, like the oozing of sap from a tree,

and then faster, until it is pouring, a tide of red flooding
out from the edges of vision and swallowing what might

have been, covering whatever it was that was hiding
out there, everywhere, since they came to the forest

whose spirit, a fugitive,
unprovisioned and naked, had fled.

C. D. Wright ～

from *Deepstep Come Shining*

Meanwhile the cars continued in a persistent flow down
Closeburn Road.

The refrain of the rain would be a movement up and down the
clefs of light.

Chlorophyll world. July. Great goblets of magnolialight.

Her head cooling against the car glass. The mind apprehends
the white piano, her mother. Who played only what she chose,
who chose only to play "Smoke Gets in Your Eyes."

A stadium emptied. The ruby progression of taillights. The
eyes' ability to perceive a series of still images as continuous
motion. Time lapse.

This wasn't movie traffic. There weren't twenty people to
see *Smoke.*

At the drive-in. When they were young. The parents were
young. The children falling asleep on the hood with the motor
warm. Coating the ornamental swan with their prints. The
projectionist's private life: shadows animating a wall.

"Never avert your eyes." (Kurosawa)

A photograph is a writing of the light. *Photo Graphein.*

More than magnolia, crepe myrtle is missed. The white bushes
especially.

Against undifferentiated dark. It is unlike night.

She will still be up when we come in. Our floating host. She will
be at the door in her pleated nightgown. Admit us into her air-
conditioned nightgown. Her glory cloud.

*

In the seclusionary cool of the car the mind furnishes a high-
ceilinged room with a white piano. Seldom struck. Color
sensations. In which the piano floats on a black marble lake,
mute swan in a dark room. Beyond the windshield the land
claims saturate levels of green. Illuminating figures and
objects. Astonishing our earthliness. I was there. I know.

*

Everyone in their car needs love. Car love. Meat love. Money
love. Pass with care.

Deepstep, Baby. Deepstep.

The boneman said he would take the blinded to the river. With
a mirror. And then what.

The boneman said he would take the blinded into a darkened
room. And then put a hot-herb poultice on their sightless face.

Mullein for this mullein for that. We called it flannel.

Then leave them there.

The baby sister of the color photographer had a baby girl in the
hills. Born with scooped-out sockets in the head. Born near the
tracks they sprayed with Agent Orange. The railroad's denials,
ditto the army's.

They would have been blue. The eyes. She did not have. Blue
as the chicory in yonder ditch.

> We see a little farther now and a little farther still
>
> She said her lights would be on and they were
>
> Groping around the sleeping house in our gowns
>
> Peeping into the unseen

Beautiful things fill every vacancy

Ripcord Lounge is up on the right. 32° beer. A little past the
package store. Suddenly I have the feeling of a great victory.
A delirious brilliance.

All around in here it used to be so pretty.

The boneman's bobcat. Its untamable eyes in the night. Did you
know a ghost has hair. A ghost has hair. That's right.

Peaches and fireworks and red ants.
Now do you know where you are.

I boarded with a suitcase of Blackbeard fireworks. I had
forgotten about the Unabomber. They shook me down.
Confiscated my sparklers, my Roman candles, my ladyfingers.

Make a left just beyond Pulltight Road.

The land obtained in exchange for two blind horses. This land
became known as Wrens.

> Merely listening

> After the rain the trees smell so pleased

> The hale sleep naked atop the sheets

> We leave the deck for the lawn

> The grasses licking our feet

> A semicircle of chairs opens a parenthesis

> In the direction of the lightsource

> We see a little farther now and a little farther still

> Peeping into the unseen

Why is she so kind. Our floating host. Why am I so stingy
and vain,

A baseball diamond in every hamlet.

The waitress in hairnets. Nurse-caps. Employees must pluck
out an eye before returning to work.

Cold eyes are bad to eat.

You lied. She doesn't have air-conditioning. She is long in bed.
Note on the fridge: Vanilla yogurt inside. See you in the
morning, girls. How did you like *Smoke*. No one should know
the hour or the day.

We will become godlike.

Open the window. That the glory cloud may come and go.

Inside the iris of time, the iridescent dreaming kicks in. Turn off
that stupid damn machine.

Kepler's invention of the *camera lucida* fell into oblivion some
two hundred years. There is no avoiding oblivion.

Where does this damn stupid thing go. For god's sake. Are you
sure you want to wear that.

Especially in this one-stoplight town. Watch out for "the swerve
of smalltown eyes." (Agee) Feel them trained on you in unison.

Boiled peanuts. Now that *is* an acquired taste.

Once the eye is enucleated. Would you replace it with wood,
ivory, bone, shell, or a precious stone. Who invented the glass
eye. Guess. The Venetians. Of course.

Go to Venice; bring me back a mason jar of glass eyes. They
shall multiply like shadflies.

Contributors ~

Marjorie Agosin was raised in Chile and settled with her family in the United States in the early 1970s. She is the author of twelve collections of poetry and the recipient of distinguished prizes in the fields of literature and human rights, including The Latino Literature Prize and the Letras de Oro Prize (both 1995) and the United Nations Leadership Award in the field of Human Rights (1998). She is professor of Spanish at Wellesley College.

Ai received the National Book Award for Poetry in 1999. She teaches at the University of Oklahoma.

Susan Aizenberg's first collection of poems, *Peru*, appeared in the second volume of *Take 3: AGNI New Poets Series* (Graywolf, 1997). She is poetry editor of *The Nebraska Review* and teaches creative writing and English at Creighton University in Omaha, Nebraska.

Sandra Alcosser's *Except by Nature* received numerous awards, including the James Laughlin Award from the Academy of American Poets. James Tate selected *A Fish to Feed All Hunger* to be the Associated Writing Programs Award Series winner in poetry. Alcosser directs the graduate writing program at San Diego State University.

Elizabeth Alexander is the author of two collections of poetry, *The Venus Hottentot* (University Press of Virginia) and *Body of Life* (Tia Chucha Press).

Pamela Alexander is a Yale Younger Poet; her third book, *Inland*, won the Iowa Prize in 1997. She codirects the creative writing program at Oberlin College and is poetry columnist for *The Boston Book Review*. She and her husband divide their time between Ohio and Arizona.

Julia Alvarez is the author of three novels, *How the Garcia Girls Lost Their Accents* (Algonquin Books and Plume Paperback), *In the Time of the Butterflies* (Algonquin Books and Plume Paperback), and *Yo!* (Algonquin Books and Plume Paperback), and of two books of poetry, *The Other Side / El Otro Lado* (Dutton and Plume Paperback) and *Homecoming: New and Collected Poems* (Plume Paperback). Her awards include a NEA grant and a fellowship from the Ingram Merrill Foundation. In 1996, her poetry was selected by the New York Public Library for its 100th Anniversary exhibit, "The Hand of the Poet: Original Manuscripts by 100 Masters, From John Donne to Julia Alvarez."

Angela Ball's books of poetry include *Kneeling Between Parked Cars, Possession, Quartet,* and *The Museum of the Revolution: 58 Exhibits.* She lives in Hattiesburg, Mississippi, where she teaches in the Center for Writers at the University of Southern Mississippi.

Dorothy Barresi is the author of *All of the Above,* which won the Barnard College New Women Poets Prize, and *The Post-Rapture Diner,* which won an American Book Award. She is a regular contributor to *The Gettysburg Review* and is director of the Creative Writing Program at California State University at Northridge.

Robin Becker's most recent collection of poems, *The Horse Fair,* was published in March 2000 by the University of Pittsburgh Press. Winner of the 1996 Lambda Literary Award in Lesbian Poetry for *All-American Girl,* Becker teaches in the M.F.A. program at Penn State.

Erin Belieu is the author of *Infanta,* which was a selection of the National Poetry Series in 1995, and her recent collection, *One Above & One Below,* both published by Copper Canyon Press. She received an M.F.A. from Ohio State and an M.A. in poetry from Boston University. She has been a visiting professor at Washington University and Kenyon College and is currently on the Creative Writing Faculty at Ohio University in Athens.

Linda Bierds is the author of seven books, most recently *The Profile Makers.* Her numerous awards include an NEA grant, an Ingram Merrill Foundation Fellowship, and a Guggenheim Foundation Fellowship. She is a professor at the University of Washington.

Chana Bloch is the author of *The Secrets of the Tribe, The Past Keeps Changing* and the prize-winning *Mrs. Dumpty,* and is cotranslator of the biblical Song of Songs and of the Israeli poets Yehuda Amichai and Dahlia Ravikovitch. She teaches at Mills College.

Michelle Boisseau is the author of *Understory* (Northeastern University Press, 1996), *No Private Life* (Vanderbilt University Press, 1990), and *East of the Sun and West of the Moon* (St. Louis Poetry Center, 1989). Among her many awards are an NEA Fellowship and a Samuel French Morse Poetry Prize.

Catherine Bowman was born in El Paso, Texas. She is the author of two collections, *1–800-HOT-RIBS* (Gibbs Smith, 1993) and *Rock Farm* (Gibbs Smith, 1996). *1–800-HOT-RIBS* has been reprinted in the Carnegie Mellon Classic Contemporary Poetry Series 2000. She teaches at Indiana University in Bloomington.

Lucie Brock-Broido is the author of two collections of poetry, *A Hunger* and *The Master Letters,* both from Knopf. She is Director of Poetry in the School of the Arts at Columbia University and lives in New York City and in Cambridge, Massachusetts.

Olga Broumas is the author of nine books of poetry and collaborations. Her most recent is *Rave: Poems 1975–1999* (Copper Canyon, 1999). She is also the author of two books of translations of the Greek poet Odysseas Elytis. Broumas, whose awards include the Yale Younger Poet Prize, the Guggenheim, and, recently, the Lambda Literary Award, is poet-in-residence and director of the writing program at Brandeis University.

Teresa Cader is the author of *Guests* (Ohio State University Press, 1991), which won the Norma Farber First Book Award from the Poetry Society of America and *The Journal* Award in Poetry. Her second book, *The Paper Wasp,* was published by TriQuarterly Books / Northwestern University Press in 1999. A long poem from that collection won the George Bogin Memorial Award in 1997. She has won awards from the NEA, the Massachusetts Cultural Council, and the Radcliffe Institute for Advanced Study.

Marilyn Chin's books of poems include *The Phoenix Gone, The Terrace Empty,* and *Dwarf Bamboo.* She was featured in *The Language of Life,* Bill Moyers's PBS series on poetry. She has won many awards, including two from the NEA, three Pushcarts, a Stegner Fellowship, the PEN / Josephine Miles Award, and a Fulbright Fellowship to Taiwan. She teaches in the M.F.A. program at San Diego State University.

Lucille Clifton's new collection, *Blessing the Boats: New and Selected Poems, 1988 2000 was published in April 2000* by BOA Editions. Clifton was named Chancellor of The Academy of American Poets in 1999.

Judith Ortiz Cofer is the author of two collections of poetry, *Terms of Survival* and *Reaching for the Mainland;* the novel *The Line of the Sun;* a collection of poetry and essays, *Silent Dancing;* and of *The Latin Deli: Prose and Poetry.* Among her numerous awards are fellowships from the NEA and the Witter Bynner Foundation. She is currently Franklin Professor of English and Creative Writing at the University of Georgia.

Martha Collins's volumes of poetry include *Some Things Words Can Do* (1998), *The Arrangement of Space* (1991), and *The Catastrophe of Rainbows* (1985). She is the recipient of fellowships from the NEA, the Ingram Merrill Foundation, and the Bunting Institute, and has cotranslated, with the author, a collection of poems by the Vietnamese poet Nguyen Quang Thieu. She founded the creative writing program at the University of Massachusetts–Boston, and currently codirects the creative writing program at Oberlin College, where she edits the journal *FIELD*.

Jane Cooper was State Poet of New York 1995–1997. Her fifth book, *The Flashboat: Poems Collected and Reclaimed*, was recently published by W. W. Norton.

Kate Daniels was born in Richmond, Virginia, in 1953. She is the author of three volumes of poetry, and the editor of Muriel Rukeyser's selected poems. She lives in Nashville, Tennessee, where she teaches in the English Department at Vanderbilt University.

Madeline DeFrees' chapbook, *Double Dutch*, appeared from Red Wing Press in 1999. Author of six full-length collections, she lives and writes in Seattle. She left the convent in 1973, dispensed from her vows.

Toi Derricotte, born in Detroit, Michigan, has published four books of poetry and a memoir. Her latest book, *Tender* (University of Pittsburgh Press), received the Paterson Poetry Prize in 1998. Her memoir, *The Black Notebooks* (W. W. Norton, 1997), was chosen by the *New York Times* to be a notable book of the year. She is a two-time winner of fellowships from the NEA and currently teaches at the University of Pittsburgh.

Deborah Digges has written three books of poetry. The most recent, *Rough Music,* won the Kingsley-Tufts Prize.

Rita Dove served as Poet Laureate of the United States from 1993 to 1995. She has received numerous literary awards, including a Pulitzer Prize in Poetry, the Heinz Award, and the Charles Frankel Prize / National Humanities Medal. She is the author of seven collections of poetry, including *Selected Poems* (1993) and *On the Bus with Rosa Parks* (1999). She is currently professor of English at the University of Virginia.

Nancy Eimers is the author of two volumes of poetry, *No Moon* (Purdue University Press, 1997) and *Destroying Angel* (Wesleyan University Press, 1991). She is the recipient of two NEA fellowships and a 1998 Whiting Writers Award and teaches at Western Michigan University.

Lynn Emanuel is the author of three books of poetry, *Hotel Fiesta, The Dig,* and *Then, Suddenly.* Currently, she is professor of English at the University of Pittsburgh, Director of the Writing Program, and Director of the Pittsburgh Contemporary Writers Series. She has been a poetry editor for the Pushcart Prize Anthology, a member of the Literature Panel for the NEA, and is a judge for the James Laughlin Award from the Academy of American Poets.

Angie Estes is the author of *The Uses of Passion* (Gibbs Smith, 1995), winner of the Peregrine Smith Poetry Prize. Poems from her new manuscript are appearing in *TriQuarterly* and *The Paris Review.* She teaches at California Polytechnic State University–San Luis Obispo and at Ohio State.

Kathy Fagan is the author of the National Poetry Series selection *The Raft* and, most recently, *MOVING & ST RAGE,* winner of the 1998 Vassar Miller Prize for Poetry. She teaches in the M.F.A. program at Ohio State, where she also coedits *The Journal.*

Candice Favilla was born in 1949 in the farming community of Chico, California. She is the author of *Cups* (University of Georgia Press), and has been published in *The New Republic, Denver Quarterly,* and the *Los Angeles Times Book Review.*

Carolyn Forché's first collection of poetry, *Gathering the Tribes* (Yale University Press, 1976), won the Yale Series of Younger Poets Award. She is also the author of two other collections, *The Country Between Us* (Harper and Row, 1982) and *The Angel of History* (HarperCollins, 1994), as well as editor of the anthology *Against Forgetting: Twentieth Century Poetry of Witness* (W. W. Norton, 1993). She has been awarded a Guggenheim Foundation Fellowship, three NEA Fellowships, and a Lannan Foundation Literary Award. She teaches in the M.F.A. program at George Mason University.

Alice Fulton's books of poems include *Sensual Math* (W. W. Norton), *Powers Of Congress, Palladium,* and *Dance Script With Electric Ballerina.* A collection of essays, *Feeling as a Foreign Language: The Good Strangeness of Poetry*, was published by Graywolf Press in 1999.

Tess Gallagher is a poet, short-story writer, and essayist who writes in Sky House, which she designed and built in her birthplace, Port Angeles, Washington. Her most recent books are her essays, *Soul Barnacles: Ten More Years with Ray* (University of Michigan Press, 2000); her short-story collection, *At the Owl Woman Saloon* (Simon & Schuster, 1999); and her poems in *Portable Kisses* (1996), and *My Black Horse: New and Selected Poems* (1995), *Moon Crossing Bridge* (1992), and *Amplitude, New and Selected Poems* (1987, reprinted 1999), the last two from Graywolf Press.

Amy Gerstler's most recent book of poems is *Crown of Weeds.* Her book *Medicine* was published by Penguin Putnam in 2000. She teaches in the writing program at Antioch University West in Los Angeles, and at Art Center College of Design in Pasadena.

Patricia Goedicke is the author of twelve books of poetry, the most recent of which is *As Earth Begins to End.* She teaches at the University of Montana in Missoula, and has received, among other honors, a Rockefeller Foundation grant to study at the Villa Serbelloni in Bellagio, Italy.

Beckian Fritz Goldberg is the author of *Body Betrayer* (Cleveland State University Poetry Center, 1991), *In the Badlands of Desire* (Cleveland State University Poetry Center, 1993) and *Never Be the Horse* (University of Akron Press, 1999). She teaches creative writing at Arizona State University.

Jorie Graham is the author of eight collections of poetry, including *Swarm* (2000), *The Errancy* (1997), and *The Dream of the Unified Field: Selected Poems 1974–1994*, which won a Pulitzer Prize. Her many honors include a John D. and Catherine T. MacArthur Fellowship and the Morton Dauwen

Zabel Award from The American Academy and Institute of Arts and Letters. She is a member of the permanent faculty of the University of Iowa Writers' Workshop, and was elected Chancellor of The Academy of American Poets in 1997.

Linda Gregerson is the author of *Fire in the Conservatory* (Dragon Gate) and *The Woman Who Died in Her Sleep* (Houghton Mifflin), as well as a volume of criticism, *The Reformation of the Subject: Spenser, Milton, and the English Protestant Epic* (Cambridge University Press). Her collection of essays on contemporary American poetry, *Negative Capability*, will be published in 2001 by the University of Michigan Press in its Poets on Poetry Series.

Linda Gregg has just published her fifth book, *Things and Flesh* (Graywolf Press). All of her poems included here are from that book.

Marilyn Hacker is the author of nine books of poems, most recently *Squares and Courtyards* (W. W. Norton, 2000). She received the Lenore Marshall Prize of the Academy of American Poets and a Lambda Literary Award for *Winter Numbers* in 1995. She lives in New York City and Paris.

Rachel Hadas is the author of many books of poetry, essays, and translations. *Halfway Down the Hall: New and Selected Poems* appeared in 1998 from Wesleyan University Press. Hadas lives in New York City with her husband and son and teaches at the Newark campus of Rutgers University.

Kimiko Hahn is the author of five collections of poetry, including *Mosquito & Ant, Volatile, Earshot,* and *The Unbearable Heart,* which received an American Book Award. A recipient of fellowships from the NEA and the New York Foundation for the Arts, she recently received a Lila Wallace-Reader's Digest Writer's Award. Hahn is an associate professor in the English Department at Queens College (CUNY) and lives in New York City.

Susan Hahn's books of poetry are *Harriet Rubin's Mother's Wooden Hand* (1991), *Incontinence* (1993) and *Confession* (1997), all published by the University of Chicago Press. She is editor of *TriQuarterly* magazine and coeditor of TriQuarterly Books.

Brenda Hillman is the author of five books of poetry—*White Dress, Fortress, Death Tractates, Bright Existence,* and *Loose Sugar*—all published by Wesleyan University Press. Her work has appeared in numerous periodicals and anthologies. She teaches at Saint Mary's College in Moraga, California.

Jane Hirshfield is the author of four books of poetry, most recently *The Lives of the Heart*. The recipient of fellowships from the Guggenheim and Rockefeller foundations as well as other honors, she currently teaches in the Bennington M.F.A. Writing Seminars.

Linda Hogan, a Chickasaw, was born in Denver, Colorado. Her writings include six volumes of poetry, two volumes of short stories, two novels, and a book of essays. She is associate professor of American Indian studies at the University of Minnesota.

Janet Holmes is the author of *The Green Tuxedo* and *The Physicist at the Mall*. Her third book, *Humanophone*, will appear in spring 2001 from the University of Notre Dame Press. She teaches in the M.F.A. program at Boise State University.

Fanny Howe is both a poet and a writer of fiction. Her *Selected Poems* have just been published by University of California Press. Other books of poetry include *One Crossed Out* (Graywolf Press), *The End* (Littoral Books), and *The Vineyard* (Lost Roads). Her most recent novels, including *Nod*, which won a New American Writing Award in 1999, have been published by Sun and Moon Books.

Marie Howe has published two books of poems: *The Good Thief* (Persea) and *What The Living Do* (W. W. Norton). She lives in New York City.

Lynda Hull was born in Newark, New Jersey, in 1954. She taught at several universities, among them Brandeis and The M.F.A. in Writing Program of Vermont College. She was the author of three collections of poetry: *Ghost Money* (1986), *Star Ledger* (1991), and *The Only World* (1995). She died in an automobile accident in 1994.

Barbara Jordan is the author of *Trace Elements* (Penguin) and *Channel* (Beacon, 1990). She has been awarded the Barnard New Women Poets Prize, an NEA Fellowship, and a Massachusetts Artists Foundation Fellowship. She teaches at the University of Rochester.

Allison Joseph is the author of three books of poems: *What Keeps Us Here* (Ampersand Press, 1992), Soul Train (Carnegie-Mellon University Press, 1997), and *In Every Seam* (University of Pittsburgh Press, 1997). She is an associate professor of English at Southern Illinois University in Carbondale,

Illinois, where she serves as poetry editor of *Crab Orchard Review* and director of the Young Writers Workshop.

Brigit Pegeen Kelly teaches in the Creative Writing Program at the University of Illinois at Champaign-Urbana. Her first book of poems, *To the Place of Trumpets,* was published by the Yale University Press in 1988. Her second book, *Song,* was published by Boa Editions in 1995.

Jane Kenyon was born in 1947 and died of leukemia in 1995. She published four books of poems in her lifetime. Her new and selected poems, *Otherwise,* appeared in 1996.

Mary Kinzie is a poet and critic who founded the creative writing program at Northwestern. She is the author of five volumes of poems, including *Summers of Vietnam, Autumn Eros,* and *Ghost Ship,* and three volumes of critical prose, including *The Cure of Poetry in an Age of Prose* and *A Poet's Guide to Poetry.*

Carolyn Kizer won the Pulitzer Prize for *Yin* in 1985. The complete version of "Pro Femina," described as "a first-wave feminist ur-text" (*Publishers Weekly*), is now in a chapbook published by BKMK Press. Her collected poems appeared from Copper Canyon Press in late 2000.

Maxine Kumin is the author of several collections of poetry, including *Up Country* (1972), for which she won a Pulitzer Prize, and, most recently, *Nurture* (1989), *Looking for Luck: Poems* (1992), and *Connecting the Dots: Poems* (1996). She has also published several novels, collections of essays and short stories, and more than twenty children's books.

Ann Lauterbach's books include *Many, Times, But Then* (University of Texas Press, 1979), *Before Recollection* (Princeton University Press, 1987), *Clamor* (Viking Penguin, 1991), *And For Example* (Viking Penguin, 1994), and *On a Stair* (Penguin, 1997). She has received grants from the New York State Foundation for the Arts, the Ingram Merrill Foundation, and the Guggenheim Foundation. She also received a John D. and Catherine T. MacArthur Fellowship in 1993. She currently teaches at Bard College.

Dorianne Laux is the author of two collections of poetry from BOA Editions, *Awake* (1990) and *What We Carry* (1994), which was a finalist for the National Book Critics Circle Award. She is also coauthor, with Kim Addonizio, of *The Poet's Companion: A Guide to the Pleasures of Writing Poetry* (W. W. Norton, 1997).

Cleopatra Mathis was born and raised in Louisiana, and has written four books of poems, all published by Sheep Meadow Press. Her forthcoming collection is called *What to Tip the Boatman?* She teaches at Dartmouth College.

Gail Mazur's books of poems include *Nightfire, The Pose of Happiness, The Common,* and *They Can't Take That Away From Me* (University of Chicago Press, 2001). She is the founding director of The Blacksmith House Poetry Center and on the faculty of Emerson College's Graduate Writing Program. She lives in Cambridge and Provincetown, Massachusetts.

Heather McHugh is Milliman Distinguished Writer-in-Residence at the University of Washington in Seattle for two-thirds of each year, and at other times works with students in the low-residency M.F.A. program for Writers at Warren Wilson College in Asheville, North Carolina. Her most recent books are a collection of poems, *The Father of the Predicaments,* and a translation, *Glottal Stop: 101 Poems by Paul Celan,* with husband and cotranslator Nikolai Popov.

Lynne McMahon's books of poetry include *Faith* (Wesleyan University Press), *Devolution of the Nude* (David R. Godine), and *The House of Entertaining Science* (David R. Godine). She is professor of English at the University of Missouri.

Sandra McPherson is the author of nine books of poetry, the most recent being *A Visit to Civilization,* forthcoming from Wesleyan University Press. She is professor of English at University of California at Davis, and founder of Swan Scythe Press, a poetry chapbook publisher.

Jane Miller's newest collection of poetry is *Wherever You Lay Your Head* (Copper Canyon Press). Among earlier collections are *Memory at These Speeds: New and Selected Poems, The Greater Leisures,* and *August Zero.*

Susan Mitchell's most recent books are *Erotikon* and *Rapture,* a National Book Award finalist and winner of the Kingsley Tufts Poetry Award. Her honors include fellowships from the Guggenheim and Lannan foundations.

Thylias Moss is the author of six volumes of poetry, a memoir, and a book for children. Her second book of poetry was shortlisted for the National

Book Critics Circle Award and her fourth won the National Poetry Series Open Competition. She has won a John D. and Catherine T. MacArthur Fellowship, a Guggenheim Fellowship, a Whiting Writer's Award, and a Witter Bynner Prize. She teaches at the University of Michigan.

Lisel Mueller has published seven volumes of poetry, most recently *Alive Together*, which won the 1997 Pulitzer Prize. She has also translated the poetry of Marie Louise Kaschnitz. She lives in Chicago.

Laura Mullen is the author of two collections of poetry, *The Surface* and *After I Was Dead*, as well as a book-length work, *The Tales of Horror*. She teaches at Colorado State University.

Carol Muske has published six books of poems. The most recent is *An Octave Above Thunder: New and Selected Poems* (Penguin, 1997). She has also authored two novels and a collection of essays, *Women & Poetry* (University of Michigan Press, 1997). She is professor of Creative Writing at the University of Southern California.

Marilyn Nelson's books include two National Book Award finalists. Her latest collection won the 1998 Poets' Prize. She teaches at the University of Connecticut.

Alice Notley was born in Bisbee, Arizona. She is the author of twenty-two books of poetry, the most recent of which is *Mysteries of Small Houses* (Penguin, 1998).

Naomi Shihab Nye was born in St. Louis in 1952, of a Palestinian father and American mother, and has lived in San Antonio, Texas, since 1967. Her books include *Fuel* (poems), *Habibi* (a novel for teens), *Sitti's Secrets* (a picture book), *What Have You Lost?* (an anthology of poems), and *The Space Between Our Footsteps: Poems & Paintings from the Middle East.*

Sharon Olds teaches at New York University. Her sixth book, *Blood, Tin, Straw,* was released by Knopf in 1999. She is currently the New York State Poet Laureate.

Jacqueline Osherow is the author of four books of poetry, most recently *Dead Men's Praise* (Grove, 1999). She has received fellowships from the John Simon Guggenheim Foundation, the NEA, and the Ingram Merrill Foundation, as well as the Witter Bynner Prize from the American Academy and Institute of Arts and Letters.

Alicia Suskin Ostriker is a poet and critic, twice nominated for a National Book Award, author of nine volumes of poetry, including *The Little Space: Poems Selected and New* (1998). She is also the author of *Stealing the Language: The Emergence of Women's Poetry in America.*

Linda Pastan's tenth book of poems, *Carnival Evening: New and Selected Poems, 1968–1998,* was published by Norton and was a finalist for the National Book Award. From 1991 to 1994 she served as Poet Laureate of Maryland.

Molly Peacock is one of the originators of Poetry in Motion on the nation's subways and buses. Her most recent book is *How to Read a Poem & Start a Poetry Circle.* She is the author of four books of poems, including *Raw Heaven, Take Heart,* and *Original Love,* as well as a memoir, *Paradise Piece by Piece.* A Danforth, Ingram Merrill, and Woodrow Wilson Foundation Fellow, her poems have appeared in *The New Yorker, The Nation, The New Republic, The Paris Review,* and other leading literary journals. She currently serves as copresident of the Poetry Society of America and Poet-in-Residence at the Cathedral of St. John the Divine.

Lucia Perillo has published three books of poetry: *Dangerous Life* (Northeastern University Press, 1989), *The Body Mutinies* (Purdue University Press, 1996), and *The Oldest Map With the Name America* (Random House, 1999).

Marie Ponsot is the author of four books of poetry: *True Minds, Admit Impediment, The Green Dark* and *The Bird Catcher.* Her awards include the National Book Critics Circle Award, the Delmore Schwartz Memorial, and an NEA Fellowship. She is professor emerita of English at Queens College (CUNY).

Minnie Bruce Pratt's second book of poetry, *Crime Against Nature,* was chosen as the 1989 Lamont Poetry Selection by the Academy of American Poets, and received the American Library Association's Gay and Lesbian Book Award for Literature. She is coauthor of the classic feminist essay "Identity: Skin Blood Heart" in *Yours in Struggle: Three Feminist Perspectives on Anti-Semitism and Racism.* Her most recent book is *Walking Back Up Depot Street* (Pitt Poetry Series). She can be reached at www.mbpratt.org.

Claudia Rankine is the author of three collections of poetry: *PLOT, The End of the Alphabet,* and *Nothing in Nature Is Private.* She teaches at Barnard College.

Hilda Raz is editor of *Prairie Schooner* and professor of English at the University of Nebraska. Her most recent books are *Divine Honors* (poems) and *Living On the Margins: Women Writers on Breast Cancer* (essays).

Martha Rhodes is the author of *At the Gate,* a poetry collection published by Provincetown Arts Press. She is a founding editor of Four Way Books and director of the CCS Reading Series in New York City.

Adrienne Rich was born in Baltimore in 1929. She has lived since 1984 in California. Her most recent volume of poetry is *Midnight Salvage;* of prose, *What Is Found There: Notebooks on Poetry and Politics.*

Mary Ruefle grew up in Nebraska and Belgium and attended Bennington College. She has published five books of poetry and has received many awards for her work.

Kay Ryan is the author of five books of poetry, most recently *Say Uncle* (Grove Press, 2000). She lives in Marin County, California.

Mary Jo Salter is the author of four collections of poetry, most recently *A Kiss in Space* (Knopf, 1999). Her many awards include an Amy Lowell Travelling Scholarship and a Lamont Selection for her second book, *Unfinished Painting* (1989). She is an Emily Dickinson Lecturer in the Humanities at Mount Holyoke College.

Leslie Scalapino is the author of numerous books of poetry, essays, drama, and fiction. The most recent include *New Time* (Wesleyan University Press, 1999), *The Public World / Syntactically Impermanence* (Wesleyan University Press, 1999), *The Front Matter, Dead Souls* (Wesleyan University Press, 1996), and *Defoe* (Sun & Moon Press, 1994).

Grace Schulman's new book of poems, *The Paintings of Our Lives,* is forthcoming from Houghton Mifflin. Earlier poetry collections include *For That Day Only, Hemispheres,* and *Burn Down the Icons.*

Maureen Seaton's third book of poems, *Furious Cooking* (Iowa, 1996), won the Iowa Prize and the Lambda Award. Her fourth collection is forthcoming from BOA Editions. Recipient of an NEA award and twice of the Pushcart Prize, who is currently Artist-in-Residence at Columbia College in Chicago.

Rebecca Seiferle's *The Music We Dance To* was a Pulitzer Prize nominee, and the title poem won the 1998 Cecil Hemley Award from the Poetry Society of America. "Welcome to Ithaca" will be included in *The Best American Poetry 2000*. Her previous collection, *The Ripped-Out Seam* (Sheep Meadow, 1993), won the Bogin Memorial Award from the Poetry Society of America, the Writers' Exchange Award from Poets & Writers, and the Writers' Union Poetry Prize. Her translation of Cesar Vallejo's *Trilce* (Sheep Meadow, 1992) was the only finalist for that year's PenWest Translation Award.

Vivian Shipley, editor of *Connecticut Review* and Distinguished Professor at Connecticut State University, teaches at Southern CSU. Author of five books of poetry, including *Devil's Lane* and *Crazy Quilt*, she lives in North Haven with her husband, Ed Harris.

Aleda Shirley is the author of *Long Distance* (Miami University Press, 1996) and *Chinese Architecture* (University of Georgia Press, 1986) and the editor of *The Beach Book: A Literary Companion* (Sarabande Books, 1999). She lives in Jackson, Mississippi.

Betsy Sholl's most recent books are *The Red Line* and *Don't Explain*. She's the recipient of an NEA fellowship, the Associated Writing Programs' Award in Poetry, and the Felix Pollak Prize in Poetry from the University of Wisconsin. She teaches in the M.F.A. program at Vermont College.

Maurya Simon is the recipient of a 1999 NEA fellowship in poetry, as well as the author of four volumes of poetry, most recently *The Golden Labyrinth* (University of Missouri Press, 1995). Her fifth book, *WEAVERS*, based on a series of paintings by Los Angeles artist Baila Goldenthal, is forthcoming from Blackbird Press in 2000. She teaches creative writing at the University of California at Riverside and lives in the Angeles National Forest.

Cathy Song is the author of *Picture Bride* (Yale University Press), *Frameless Windows, Squares of Light* (W. W. Norton), and *School Figures* (University of Pittsburgh Press).

Elizabeth Spires, born in Lancaster, Ohio, in 1952, is the author of *Globe, Swan's Island, Annonciade,* and *Worldling,* and several books for children, including *The Mouse of Amherst*. The recipient of a Guggenheim Fellowship, a Whiting Award, and the Witter Bynner Prize, she is a professor at Goucher College in Baltimore.

Pamela Stewart's most recent book is *The Red Window* (University of Georgia Press, 1997). She co-owns and works on an exotic fiber animal farm in western Massachusetts.

Susan Stewart is the author of three books of poems, most recently *The Forest* (University of Chicago Press). Her cotranslation, with Wesley Smith, of Euripides' *Andromache*, was published by Oxford University Press in 2000, and a new prose study, *Poetry and the Fate of the Senses*, will be published by the University of Chicago Press in Autumn 2001. She teaches poetry and aesthetics at the University of Pennsylvania.

Ruth Stone is professor of English at the State University of New York at Binghamton. Her most recent book, *Ordinary Words* (Paris Press, 1999), received the National Book Critics Circle Award for Poetry.

Stephanie Strickland's manuscript "V" won the 2000 Alice Fay di Castagnola Award. Her "Ballad of Sand and Harry Soot" won the 1999 Boston Review prize, and its Web version was chosen for an About.com Best of the Net award. She is the author of *True North* (1997), *True North* (hypertext, 1998), *The Red Virgin: A Poem of Simone Weil* (1993), and *Give the Body Back* (1991).

Terese Svoboda's poetry has been published in *The Paris Review*, *The New Yorker*, *APR*, *Grand Street*, and *The New Republic*. Her most recent book of poetry is *Mere Mortals* (University of Georgia Press).

Ann Townsend's first collection of poems, *Dime Store Erotics*, won the Gerald Cable Prize and was published in 1998. Her awards include the "Discovery" / The Nation Prize for poetry, a Pushcart Prize, and a grant from the Ohio Arts Council. She teaches at Denison University in Granville, Ohio.

Chase Twichell has published five books of poetry, the most recent of which is *The Snow Watcher* (Ontario Review Press, 1998). She is editor of Ausable Press and teaches in the M.F.A. program at Warren Wilson College in Swannanoa, North Carolina.

Leslie Ullman is the author of three poetry collections, most recently *Slow Work Through Sand* (University of Iowa Press, 1998). She teaches at University of Texas at El Paso and in the M.F.A. program at Vermont College.

Jean Valentine lives and works in New York City. She is the author of eight books of poetry, most recently *The Cradle of the Real Life* (Wesleyan University Press).

Mona Van Duyn lives in St. Louis and has published nine books of poetry, most recently *Firefall* (Knopf). In 1992–1993 she served as U.S. Poet Laureate. Books of hers have received, among many other awards, the National Book Award, the Bollingen Prize, and the Pulitzer Prize.

Ellen Bryant Voigt's most recent book is *The Flexible Lyric*, a collection of essays. She has received Guggenheim and Lila Wallace fellowships, and *Kyrie*, her fifth volume of poetry, was a finalist for the National Book Critics Circle award.

Belle Waring has written two collections of poems: *Refuge* (University of Pittsburgh Press), cited by *Publishers Weekly* as a "best book" of 1990, and *Dark Blonde* (Sarabande Books), winner of the 1997 Larry Levis Prize.

Rosanna Warren is Emma MacLachlan Metcalf Professor of the Humanities at Boston University. Her most recent books are a verse translation of Euripides' *Suppliant Women* and a book of poems, *Stained Glass*.

Rachel Wetzsteon is the author of two books of poems, *The Other Stars* and *Home and Away*, both published by Penguin. She recently received a doctorate in English from Columbia, and currently teaches at Barnard and the Unterberg Poetry Center of the Ninety-Second Street Y.

Susan Wheeler is the author of three collections of poems: *Bag 'o' Diamonds*, *Smokes*, and *Source Codes*. She currently teaches at Princeton University and in the graduate creative writing program at New School University in New York City. Recipient of fellowships from the Guggenheim Foundation and the New York Foundation for the Arts, she has appeared in five editions of *The Best American Poetry*.

Eleanor Wilner is the author of five volumes of poetry, including *Otherwise* (1993) and *Sarah's Choice* (1989). Her most recent book is *Reversing the*

Spell: New and Selected Poems (Copper Canyon, 1998). Her many awards include a grant from the John D. and Catherine T. MacArthur Foundation. She teaches in the M.F.A. program at Warren Wilson College.

C. D. Wright's most recent title is *Deepstep Come Shining* (Copper Canyon, 1998). She is currently working in collaboration with photographer Deborah Luster on a project titled *One Big Self: Prisoners of Louisiana*. Wright lives in Rhode Island with her husband and son.

Acknowledgments ∼

Marjorie Agosin "The Obedient Girl," "Fear," "Fear II" and "Night" by Marjorie Agosin. Translated by Celeste Kostopulos-Cooperman. From *An Absence of Shadows*. Published by White Pine Press, 1998. Used by permission of the publisher.

Ai "Chance," "Charisma" and "The Paparazzi" from *Vice: New and Selected Poems* by Ai. Copyright © 1999 by Ai. Used by permission of W. W. Norton & Co., Inc.

Susan Aizenberg "Art" copyright © 1997 by Susan Aizenberg. Reprinted from *Take Three: 2*, published by Graywolf Press, St. Paul, MN with permission of the author. "Meeting the Angel" and "Kiss" reprinted by permission of the author.

Sandra Alcosser "My Number," "Dancing The Tarantella At The County Farm" and "By The Nape" copyright © 1998 by Sandra Alcosser. Reprinted from *Except by Nature* with the permission of Graywolf Press, St. Paul, MN.

Elizabeth Alexander "Apollo," "Affirmative Action Blues (1993)" and "Equinox" reprinted by permission of the author.

Pamela Alexander "Manners," "Understory," "Look Here" and "Soon" reprinted from *Inland* with permission of the University of Iowa Press.

Julia Alvarez "Bilingual Sestina" and "Estel" from *The Other Side/El Otro Lado*. Copyright © 1995 by Julia Alvarez. Published by Dutton, a division of Penguin USA. Reprinted by permission of Susan Bergholz Literary Services, New York. All rights reserved.

Angela Ball "The Dance Pianist," "The Man in a Shell" and "The Kiss" reprinted from *Possession* by permission of Red Hen Press.

Dorothy Barresi "When I Think About America Sometimes (I Think of Ralph Kramden)" is from *The Post-Rapture Diner* by Dorothy Barresi, copyright © 1996. Reprinted by permission of the University of Pittsburgh Press.

Robin Becker "The Crypto-Jews" and "A History of Sexual Preference" are from *All-American Girl* by Robin Becker, copyright © 1996. "Late Words for My Sister" and "Dog-God" are from *The Horse Fair* by Robin Becker, copyright © 2000. Reprinted by permission of the University of Pittsburgh Press.

Erin Belieu "Erections" reprinted from *Infanta*, copyright © 1995 by Erin Belieu. "Your Character Is Your Destiny," "Choose Your Garden" and "Lovely" reprinted from *One Above & One Below*, copyright © 2000 by Erin Belieu. Reprinted by permission of Copper Canyon Press, PO Box 271, Port Townsend, WA 98368.

Linda Bierds "Vespertilio," "Lawrence and Edison in New Jersey: 1923," "Depth of Field" and "After-Image" from *The Profile Makers* by Linda Bierds. Copyright © 1997 by Linda Bierds. Reprinted by permission of Henry Holt and Co., LLC.

Chana Bloch "Act One," "How the Last Act Begins" and "Puzzle Pieces" from *Mrs. Dumpty, copyright © 1998 by Chana Bloch. Reprinted by permission of The University of Wisconsin Press.*

Michelle Boisseau "Fog," "—Cassiopeia at Noon" and "Sleeplessness:" reprinted by permission of Northeastern University Press.

Catherine Bowman "Demographics," "From *The El Paso Times* 'World of Women'" and "Heart" reprinted by permission of the author.

Lucie Brock-Broido "Her Habit," "Prescient" and "Housekeeping" from *The Master Letters* by Lucie Brock-Broido. Copyright © 1995 by Lucie Brock-Broido. Reprinted by permission of Alfred A. Knopf, a Division of Random House Inc.

Olga Broumas "Lumens" and "Photo Genic" reprinted from *Perpetua*, copyright © 1989 by Olga Broumas. Reprinted by permission of Copper Canyon Press, PO Box 271, Port Townsend, WA 98368.

Teresa Cader "Sprit Papers" and "Empress Shōku Invents Printing in 770" reprinted from *Paper Wasp*, a TriQuarterly Book. Evanston: Northwestern University Press, 1998.

Marilyn Chin "Composed Near the Bay Bridge," "Beijing Spring" and "Autumn Leaves" by Marilyn Chin were published in *The Phoenix Gone, The Terrace Empty*. Copyright © 1994 by Marilyn Chin. Reprinted with permission from Milkweed Editions, www.milkweed.org.

Lucille Clifton "hag riding," "blake," "to michal" and "what did she know, when did she know it" copyright © 1996 by Lucille Clifton. Reprinted from *The Terrible Stories*, poems by Lucille Clifton, with the permission of BOA Editions, Ltd.

Judith Ortiz Cofer "Photographs of My Father," "Letter from Home in Spanish" and "from Three Poems in Memory of Mamè; (Grandmother): Cold As Heaven" from *Reaching For The Mainland*, copyright © 1995 by Judith Ortiz Cofer. Reprinted by permission of Bilingual Press/Editorial Bilingë, Arizona State University, Tempe, AZ.

Martha Collins "The Border" and "Lies" reprinted by permission of The Sheep Meadow Press. "Out Of My Own Pocket" and "Like Her Body The World" reprinted by permission of the author.

Jane Cooper "My Mother in Three Acts," "Estrangement," "Hotel de Dream" and "Childhood in Jacksonville, Florida" from *The Flashboat: Poems Collected and Reclaimed* by Jane Cooper. Copyright © 2000 by Jane Cooper. Used by permission of W. W. Norton & Co., Inc.

Kate Daniels "Prayer to the Muse of Ordinary Life" and "After Reading Reznikoff" reprinted by permission of Louisiana State University Press from *Four Testimonies: Poems* by Kate Daniels. Copyright © 1998 by Kate Daniels.

Madeline DeFrees "In the Locker Room," "In the middle of Priest Lake" and "Blueprints" reprinted by permission of Lynx House Press.

Toi Derricotte "Bookstore," "Black Boys Play the Classics," "For Black Women Who Are Afraid" and "For Sister Sue Ellen and Her Special Messenger" are from *Tender* by Toi Derricotte, copyright © 1997. Reprinted by permission of the University of Pittsburgh Press.

Deborah Digges "Rough Music," "Akhmatova" and "Five Smooth Stones" from *Rough Music* by Deborah Digges. Copyright © 1995 by Deborah Digges. Reprinted by permission of Alfred A. Knopf, a Division of Random House Inc.

Rita Dove "History," "Exit" and "Blue Days" from *Mother Love* by Rita Dove. Copyright © 1995 by Rita Dove. "Rosa" and "Götterdämmerung" from *On the Bus with Rosa Parks* by Rita Dove. Copyright © 1999 by Rita Dove. Used by permission of W. W. Norton & Co., Inc.

Nancy Eimers "Morbid," "A Night without Stars" and "No Moon" from *No Moon*, copyright © 1997 by Nancy Eimers. Reprinted by permission of the Purdue University Press.

Lynn Emanuel "The Corpses," "Halfway Through the Book I'm Writing," and "In English in a Poem" are from *Then, Suddenly—* by Lynn Emanuel, copyright © 1999. Reprinted by permission of the University of Pittsburgh Press.

Angie Estes "Now and Again: An Autobiography of Basket" and "The Annunciation in an Initial R" reprinted by permission of the author.

Kathy Fagan "Moving & St Rage," "Revisionary Instruments I" and "*She Attempts to Tell the Truth About True Romance*" from *Moving & St Rage*. Reprinted by permission of the author.

Candice Favilla "West Texas Rain Journal" and "Red Clay" are reprinted from *Cups* by Candice Favilla with permission of The University of Georgia Press.

Carolyn Forché "Elegy," "The Testimony of Light" and "The Garden Shukkei-en" from *The Angel of History* by Carolyn Forché. Copyright © 1994 by Carolyn Forché. Reprinted by permission of HarperCollins Publishers, Inc.

Alice Fulton "Wonder Bread" (excerpted from "My Last TV Campaign: A Sequence"), "Take: A Roman Wedding" (excerpted from "Give: A Sequence Re-imagining Daphne & Apollo") and "= =" from *Sensual Math* by Alice Fulton. Copyright © 1995 by Alice Fulton. Used by permission of W.W. Norton & Co., Inc. and the author.

Tess Gallagher "Trace, In Unison," "Fresh Stain," "Valentine Delivered by a Raven" and "Un Extraño" copyright © 1992 by Tess Gallagher. Reprinted from *Moon Crossing Bridge* with the permission of Graywolf Press, St. Paul, MN.

Amy Gerstler "Siren," "The Nature of Suffering," "Saints" and "House-bound" reprinted by permission of the author.

Patricia Goedicke *"Lacrimae Rerum,"* "From the Boat," "The Ground Beneath Us" and "And Yet" reprinted from *As Earth Begins to End*, copyright © 2000 by Patricia Goedicke. Reprinted by permission of Copper Canyon Press, PO Box 271, Port Townsend, WA 98368.

Beckian Fritz Goldberg "My Bomb," "Swallower" and "Rebirth" from *Never Be the Horse*, copyright © by Beckian Fritz Goldberg. Reprinted by permission of The University of Akron Press.

Jorie Graham "Thinking," "The Guardian Angel of Not Feeling," "Willow in Spring Wind: A Showing" and "Of the Ever-Changing Agitation in the Air" from *The Errancy* by Jorie Graham. Copyright © 1997 by Jorie Graham. Reprinted by permission of HarperCollins Publishers, Inc.

Linda Gregerson "Saints' Logic," "Line Drive Caught by the Grace of God" and "Mother Ruin" from *The Woman Who Died In Her Sleep* by Linda Gregerson. Copyright © 1996 by Linda Gregerson. Reprinted by permission of Houghton Mifflin Co. All rights reserved.

Linda Gregg "The Limits of Desire," "Stuff," "Fish Tea Rice," "The Tree Falling in a Vacant Forest" and "The Unknowing" copyright © 1999 by Linda Gregg. Reprinted from *Things and Flesh* with the permission of Graywolf Press, St. Paul, MN.

Marilyn Hacker "The Boy," "Twelfth Floor West ," "Invocation" and "Broceliande" from *Squares and Courtyards* by Marilyn Hacker. Copyright © 2000 by Marilyn Hacker. Used by permission of W. W. Norton & Co., Inc.

Rachel Hadas "Still Life In Garden," "Shells," "On That Mountain," "Falcon" and "Mutability" from *Halfway Down the Hall: New and Selected Poems*, copyright © 1998, Wesleyan University Press by permission of University Press of New England.

Allison Joseph "Soul Train" and "Wedding Party" reprinted by permission of Carnegie Mellon University Press.

Brigit Pegeen Kelly "Song," "Petition," "Botticelli's St. Sebastian" and "Wild Turkeys: The Dignity of the Damned" copyright © 1995 by Brigit Pegeen Kelly. Reprinted from Song, poems by Brigit Pegeen Kelly, with the permission of BOA Editions, Ltd.

Jane Kenyon "Dutch Interiors," "Having It Out with Melancholy" and "August Rain, After Haying" copyright © 1996 by the Estate of Jane Kenyon. Reprinted from *Otherwise: New & Selected Poems* with the permission of Graywolf Press, St. Paul, MN.

Mary Kinzie "The Bolt" and "Beautiful Days" from *Ghost Ship* by Mary Kinzie. Copyright © 1996 by Mary Kinzie. Reprinted by permission of Alfred A. Knopf, a Division of Random House Inc.

Carolyn Kizer "Twelve O'Clock" "Reunion," "Fearful Women," "Ingathering" and "Election Day, 1984" reprinted from *Harping On,* copyright © 1996 by Carolyn Kizer. Reprinted by permission of Copper Canyon Press, PO Box 271, Port Townsend, WA. 98368.

Maxine Kumin "Early Thoughts of Winter," "Almost Spring, Driving Home, Reciting Hopkins" and "October, Yellowstone Park" copyright © 1992, from *Connecting the Dots* by Maxine Kumin. Copyright © 1996 by Maxine Kumin. "Credo" from *Looking for Luck* by Maxine Kumin. Copyright © 1992 by Maxine Kumin. Used by permission of W. W. Norton & Co., Inc.

Ann Lauterbach "Meanwhile the Turtle," "Werner Herzog 68 / Iowa City 88" and "How Things Bear Their Telling" from *Clamor* by Ann Lauterbach, copyright © 1991 by Ann Lauterbach. Used by permission of Viking Penguin, a division of Penguin Putnam Inc.

Dorianne Laux "This Close," "What I Wouldn't Do," "Homecoming" and "The Thief" copyright © 1994. Reprinted from *What We Carry,* poems by Dorianne Laux, with the permission of BOA Editions, Ltd.

Cleopatra Mathis "Blues: Late August," "The Angels" and "*from* Lessons" reprinted by permission of The Sheep Meadow Press.

Somebody Else" and "After I Was Dead" from *After I Was Dead* reprinted by permission of The University of Georgia Press.

Carol Muske "Like This," "Miracles," "At the School for the Gifted" and "Blue Rose" reprinted from *An Octave Above Thunder* by Carol Muske, copyright © 1997 by Carol Muske. Used by permission of Penguin, a division of Penguin Putnam Inc.

Marilyn Nelson "How I Discovered Poetry," "Juneteenth," "Chosen," "The Sacrament of Poverty" and "Lovesong" reprinted by permission of Louisiana State University Press from *The Fields of Praise: New and Selected Poems* by Marilyn Nelson. Copyright © 1997 by Marilyn Nelson.

Alice Notley "A Baby Is Born Out of a White Owl's Forehead—1972," "I— Towards a Definition" and "Mysteries of Small Houses" reprinted from *Mysteries of Small Houses* by Alice Notley, copyright © 1998 by Alice Notley. Used by permission of Viking Penguin, a division of Penguin Putnam Inc.

Naomi Shihab Nye "Steps," "Across the Bay," "Vocabulary of Dearness," "I Still Have Everything You Gave Me" and "Fuel" copyright © 1998 by Naomi Shihab Nye. Reprinted from *Fuel*, poems by Naomi Shihab Nye, with the permission of BOA Editions, Ltd.

Sharon Olds "First," "Her First Week" and "Lifelong" from *The Wellspring* by Sharon Olds. Copyright © 1996 by Sharon Olds. "The Promise" from *Blood, Tin, Straw* by Sharon Olds. Copyright © 1999 by Sharon Olds. Reprinted by permission of Alfred A. Knopf, a Division of Random House Inc.

Jacqueline Osherow "Phantom Haiku/Silent Film," "Ghazal: Comet" and "Villanelle from a Sentence in a Poet's Brief Biography" from *Dead Men's Praise*. Used by permission of Grove/Atlantic, Inc. Copyright © 1999 by Jacqueline Osherow.

Alicia Suskin Ostriker "The Studio (Homage to Alice Neel)," "The Boys, the Broom Handle, the Retarded Girl," "Excerpts from 'The Mastectomy Poems'" and "Millennial Polka" are from *The Little Space: Poems Selected and New* by Alicia Ostriker, copyright © 1998. Reprinted by permission of the University of Pittsburgh Press.

Linda Pastan "An Early Afterlife," "Agoraphobia" and "Self-Portrait" from

Carnival Evening: New and Selected Poems 1968–1998 by Linda Pastan. Copyright © 1998 by Linda Pastan. Used by permission of W. W. Norton & Co., Inc.

Molly Peacock "Why I Am Not a Buddhist," "The Purr," "The Fare" and "Matins" from *Original Love* by Molly Peacock. Copyright © 1995 by Molly Peacock. Used by permission of W. W. Norton & Co., Inc.

Lucia Perillo "For Edward Hopper, from the Floor," "Lament in Good Weather" and "For I Have Taught the Japanese" from *The Oldest Map With the Name America* by Lucia Perillo. Copyright © 1999 by Lucia Perillo. Reprinted by permission of Random House, Inc.

Marie Ponsot " 'I've Been Around: It Gets Me Nowhere.' " "One Is One," "The Story After the Story," " '*Trois Petits Tours et Puis . . .* ' " and "Winter" from *The Bird Catcher* by Marie Ponsot. Copyright © 1998 by Marie Ponsot. Reprinted by permission of Alfred A. Knopf, a Division of Random House Inc.

Minnie Bruce Pratt "Shades," "The White Star" and "Eating Clay" are from *Walking Back Up Depot Street* by Minnie Bruce Pratt, copyright © 1999. Reprinted by permission of the University of Pittsburgh Press.

Claudia Rankine Four sections from "Testimonial" reprinted from *The End of the Alphabet*, copyright © 1998 by Claudia Rankine. Used by permission of Grove/Atlantic, Inc.

Hilda Raz "Before John and Maria's Wedding," "Volunteers" and "Fast Car on Nebraska I-80: Visiting Teacher" reprinted by permission of the author.

Martha Rhodes "Behind Me," "Bare Windows," "Inside Father's Pockets," "All the Soups" and "The Robe" reprinted from *At the Gate* by permission of Provincetown Arts Press.

Adrienne Rich "In Those Years" and "What Kind of Times Are These" from *Dark Fields of the Republic: Poems 1991–1995* by Adrienne Rich. Copyright © 1995 by Adrienne Rich. "Letters to a Young Poet" from *Midnight Salvage: Poems 1995–1998* by Adrienne Rich. Copyright © 1999 by Adrienne Rich. Used by permission of the author and W. W. Norton & Co., Inc.

Mary Ruefle "Controlling Factors," "School of Denial," "Minor Figure" and "Stopwatch" reprinted by permission of Carnegie Mellon University Press.

Kay Ryan "Why Isn't It All More Marked," "The Woman Who Wrote Too Much," "Surfaces," "If She Only Had One Minute" and "Elephant Rocks" reprinted from *Elephant Rocks*, copyright © 1996 by Kay Ryan. Used by permission of Grove/Atlantic, Inc.

Mary Jo Salter "A Rainbow Over the Seine," "Distance," "Absolute September" and "Liam" from *A Kiss in Space* by Mary Jo Salter. Copyright © 1999 by Mary Jo Salter. Reprinted by permission of Alfred A. Knopf, a Division of Random House Inc.

Leslie Scalapino from *New Time*, copyright © 1999, Wesleyan University Press by permission of University Press of New England.

Grace Schulman "False Move," "Crossing the Square," "Notes from Underground: W. H. Auden on the Lexington Avenue IRT" and "Two Trees" reprinted by permission of The Sheep Meadow Press.

Maureen Seaton *"Malleus Maleficarum 4,"* "Tagging," *"Cannibal Women in the Avocado Jungle of Death"* and "The Man Who Killed Himself to Avoid August" reprinted from *Furious Cooking* by Maureen Seaton with permission of the University of Iowa Press.

Rebecca Seiferle "Welcome to Ithaca," "The Catch" and "Mother Tongue" reprinted by permission of The Sheep Meadow Press.

Vivian Shipley "At Fifty," "The Faithful Daughter Dreams of Spring Break While Installing a Bird Feeder for Her Mother by a Window in the Courtyard of Safe Harbour" and "A Heart With Little or No Bedrock for Anchor" reprinted by permission of the author.

Aleda Shirley "Late Night Radio" and "Long Distance" reprinted from Long Distance, copyright © 1996, by permission of Miami University (OH) Press.

Betsy Sholl "Something to Say" from *The Red Line* by Betsy Sholl, copyright © 1992. Reprinted by permission of the University of Pittsburgh Press. "To The Dregs" and "The Past" from *Don't Explain*, copyright © 1997 by Betsy Sholl. Reprinted by permission of The University of Wisconsin Press.

Maurya Simon "All Souls' Day," "Coward," "Doomsday" and "The Search" printed by permission of the author.

Cathy Song "Journey," "Leaf" and "Golden" are from *School Figures* by

Cathy Song, copyright © 1994. Reprinted by permission of the University of Pittsburgh Press.

Elizabeth Spires "Worldling," "The Robed Heart" and "The Rock" from *Worldling* by Elizabeth Spires. Copyright © 1995 by Elizabeth Spires. Used by permission of the author and W. W. Norton & Co., Inc.

Pamela Stewart "August," "What It's For," "Martin" and "Against Silence" reprinted from *The Red Window* by Pamela Stewart with permission of The University of Georgia Press.

Susan Stewart "The Arbor 1937" from *The Forest* by Susan Stewart. Copyright © 1995 by the University of Chicago. All rights reserved.

Ruth Stone "Hummingbirds," "Earth Quake," "Up There," "Reading" and "So Be It" from *Ordinary Words*. Copyright © 1999 by Ruth Stone. Reprinted by permission of Paris Press.

Stephanie Strickland "Absent from Dances, 1925," "Fig Tree," "Gustave Thibon, *How Simone Weil Appeared to Me/2*," "Gustave Thibon, *How Simone Weil Appeared to Me/3*," "Gustave Thibon, *How Simone Weil Appeared to Me/4*," "Gustave Thibon, *How Simone Weil Appeared to Me/5*" and "Intact" from *The Red Virgin: A Poem of Simone Weil*, copyright © 1993 by Stephanie Strickland. Reprinted by permission of The University of Wisconsin Press.

Terese Svoboda "The Goddess Corn Finds Her Dress in Disarray," "Appomattox" and "Epithalamion" reprinted from *Mere Mortals* by Terese Svoboda with permission of The University of Georgia Press.

Ann Townsend "Purple Loosestrife," "Rouge" and "Outdoor Chums in the Forest" from *Dime Store Erotics*. Copyright © 1998 by Ann Townsend. Reprinted by permission of Silverfish Press.

Chase Twichell "Tea Mind," "Kerosene," "Private Airplane," "My Taste for Trash" and "Horse" reprinted from *The Snow Watcher* by permission of Ontario Review Press.

Leslie Ullman "Rose Quartz," "1945" and "Resolve" reprinted from *Slow Work Through Sand* by Leslie Ullman with permission of the University of Iowa Press.

Jean Valentine "X," "The One You Wanted to Be Is the One You Are," "The First Station," "The Under Voice," "American River Sky Alcohol Father," "Death Asphodel" and "Yield Everything, Force Nothing" from *The River at Wolf.* Alice James Books, 1992.

Mona Van Duyn "One Strategy for Loving the World," "Late Flight of the Love God" and "Poets in Late Winter" from *Firefall* by Mona Van Duyn. Copyright © 1992 by Mona Van Duyn. Reprinted by permission of Alfred A. Knopf, a Division of Random House Inc.

Ellen Bryant Voigt "[All ears, nose, tongue and gut,]," "[When does childhood end? Mothers]," "[Nothing would do but that he dig her grave]," "[My brothers had it, my sister, parceled out]," "[Dear Mattie, Pug says even a year of camp]," "[Hogs aren't pretty but they're smart]," "[All day, one room: me, and the cherubim]" and "[Maybe the soul is breath. The door shut,]" from *Kyrie* by Ellen Bryant Voigt. Copyright © 1995 by Ellen Bryant Voigt. Used by permission of W. W. Norton & Co., Inc.

Belle Waring "Look," "So Get Over It, Honey" and "Baltazar Beats His Tutor at Scrabble" are reprinted from *Dark Blonde* by Belle Waring, published by Sarabande Books, Inc. Copyright © 1997 by Belle Waring. Reprinted by permission of Sarabande books and the author.

Rosanna Warren "Hagar," "His Long Home" and "Song" copyright © 1991 by Rosanna Warren. "Man, That Is Born of A Woman" from *Stained Glass* by Rosanna Warren. Copyright © 1993 by Rosanna Warren. Used by permission of W. W. Norton & Co., Inc.

Rachel Wetzsteon "Learning from the Movies," "Thoughts While Walking" and "Surgical Moves" reprinted from *Home and Away* by Rachel Wetzsteon, copyright © 1998 by Rachel Wetzsteon. Used by permission of Penguin, a division of Penguin Putnam Inc.

Susan Wheeler "He or She That's Got the Limb, That Holds Me Out On It" and "Song for the Spirit of Natalie Going" from *Smokes* by Susan Wheeler, copyright © 1998 by Susan Wheeler. Reprinted by permission of Four Way Books, Marshfield, MA 02050. "That Been to Me My Lives Light and Saviour" printed by permission of the author.

Eleanor Wilner "You, Failed Pronoun," "Judgment," "Her Body is Private," "All the Wide Grin of Him" and "Abstraction" reprinted from *Reversing the*

Index ～